Nich

GUID
GREEK
ISLANDS

The practical pocket guide to more than
50 holiday islands

ROBERT NICHOLSON PUBLICATIONS

A Nicholson Guide

First published 1986

© **Robert Nicholson Publications Limited 1986**
Maps © Robert Nicholson Publications Limited 1986
Town plans © Robert Nicholson Publications Limited 1986

Researched and written by **Martha Ellen Zenfell**

Maps by **David Perrott**
Design by Bob Vickers
Line drawings by Rodney Paull
Art & architecture by Louise Cavanagh with illustrations by
Towler Cox

The publishers and the author gratefully acknowledge the
generous assistance of Olympic Holidays, 17 Old Court Place,
London W8 4PL, who fly from 11 UK airports to 22 different
Greek islands; the National Tourist Organisation of Greece for
their co-operation in providing information; and Clio Mamalaki for
compiling the vocabulary.

The author would also like to extend special thanks to
John Wilcock.

Robert Nicholson Publications Ltd
62–65 Chandos Place
London WC2N 4NW

Phototypeset in England by Input Typesetting Limited
London SW19 8DR

Printed and bound in Great Britain by
Chorley & Pickersgill Ltd, Leeds and London

ISBN 0 905522 94 X

Contents

Greece and the islands

Using the guide

The islands covered in this guide are presented in alphabetical order within their individual groups; namely the Cyclades, the Dodecanese, the Ionian, the North East Aegean, the Saronic and the Sporades. The two largest islands, Crete and Evia, appear separately as they are not part of island chains.

At the front of the book there is a double-page orientation map of all the islands. Throughout the gazetteer, individual island maps complement the text, pinpointing all the main places of holiday interest.

For ease of reference, all the practical information relating to each island, including essential telephone numbers, air and ferry links, is shown in a tinted box. In many instances, the main islands have satellites – usually smaller and less developed islands, but still easily accessible – these also appear in tinted box which come at the end of the main island description. Under **Ports & towns**, the main port (where most visitors will arrive) is listed first, with all other ports, towns and villages following alphabetically thereafter. Museums, monasteries, ancient monuments and spectacular natural features are included under the topic heading **Sights**. The word Charge at the end of an entry denotes an admission fee. Opening times, in italic, are also given at the end of individual entries. While these times were correct at the time of going to press, they are subject to change, and it is always advisable to check locally before embarking on a long excursion.

At the back of the book, there is a reference section which includes a fully illustrated guide to the main periods of Greek art and architecture, as well as a 370-word vocabulary for basic communication.

A note on place names and spelling

English spellings of Greek place names present problems, as usually several alternatives exist. Except in the case of very well-known places, e.g. Crete, Corfu and Athens, the phonetic spelling has been used. Stress is a very important feature of the Greek language. This is indicated by an accent (ʹ) over the letter(s) to be emphasised.

Key to symbols on maps & town plans

⊠	Post office	🚌	Bus station	∴	Sight
☏	OTE office	✳	Windmill	⚓	Beach
🚍	Tourist police	✗	Airport	∩	Cave
$	Bank	╪	Monastery/church	∧	Campsite

Introduction

Where to go

Everyone will have their own ideas of what they want from a Greek island holiday. All the islands have something to offer, whether it be beautiful scenery, good beaches, spectacular ancient sites, lively nightlife, remoteness, tranquillity or just traditional Greek atmosphere and excellent hospitality. This book covers 50 islands in detail. The following groupings are designed to give you a general guide to each island's overall appeal and should help you to make the ideal choice.

For family holidays

Aegina, Corfu, Crete, Evia, Kefalonia, Kos, Naxos, Paros, Paxi, Poros, Rhodes, Santorini, Skiathos, Spetsai, Skyros, Thassos, Zante.

For ancient sites

Aegina, Crete, Delos, Evia, Ithaca, Kos, Lesbos, Naxos, Rhodes, Samos, Samothrace, Santorini.

For fun seekers

AntiParos, Corfu, Crete, Hydra, Ios, Kos, Mykonos, Paros, Rhodes, Samos, Skiathos, Zante.

For more tradition, less tourism

Alonnisos, Amorgos, Astipalea, Donoussa, Folegandros, Halki, Ithaca, Kalymnos, Kefalonia, Kea, Kythnos, Lemnos, Lesbos, Leros, Lipsi, Nissiros, Patmos, Pserimos, Salamis, Serifos, Sifnos, Skopelos, Syros, Spetsai, Symi, Tilos, Tinos.

When to go

The holiday season lasts from April to October. Rhodes and Crete are warm all year round, although swimming in winter is only for the hardy. The rain which keeps Corfu so green begins in September and continues until spring. Corfu is gorgeous in the rain, but most people come to Greece primarily for the sun. July and August are not the best months for independent travellers; ferries are over-full, available accommodation on many islands is almost non-existent and most resorts are crowded. Those who book a package or hotel in advance should avoid the Cyclades during this period if they want a touch of privacy. June and September are ideal months, as amenities are in full swing but the numbers of people using them depleted. April and October are also good months, but expect cloudy skies on a few days at least. In April and October it is best to stick to the major tourist islands as most of the others will have shut up shop for the winter. The islands are not equipped for rain and cold weather. There is no central heating, and a deserted Greek island off-season is more a romantic idea than a practical one.

Climate

The Greek islands have a Mediterranean climate with hot dry summers and warm wet winters. From May to August the *meltemi*, a cool northerly wind can provide welcome relief from the intense heat, but also makes waters choppy. The north-easterly *gregos* blows in the Saronic islands.

Getting there

By air

Scheduled flights Both British Airways and Olympic Airways schedule several flights daily to/from Athens. Direct flights can also be made to Crete, Rhodes, Corfu and Kos. There are connecting flights (via Athens) to Skiathos, Santorini, Mykonos, and a few other islands. Check with a travel agent for details.

British Airways

75 Regent St, London W1. Tel 01-897 4000. *Open 07.00–22.45 Mon-Sat; 08.00–20.00 Sun & hols.*

10 Othonos St, Athens 10557. Tel 01-3250601/610. *Open 08.00–18.00 Mon–Fri; 08.00–16.00 Sat. Closed Sun & hols.*

Olympic Airways

141 New Bond St, London W1. Tel 01-493 7262. *Open 09.00–18.00 Mon–Fri; 09.00–13.00 Sat. Closed Sun & hols.*

6 Othonos St, Athens. Tel 01-9292555. *Open 08.00–15.00 Mon–Fri.*

Charter flights The lowest fares can be found on charter flights. Check both national and local newspapers and magazines for a list of agencies, then call as many as patience will allow to get the most competitive price. Flexibility in arrival/departure dates is a great help. Due to Greek law, all tickets must be accompanied by an 'accommodation voucher'. Although the hotel probably exists, any reservation in your name will not, and you should ignore it. Tickets are usually valid for between one and three weeks only.

Package tours In the last few years an ever-increasing number of companies have put together package tours to Greece. This type of holiday is especially good for anyone with children, as it eliminates much of the worry about getting to the islands. Due to the lack of high-rise hotels (bar Athens, Crete, Rhodes and Corfu), accommodation is likely to be in clean, neat, two-storey villas, pensions or tavernas. One of the most popular companies specialising in vacations to Greece is Olympic Holidays, 17 Old Court Pl, London W8 4PL. Tel 01-727 8050; reservations 01-229 2411. Olympic Holidays fly from 11 UK airports to 22 different Greek islands, providing a wide range of accommodation, plus cruises and tours.

By train

Travelling from London (Victoria Station) to Athens by train takes three and a half days and involves numerous changes. Go prepared with provisions, comfortable clothes and books to read. Routes are generally via France

Climate

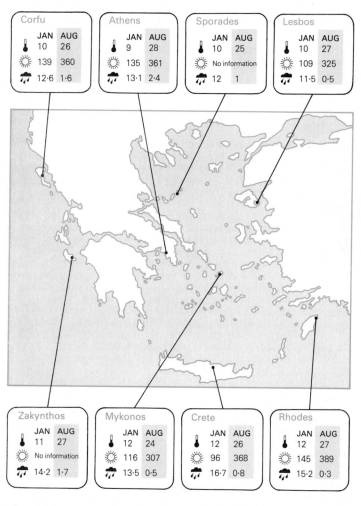

Corfu

	JAN	AUG
🌡	10	26
☀	139	360
🌧	12·6	1·6

Athens

	JAN	AUG
🌡	9	28
☀	135	361
🌧	13·1	2·4

Sporades

	JAN	AUG
🌡	10	25
☀	No information	
🌧	12	1

Lesbos

	JAN	AUG
🌡	10	27
☀	109	325
🌧	11·5	0·5

Zakynthos

	JAN	AUG
🌡	11	27
☀	No information	
🌧	14·2	1·7

Mykonos

	JAN	AUG
🌡	12	24
☀	116	307
🌧	13·5	0·5

Crete

	JAN	AUG
🌡	12	26
☀	96	368
🌧	16·7	0·8

Rhodes

	JAN	AUG
🌡	12	27
☀	145	389
🌧	15·2	0·3

🌡 Average temperature C°   ☀ Sunshine hours each month   🌧 Days of rain each month

and Italy, then by ferry to Corfu, or through Belgium, Germany and Yugoslavia. Tickets and information are available from principal British Rail Travel Centres or from accredited Continental rail travel agencies. Anyone under 26 can travel at a reduced rate using an InterRail card purchased from Transalpino, 71–75 Buckingham Palace Rd, London SW1. Tel 01-834 9656

By coach

Up to four coaches weekly go from London to Athens; the journey lasts two and a half days, with breaks only for food and toilet requirements. There are reduced rates for children. Tickets and information from Victoria Coach Station, 164 Buckingham Palace Rd, London SW1. Tel 01-730 0202.

By ship

Ferries, both car and passenger, sail to Corfu or Patras on the Greek mainland from the Italian ports of Ancona, Bari and Brindisi. Brindisi is by far the most popular departure port, and the journey can be a pleasant overnight experience, providing a berth is booked. If planning to take this route, arrive early at Brindisi because sleeping space is limited on many ships. Steamers also sail to Piraeus on an irregular basis from Marseilles, Naples, Venice, Barcelona, Turkey, Egypt, the Lebanon, Russia and Yugoslavia.

By yacht

Sailing is one of the best ways of exploring the Greek islands. There are 27 officially designated ports of entry. Yachts entering Greek waters must fly the code flag Q until cleared by the port authorities. The Greek flag should also be flown as a courtesy. Upon arrival, the port authority *Limenarkion* issues all yachts with a transit log permitting unlimited travel in Greek waters. These documents must be produced when purchasing spares, fuel or other duty-free goods. Greek radio transmits weather bulletins in English. On Athens radio, frequency 2590, broadcast times are *07.03, 09.33, 15.03, 21.03* (Greek & English); on frequency 418 broadcast times are *03.48, 06.18, 09.18, 15.18, 20.48* (English only). On Corfu radio, frequency 2830, broadcast times are *07.03, 09.03, 15.33, 21.33* (Greek & English); on frequency 421, broadcast times are *04.18, 06.18, 09.48, 15.48, 21.18* (English only).

Passports & visas

Citizens of the United Kingdom, Eire, the EEC, the United States, Canada, Australia, and New Zealand can stay in Greece for up to three months by presenting a valid passport upon arrival. No visa is necessary. South Africans can stay for up to eight weeks. If you want to stay longer than three months, you must register at the Athens Alien Department, 9 Chalkokondyli Street, or at the nearest police station, and apply for a special residence permit. No foreigner is permitted to work in Greece without having obtained a work permit before entering the country. Penalties for working illegally can be severe.

Information centres

National Tourist Organisation of Greece

The National Tourist Organisation of Greece (NTOG) operates state-owned information centres in Athens, on major islands and in some foreign countries. They can provide maps, lists of accommodation and colour brochures, as well as helping with general enquiries. If possible, it is a good idea to visit the office in your own country beforehand to gather information.

Offices abroad

United Kingdom 195–197 Regent St, London W1R 8DR. Tel 01-734 5997, Telex 21122

Australia 51–57 Pitt St, Sydney, NSW 2000. Tel (02) 241 1663/4, Telex 111816

Canada 2 Place Ville Marie, Esso Plaza, Montreal, Quebec H3B 2C9. Tel (514) 871-1535, Telex 60021

USA 168 North Michigan Av, Chicago, Illinois 60601. Tel (312) 782-1084, Telex 283468; 611 West Sixth St, Los Angeles, California 90017. Tel (213) 626-6696, Telex 686441; 645 Fifth Av, Olympic Tower, New York, NY 10022. Tel (212) 421-5777, Telex 66489

Greece

Athens Head office, 2 Amerikis St. Tel 01-3223111/9, Telex 5832; East Terminal, Eliniko Airport. Tel 01-9799500

Piraeus Zea Marina. Tel 01-4135716/730

Corfu Administration Bldg, Corfu Town. Tel (0661) 39730

Crete 6 Akti Tombazi, Chania. Tel (0821) 28724; 1 Xanthoudidou St, Heraklion. Tel (081) 222487/8

Kefalonia Argostoli. Tel (0671) 22847

Kos Akti Koundourioti, Kos Town. Tel (0242) 28724

Rhodes 5 Archbishop Makarios/Papagou Sts, Rhodes Town. Tel (0241) 23655 & 23255

Tourist Police

The Tourist Police are a division of the regular Greek police department, whose sole function is to deal with tourist enquiries. Most islands have a Tourist policeman, even those with NTOG offices and information centres. Tourist policemen speak English and can provide lists of accommodation. The headquarters are either on the waterfront of the main port or a short distance away. On some of the smaller islands, the Tourist Police only operate during the peak holiday season. This is indicated in the text as s.o. (summer only) after the telephone number.

Harbour Police

Most islands have Harbour Police, whose function it is to monitor sea traffic. They are the only people on each island who can give accurate information on the mysterious movements of the car ferries; both on frequency and the estimated time of arrival. Less accustomed to dealing with the public than the Tourist Police, they are nevertheless helpful. If making telephone enquiries, ask someone who speaks Greek to do the talking, as they do not all speak English. Caique and excursion boat enquiries should be directed to the Tourist Police.

Tourist agencies

Lining the harbours of all the major ports are buildings sporting the sign 'tourist agency'. These are not authorised information centres, but are run by individuals who have set up privately, usually to promote excursions and/or tourist amenities of their own. Information gleaned from them will probably be accurate, but by no means comprehensive. Often there will be someone in the office who speaks English.

Information centres

A few of the more popular islands, such as Rhodes, Paros and Symi, have their own information centres. Prominently located, they are often in interesting buildings – in Paros, a windmill, on Symi, a clocktower. They operate in the same way as the Tourist Police and are good for answering general enquiries, advising on excursions and helping with accommodation.

Embassies & consulates

Embassies of all major countries are located in Athens. Hours vary, so it is best to telephone first.

Australia 13 Messogion St. Tel 01-7757651
Canada 4 Genadiou St. Tel 01-7239511
Great Britain 1 Ploutarchou St. Tel 01-7236211
South Africa 124 Kifissias Av/Iatirdou St. Tel 01-6922125
USA 91 Vasilissis Sofias St. Tel 01-7212951

There are also British consulates located on the following islands:
Corfu 2 Zambeli St, Corfu Town. Tel (0661) 30055
Crete 16 Papalexandrou St, Heraklion. Tel (081) 224102
Rhodes 23, 25th March St, Rhodes Town. Tel (0241) 27247

Medical care

Under EEC regulations it is possible for British visitors in Greece to receive free medical care. To take advantage of this, however, it is necessary to obtain a current E111 form from the DHSS before leaving home. This is not available to the self-employed or unemployed. Wise tourists will also take out medical insurance before they go. Many package tours offer medical insurance at an extra charge; this should be accepted. Make sure the policy covers the cost of an air taxi. In emergency cases, this is the speediest way off the islands or to the nearest hospital. Also ensure it covers motoring accidents, especially if you are planning to hire a car or motorbike. Usually, treatment must be paid for at the time and the money claimed back against the insurance policy at a later date.

Most islands have a doctor. The surgery is usually in the main port, *open mornings and early evenings*. Always contact the Tourist Police in case of emergency; they can direct you to the doctor or organise alternative arrangements if the doctor is not there, as is often the case. Pharmacists should be able to advise – often in English – on the treatment of minor ailments such as upset stomachs or mosquito bites. Pharmacies are easily identified by the bold symbol of a red or green cross on a white background. Most tiny islands have at least one shop which serves the same function as a chemist, even if premises are shared with the greengrocer. Two handy stand-bys for dealing with complaints, and readily available on the islands are olive oil and lemon juice. Olive oil can be used to ease sunburn, and lemon juice helps to counteract the effects of the oily Greek food. It is always a good idea to travel with basic medicines, including antiseptic cream, sunburn cream, aspirin and sticking plasters.

Money

There is no limit to the amount of foreign currency which can be brought into Greece, but only a limited amount of drachmas may be brought in from abroad. For this reason many foreign banks and airport exchange bureaux do not stock quantities of drachmas. Be sure to organise currency well in advance where possible. The East Terminal at Eliniko Airport, Athens, has a 24-hour exchange office.

Currency

The drachma (dr) is the Greek monetary unit. There are 20, 10, 5, 2 and 1 drachma coins currently in circulation. Notes come in denominations of 50, 100, 500 and 1,000 drachmas. A new 5,000 drachma note has also been issued recently. Banks tend to issue larger notes which many shops and kiosks cannot change. Ask the exchange desk for a selection of smaller notes as well.

Travellers' cheques

All banks and many large hotels will cash travellers' cheques, providing a passport is submitted. Remember to retrieve passports from the hotel desk before setting out. All major credit cards are recognised in Greece and will be accepted in some of the larger tourist shops, restaurants and hotels. It is also possible to draw cash on them, but only from certain banks. British bank cheques will be cashed in all banks displaying the EC (Eurocheque) symbol, but must be accompanied by a Eurocheque card. This is not the normal UK cheque card, but can be obtained on demand from any British bank.

Banks

The two major banks in Greece are the National Bank of Greece and the Commercial Bank of Greece. Banking hours are 08.30–13.30 Mon–Fri. In Athens and on popular islands, it is often arranged for one bank to be open on weekday evenings in the high season. Only some of the very small islands have no banking facilities at all, on others a table set up in a taverna will provide the service. Travellers' cheques can be cashed even in these makeshift premises, but credit cards cannot be used to obtain money. The National Bank of Greece has three branches in London. The addresses are: 204 Tottenham Court Rd W1, tel 01-637 0876; 50 St Mary Axe EC3, tel 01-626 3222; 6 Queensway W2, tel 01-229 1413.

OTE Telephone and Telegraph offices

All large islands and most small ones have OTE offices (Organismos
Telephikinonion Eliathos), where both long-distance and local calls can be
made. Pay at the *end* of each call. OTE offices are often *open until 23.00*
and part of the day on Sunday. Connections from the islands to Britain are
not very good, but perseverance pays off. The dialling code from Greece
to the UK is 0044. From Greece to the USA or Canada it is 001. Local calls
can be made from kiosks, some of which provide long-distance services
as well. As this is not commonly known there are fewer queues than at
OTE offices. Calls made from hotels are often subject to an extra charge;
it is cheaper to use kiosks or OTE offices.

Postal services

Stamps can be bought at post offices and most kiosks, although a small
tax might be charged by the kiosks. Overseas letters and postcards can
be sent surface or air mail. The attractive large-format postcards now
commonly sold require more postage than standard-sized postcards.
All parcels must be inspected by the post office before being sent abroad.
Do not wrap them beforehand as they will merely be unwrapped again.
Brown paper can be purchased from the post office itself or from kiosks.
Post offices
Signs denoting post offices are in bright yellow, as are post boxes
themselves. Opening hours vary, but post offices are usually *open mornings
only 07.30/08.00–13.00*.
Poste Restante
Mail can be sent to you c/o *Poste Restante*. Athens and all major islands
have at least one post office where this service operates. If on a small
island expect considerable delays in receiving mail. Remember to take a
passport as a means of identification when collecting mail.

Sundays & public holidays

All tiny islands, and many popular ones like Naxos, close down on Sundays,
church-going being the only activity engaged in. Excursion boats continue
to put into harbours on Sundays, but what the tour organisers neglect to
tell you is that nothing will be open when you arrive. One taverna might
be serving food at lunchtime, but choice is at best limited. Souvenir shops
and kiosks usually remain open in large tourist towns.

Each island has its own strictly observed saint's day or days. The
unsuspecting tourist might not be aware the day is a holiday until it is
too late; if time is important, check in advance when these days occur.
Very often, even the local boats stop running and you might get stranded.
Shops and offices are sometimes shut the afternoon before and the
morning after a religious holiday, so again it's worth checking. Two strictly
observed periods are Easter and the Assumption of the Virgin on 15

August. The Orthodox Easter usually falls later than Easter in the rest of Europe. Opening hours are inclined to vary in the weeks either side of major holidays.

Public holidays

January 1	New Year's Day
January 6	Epiphany
March 25	Independence Day
	Shrove Tuesday
	Good Friday
	Easter Monday
August 15	Assumption of the Virgin Mary
October 28	Okhi Day (when Greece said 'no' to Mussolini)
December 25	Christmas Day
December 26	St Stephen's Day

Monasteries, museums and monuments

Standard opening hours are *08.00–14.00 Mon–Sat.* Archaeological sites and museums *close on Tuesdays.* Unfortunately, few of the island sites adhere to the standard opening times; all are subject to change without notice. In the high season, most major museums and monuments reopen after siesta, or remain open through the afternoon until *16.00*; they may also *open on Sundays* during this period. Smaller museums may be *open mornings only, closing at 13.00.* Most charge admission. Open-air archaeological sites are often not restricted by opening and closing hours.

These are delightful places to visit in the evening, either to watch the sunset or stroll in the moonlight; carry a torch to find your way back. As most museums and major sites attract vast crowds in the high season, it may be worthwhile trying to go during the siesta; walking round the sites in the opposite direction from the tour guides may also make a difference.

Visiting monasteries – often beautifully situated in peaceful locations – is one of the pleasures of an island holiday. A few have facilities for overnight accommodation or even extended stays; check with the Tourist Police. Most can be visited at any time of day, but mornings or late afternoons are best. Roads rarely lead directly to the monasteries, and often a hot uphill climb is necessary. Take a sunhat and even some water, but do not wear shorts. Women should cover their arms and wear skirts; in a few places, skirts are hired out just for this purpose. It is not uncommon to be greeted by a kindly monk and offered a cool, refreshing glass of water on arrival; donations are welcome. Donations should also be given in small churches after lighting a candle or having it lit for you. If a church is locked, the nearest house or café will probably have the key. Proper dress and a respectful attitude in places of worship is always appreciated.

Laws & customs

Bargaining
Definitely not to be attempted in hotels, tavernas, kiosks or major shops. It is, however, one of the attractions when shopping in street markets (except for food) or in one of the numerous souvenir shops. Expensive purchases such as furs and jewellery should be discussed in depth; prices are inflated specifically for this purpose. Always decide beforehand how much you are willing to pay for an item, then stick to that firmly in your mind.

Nudism
Greece has over 14,000km of beaches, most of them sandy. Although it might be enjoyable to swim without a costume, nude bathing is prohibited by law, except on a very few official nudist beaches. Greeks themselves are a modest people and a flagrant disregard for their customs is not appreciated. That having been said, there are remote beaches on many of the islands where nude bathing is tolerated. Topless sunbathing is generally less frowned upon, and is practised on most beaches except those in towns. The best policy is to follow the accepted practice, whatever that might be.

Siesta
Noise, including the driving of motorbikes and scooters, is prohibited during the hours of *14.00–17.00*. This afternoon ban coincides with siesta, the traditional Greek rest period. If rest is not important, siesta can be a good time to go exploring, as most tourists will be elsewhere. Take a sunhat as the heat is fierce. Alternatively extend a leisurely lunch into the siesta. Offices and shops close during these hours, but most cafés and tavernas remain open.

Tipping
Tipping is neither mandatory nor necessarily expected in Greece. Service is included in many bills and tipping is looked upon as a reward for good service. The serving boy (as opposed to the waiter) in tavernas should be

tipped as he depends on this for his wages, otherwise gratuities of around 10% are a matter of discretion. When the bill in a café has been paid, it is customary to leave the small change on the table.

Getting around

Ferryboats

The main means of transport for getting to and around the Greek islands. Most ferries which steam out of Piraeus are car ferries, but always check before buying a ticket as some are only equipped to carry passengers and motorbikes. Car ferries have three passenger decks; passenger ferries only two. You can eat, sleep, sunbathe and listen to bouzouki music on Greek ferries, and will probably spend a great deal of time on them. The journey from Piraeus to Rhodes, for instance, can take up to 18 hours, depending on the route and the number of stops. Come prepared!

All shipping schedules are subject to change without notice. When time is important, allow at least a couple of days' grace for getting to and from an island, even longer if remote. Strikes, inclement weather and the 'hand of the gods' all play a part in the smooth running of ferryboats, so leave nothing to chance. Schedules are available on a weekly basis from the NTOG office in Syntagma Square, Athens; no need to queue. Advance schedules are listed in two monthly publications – *Key Travel Guide* and *Greek Travel Pages*, which can be purchased in Athens in the Syntagma Square area. Buying a ticket in advance is unnecessary, as it limits the choice of both boat and destination. Instead, go to Piraeus and buy direct from one of the agencies lining the harbour.

Tickets for car ferries come in three different classes: first, second and third. They may be inspected at any stage of the journey, so keep them to hand at all times. Tax is added to the ticket price and varies depending on the port of embarkation. For this reason it might be slightly cheaper to go from Piraeus to Patmos rather than vice versa. Differences, however, are not great. The first-class decks have cabins, a restaurant, carpeted floors, cushioned chairs and lots of leg room. Comfortable and tranquil. The second-class deck has similar, but less plush facilities. Although second-class has its own restaurant, some ferries allow first class dining on a second-class ticket. Food is reasonable in each. The third-class deck consists of a snack bar serving unpalatable food, a lounge with Pullman-type seats and access to the top deck which is suitable for sunbathing – take something comfortable to sit on. A third-class ticket is fine for most journeys, especially short ones. Greeks almost always travel third-class as do most people under 30 or anyone with a guitar. It is noisy and rowdy in third-class, but probably the closest to a 'real' Greek atmosphere most tourists will encounter. It should not be missed. Should the noise and general merriment get too much, a first- or second-class ticket can be bought on board by paying the difference in price. When travelling third-class, take food, books and a sleeping bag. The seats do not recline, and sleeping between them is impossible. If sunbathing, wait until the boat leaves before positioning yourself in the perfect spot to catch the sun.

Passenger ferries offer similar facilities to car ferries, though often with a snack bar instead of restaurants. The ride itself is less smooth. Berths should be booked as far ahead as possible. Even out of season, cabin space is scarce. Cabins are tiny but comfortable; showers and toilet facilities usually shared. Single passengers must expect to share with a stranger of the same sex. Always travel with an alarm clock, as pursers are too busy for wake-up calls. If you oversleep, your destination may be long-gone. There is no reimbursement and owing to the complexities of the inter-island ferries, it may take a week to reach your original destination.

Regardless of class, always travel with seasickness pills. Even the two-hour hop between Mykonos and Paros can be choppy enough to cause nausea.

Hydrofoils

Hydrofoils are twice as fast and twice as expensive as ferries. Sleek and clean, they offer refreshments on board, as well as occasional stewardess service. The enclosed space, however, can be claustrophobic and especially on the long journeys, such as to Spetsai, seasickness can occur. Hydrofoils need calmer seas than ferryboats and are prone to cancellation. Although hydrofoils were once seen as a promising alternative to time-consuming ferry journeys, they are now less common. The Paros/Mykonos/Naxos route runs rarely, if at all; Rhodes/Kos/Patmos only in the high season, providing conditions are calm. The hydrofoil link with the Saronic islands, however, is well established and popular throughout the year. Hydrofoils leave from Zea Marina, south-east of the Great Harbour in Piraeus.

Information The following telephone numbers (dialling from Athens) give information on ferry links with specific islands or island groups. Little English is spoken, so ask a Greek person to make the call. Crete (tel 4511311), Cyclades/Dodecanese (tel 4511311), Ithaca (tel 8236012), Kefalonia (tel 3632575), NE Aegean (tel 3622093), Saronic – boats (tel 4511311), Saronic – hydrofoils (tel 4527107), Sporades (tel 3622093), departures from Rafina (tel 0294 23300).

Internal flights

Olympic Airways' domestic service flies from Athens to several islands, cutting a journey which normally takes a day by ferry to 40 minutes of highly enjoyable travel. Some of the planes used on these flights are very small, holding as few as nine passengers – although there might be up to five flights daily, space is extremely limited. Do not expect to find spare seats in July and August; even out of season it is necessary to book well in advance for popular destinations. Many planes leave early in the morning and these are the ones to aim for; not only to enjoy the sunrise but to increase the chances of getting on a later flight should overbooking occur. Planes have been known to take off earlier than the scheduled time, so be prepared. Flights are very reasonably priced.

Inter-island boats

A variety of vessels is used for inter-island transport, from passenger ferries to excursion boats. These inter-island boats, known locally as *caiques*, seat anywhere from 20 to 150 people. Tickets for inter-island boats can be purchased from tour organisers on the islands, ticket booths – usually on the quay, or on the boats themselves. Arrive in good time to be sure of a place. Although boats can be privately hired on Crete and Rhodes, the cost is quite high. Fishing boats rarely venture into the open seas with passengers aboard. All small boats rock furiously in the choppy Aegean waters.

Island buses

These range from air-conditioned coaches on the larger islands to battered school buses on the smaller, remote islands. On 'tourist' islands the services are frequent and tend to run on time. This is an excellent way of sightseeing as tickets are cheap. On small islands, services are limited – often there is only one road, and the bus might or might not appear on time. Timetables – in Greek – are usually attached to a conspicuous wall or telegraph pole; the bus always honks before leaving so it is difficult to miss. On all the islands, buses are prompt at meeting the ferries; even if arriving at midnight it should be possible to catch a bus to the town. The last bus to the port is usually around *19.00*. Expect to share buses with shepherds, women with lots of shopping baskets and, occasionally, live chickens.

Island taxis

Taxis are reasonably priced, especially if sharing. Popular routes, such as
Rhodes Town to Lindos, are charged at a fixed rate. It is common on islands
with limited transport to share taxis with local people, often stopping to
pick up others on the way. Occasionally the meter is left running while
these people run errands; if you are footing the total bill, protest politely.
On some islands taxi drivers who speak English will volunteer as private
guides; this is a good way to see out-of-the-way locations, but fix the price
first. It is usual on smaller islands to pay by the kilometre as most 'taxis'
do not have meters. On the less-developed islands the bus or a farm
vehicle often doubles as a taxi after dark.

Hiring transport

Islands which provide transport for hire lose no time in informing the visitor.
The waterfront of the main port will be crammed with agencies, all
appearing competitive, but varying little in price. Firms with premises in
the back streets also charge similar prices, although service might be
more personal. Prices tend to rise in the high season and then come down
again as the tourists depart; bargaining is worth a try, but don't count on
a reduction.

   All transport should be checked carefully before rental is agreed, as wear
and tear is enormous. Check brakes and lights particularly. Depending on
the firm, petrol and local insurance are either included in the total fee, or
added as extras. Also check that your holiday insurance covers motoring
accidents. Remember to drive on the right.

Cars

Visitors to the larger islands such as Crete, Corfu, Lesbos, Rhodes and
Kefalonia, really need a car to explore properly. Many holiday companies
offer fly/drive schemes on the larger islands, but is must be remembered
that the minimum age limit for hiring cars is 23. Cars are banned
altogether on some of the very small islands such as Spetsai and Telendos.
British drivers must have a valid licence, but are not required to carry an
international driving licence. Seat belts must be worn in the front; children
must travel in the back. Hiring a car can be an expensive exercise, particularly
with added tax and insurance.

Motorbikes & scooters

By far the most popular way to travel on the islands is by motorbike,
scooter or moped. They are very versatile forms of transport, able to
tackle most rough tracks, economical on fuel and easily mastered within
half an hour. However, first-time users should still take care when riding
through unfamiliar towns. Most Cycladian towns, for example, are
constructed in tiers; one wrong turn and you might find yourself plunging
down a steep flight of steps. Otherwise, the only road hazards – apart
from traffic – are lizards, pot-holes and sand, which can blow across in
drifts several inches deep. To hire motorbikes, a valid driving licence must
be produced, but the wearing of crash-helmets is not required by law. It

is illegal to ride motorbikes and scooters in towns during the siesta
(*14.00–17.00, and after 23.00*).

Bicycles

As island terrain tends to be mountainous, cycling has not become popular,
though bicycles can be hired cheaply on the more developed islands.
They are usually allowed on the ferries free of charge.

Hitch-hiking

Hitch-hiking is not a productive way to get around the islands as cars are
scarce. However, islanders will often stop and pick up tourists anyway,
saving them a hot dusty walk, as they recognise how limited public
transport can be.

Walking

Greek islands are perfect for walkers. An after-dinner stroll along the
waterfront is mandatory for Greeks and visitors alike. On the smaller islands
walking is necessary as public transport is limited and some of the best
beaches can only be reached after an hour's trek over the foothills. Early
morning and early evening are the best time for long walks, as the midday
sun is fiercely hot and shady spots are rare. Large areas of many islands
are barren and mountainous, criss-crossed with shepherds' paths and
mainly the property of sheep and goats. These paths are excellent for
secluded walks into hills, where ancient ruins lie half-buried, rarely
discovered by the majority of beach-bound visitors. Sturdy shoes and a
water bottle are essential provisions; a sweater and a walking stick recommended. In these wilder areas snakes are sometimes a problem. They do
not attack, but may bite if disturbed. Local maps are fun to use but not to
be taken seriously. Major roads often turn out to be little more than tracks;
the tracks themselves non-existent. Although Aegean days are long,
darkness falls quickly, so be sure to time your return journey carefully. An
unsheltered night spent on a foreign mountain can be a bleak adventure.

Island-hopping

The best time to island-hop is in July and August, when all services are
fully operative. Unfortunately accommodation is extremely limited during
this period; in May, June and September when rooms are available, ferry
services are less frequent. There is no connection between the Cyclades
and the Dodecanese, for instance, until late June. Anyone travelling to
more than three islands should expect a little discomfort. Boats are often
delayed due to bad weather or lack of ticket sales, which is inconvenient
if advance bookings have been made. Much better to be flexible, going
wherever the next ferry is heading. Even out of season, accommodation
on the first night is dictated more by circumstance than choice; it is best to
travel with a sleeping bag, towel and soap, just to be on the safe side. In
any event, luggage should be kept to a minimum. Large cumbersome
suitcases are a positive disadvantage when island-hopping and exploring.
Some hotels will store luggage at no extra charge, a generous offer which
should not be refused.

It is easiest to island-hop within specific chains. The Cyclades offer the best variety, but are very crowded during the summer; ferry links are good. The Ionian islands are close together, but poorly connected. In most cases, it is necessary to return to the mainland each time. The NE Aegean islands are widely scattered and distances are great. The Dodecanese offer unlimited choice and good travel facilities; a speedy hydrofoil service connects Rhodes, Kos and Patmos in the summer months and there are numerous satellite islands to explore. The Saronic islands are excellent for those with just a few days to spare – a 'mini-hop' of all five islands can be done in three days taking the cruise from Piraeus. The Sporades are an island-hopper's dream – easily accessible, with daily ferry connections.

Island-hopper's checklist

Always a good idea to stock up at home beforehand. Most of the following items can be bought in Athens if anything has been forgotten: sunglasses, sunhat, pair of plastic shoes, pair of sturdy shoes, 1–2 pairs socks, pair of long trousers, sweater or jacket, sleeping bag, binoculars, corkscrew, suitcase trolley (if heavy luggage), alarm clock, earplugs (optional), tin opener, sharp knife, plastic fork and spoon, thermos flask, facecloth, towel, beach towel, soap, soap powder, torch, sticking plasters, antiseptic cream, portable clothes line and pegs, sink plug, seasickness pills, insect repellent and coils, aspirin, indigestion tablets, any favourite foods.

Accommodation

In recent years, accommodation on the islands has improved dramatically. Most rooms, whether in hotels or private houses, are inexpensive and good value for money. During the high season, it is always necessary to book in advance. On some of the more popular islands such as Rhodes, Mykonos and Santorini, it is also advisable to book in advance for June and September. There is a wide choice available, ranging from luxury hotels and Venetian mansions to tavernas and the occasional cell in a monastery. NTOG offices both in Athens and abroad can supply lists of accommodation. It is also possible to reserve a room through the Greek Chamber of Hotels, 2 Karageorgi Servias Street, Syntagma Square, Athens, tel 01-3237193. Reservations in writing should be addressed to 6 Aristidou Street, Athens, tel 01-3236962. Whether staying in a hotel, pension or private room, always try to ensure there is a balcony or access to a courtyard; the midday heat can be intense and ventilation becomes a priority.

Hotels

Greek hotels are divided into six classes: Luxury, A, B, C, D and E. These categories are fixed by the government, whose inspectors visit all the hotels. Although Luxury hotels are exactly that and E class hotels usually have primitive plumbing arrangements, the distinction between the other categories might not be apparent to the layman. Often the older converted mansions will receive a lower rating than the modern purpose-built hotels;

a bonus for anyone who prefers character and charm to a full range of amenities. There is a fixed price bracket for each category, and hotels in a lower class will always be cheaper than the class above. Most hotels have a high standard of cleanliness and rooms are usually spacious, though not all will have private bathrooms or washing facilities in the lower categories. Luxury, A and B class hotels will have private dining facilities, the others may only serve a light breakfast of coffee, rolls, yoghurt and honey. This will be at a small additional charge (as it is not usually included in the price of the room) and will not be insisted upon.

It is generally cheaper to stay for more than three nights in one hotel rather than moving around, as the tariff is reduced for longer stays. Tax will be added to the total bill, as will a charge for air-conditioning and a supplement for each extra bed brought into the room. During the high season, prices rise by approximately 15% and some hotels may insist on half or full board. Out of season, things are much more flexible. A single person travelling alone may be charged half, two-thirds or the full rate for a double room; single rooms are practically non-existent.

Pensions

Pensions are guest-houses, generally family-run, and often more informal than hotels with cheerful, friendly service. As with hotels, they are divided into classes A–E.

Villas

Many tour companies now offer villa holidays on the islands; a good alternative to hotels for groups of young people or families. They sleep anywhere between two and a dozen people for periods of one to three weeks. Houses or villas can also be rented privately on most of the islands, though usually for periods of one month or more. Specialist travel agents or the NTOG should have lists of villas available. The longer the stay and the more people sharing, the cheaper the overall price. On some islands, there will occasionally be snapshots in the shop windows with information on specific premises to let. Probably booked up well in advance for July and August, they can be a bargain off-season. Alternatively contact the Tourist Police, who might know of suitable premises.

Private rooms

Rooms in private houses are cheaper and often more fun to stay in than hotels. It is not possible to book them in advance. Usually owners will greet each ferry as it docks, clutching a snapshot, or a card bearing the address of their premises. Late at night, or during the high season, this is often the only way to find a room; they are much of a muchness, and it is perfectly safe to accept the first offer. Stay for one night only and then look around the following day for somewhere else; if you like the room immediately, accept for several days and negotiate a lower price. Few Greek homeowners speak English and most business is conducted on a scrap of paper, or even the palm of the hand. This is the best way to meet the islanders and see how they live. Many are overwhelming in their kindness towards their guests. A few houses sport signs to declare the owners' intentions, saying either 'Rent Room', 'Zimmer' or 'Chambre'

Camping

Camping other than on organised sites is officially illegal. However, the demand for campsites is usually much greater than their availability, and attitudes to camping rough vary from island to island. On islands such as Ios, Corfu, Thassos and Samothrace, it is accepted practice, on others, expect to be moved on by the police from time to time. One of the main concerns of the authorities is the danger of forest fires, particularly late in the season when everything is tinder-dry. If planning to camp, take extra care with camping gas cookers, matches and cigarettes.

The NTOG can supply lists of official campsites; unofficial ones, privately run and often located near beaches, are best discovered by word of mouth. Organised campsites should provide fresh water and toilet facilities, though obtaining replacement cylinders for camping gas cookers may be more of a problem. Camping with a tent is cheap; pay even less if sleeping under the stars with just a sleeping bag.

Sleeping rough

Sleeping rough is officially illegal, but the law is rarely enforced. A mild climate, soft sandy beaches and casual way of life make Greece a perfect place for sleeping under the stars. If arriving in July or August without accommodation booked, it might be the only place to sleep. It is a good idea to carry a sleeping bag, especially if island-hopping. Accommodation on the remote islands is patchy at best, but someone will always offer a flat roof on which to lay your head. From May to September it is warm enough to be without a tent, although a camping stove is a good idea, as is a foam pad and/or a groundsheet. If moved on during one of the spasmodic 'clean-up' campaigns, be generous about it and go elsewhere – the country is, after all, full of good beaches.

Practical hints

Greek plumbing Although hotel toilets have improved substantially in recent years, taverna and public toilets have not kept pace. Public toilets are rare, usually found near the harbour, and often consisting of just a hole in the ground. Pay one fee for using the hole, another for paper. Taverna toilets are often smelly and under no circumstances should the signs be ignored. In three different languages you are asked to kindly deposit used paper in a bucket to one side of the toilet.

Hot showers are a luxury found only in certain hotels and only on certain islands; Halki, for instance, has no hot water at all. At best showers will be a trickle, mildly refreshing; at worst they will splatter everything in the room with icy water. In hotels, but especially in private rooms, use water sparingly as it is often in short supply.

Electric current On remote islands the current might be 110 volts, but generally it is 220 volts. Two-pin plugs are usual, so take an adapter for shavers, travel irons and hairdryers.

Laundry The hot Greek sun ensures most drip-dry fabrics can be worn again two hours after washing; landladies can usually supply a tub or basin. If staying in D and E class hotels, take a plug, soap powder and a portable clothes line to sling over the balcony. Dry cleaning is expensive but well worthwhile if staying in a large port for three days; clothes are treated with attention and pale cottons return beautifully pressed.

Mosquitos Mosquitos are common in Greece and can be very irritating. Insect coils, strategically placed next to open windows are an effective means of combat, and even the smallest islands sell packs in chemists or grocers. Lit with a match, the coils are fragile and often break, and the smoke they produce can be almost as unpleasant for people as mosquitos. More efficient is an electric coil which burns smokeless tablets, available in Athens or from chemists on the larger islands.

Dangerous animals Scorpions and snakes are usually found only in wild, rocky areas and do not attack unless disturbed. Contact a doctor immediately if bitten or stung. The waters around the Greek islands are ideal for swimming and snorkelling. Two hazards to watch out for are the medusas (jellyfish) floating near the shore which can give a nasty sting and the spiny sea urchins found on rocky shores. If a spine lodges in the foot it can be extremely painful. Wear plastic shoes for swimming off the rocks.

Eating & drinking

At its best, Greek food is fresh, tasty and wholesome, if somewhat repetitive and lacking in variety. It does not, however, have the reputation of being one of the better European cuisines and is often described as 'swimming in oil and served only lukewarm'. While this can be true, it is more than compensated for by the freshness and good value for money.

Lamb and mutton are the types of meat most readily available. Served either grilled on a skewer (*souvláki*) or as mince in prepared dishes such as *moussaka* and *keftédes*. Charcoal-grilled chicken is delicious, as is roast suckling pig, though the latter may be harder to find. On some remote islands, goat (*katsíki*) or kid (*katsikáki*) – less tough – may be the only meat on offer.

Seafood is good and very fresh, but surprisingly expensive. Many smaller islands serve little or no fish, sending their catches instead to the lucrative markets of Crete, Rhodes, Corfu and Athens. On popular islands, red mullet (*barboúnia*) is a good, if pricey choice. Fried squid (*kalamári*), especially young squid (*kalamarákia*) is less expensive and extremely tasty, as is octopus (*oktapóthi*) and whitebait (*marídes*). Grilled swordfish is also well-worth sampling when available. Most fish is priced according to weight. Explain how much you want to spend and the appropriate amount of fish will appear on your plate.

Greek salad, doused in oil, is ubiquitous. It can either be just tomatoes or a combination of sliced cucumber, tomatoes, green peppers, onions and olives, liberally sprinkled with crumbly, white *féta* cheese (made from sheep's or goat's milk). Placed in the middle of the table, it is usually shared. Vegetables include artichokes (*angináres*), okra (*bámies*), courgettes (*kolokithákia*) and beans (*vasólia*). Aubergines (*melitzánes*) and peppers (*piperiés*) are often stuffed with meat and rice, then oven-baked.

Potatoes, rice and pasta are good for soaking up all the oil and tomato sauces; white bread is standard and is provided on the table with the cutlery. A small charge is made even if it is left untouched.

Greece grows a lot of fruit including peaches, figs, oranges, lemons, cherries, strawberries, grapes and melons. In season, the fruit is extremely good and an ideal choice for puddings or picnics. Nuts, dates and other dried fruit are available throughout the year.

In areas popular with tourists, the menu will be written in both Greek and English, possibly another language as well. There are two sets of prices, the one on the left is without tax and service charges, the one on the right is all inclusive. Even if service is included a small tip should be left for the boy (*mikró*) who clears the tables. In more remote places there will probably be no menu at all, and it is common practice to go into the kitchens to choose a dish.

Restaurants (*estiatórion*) serve oven-baked dishes and grills, and are more formal than tavernas. In general, the choice will be limited to Greek food only, though restaurants specialising in French or Italian cuisine can be found on the larger tourist islands. Tavernas also serve oven-baked dishes and charcoal grills, but menus are more limited, and the 'dish of the day' is usual fare. There will be tavernas even on the most remote islands. Not all tavernas and restaurants serve puddings, and it is traditional to go on to a *zacharoplasteíon* to buy cakes and pastries steeped in honey. The best known is *baklavá; kataífi* is also good. Ice cream and coffee may also be served at small indoor tables in the *zacharoplasteíon*. Greek cafés (*kafeneíons*) serve mainly drinks, but ice cream and a range of coffees will probably be available in the bright waterside cafés which line the harbours of most tourist resorts.

The Greeks are great snack eaters. *Galaktopoléions* sell cheese pies (*tirópita*), crusty bread, coffee, milk, rice puddings and yoghurt. The yoghurt is excellent and very creamy; served with honey for breakfast, or with nuts as a dessert. Pre-dinner drinks in *kafeneíons* or *oúzeries* – more frequented by locals – will often be accompanied by a plate of snacks

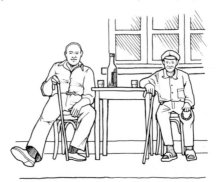

(*mezédes*). These can be anything from olives and cheese to *tsatsíki* and *taramosaláta*.

Oúzo is the national aperitif – beware, it bites back! Made locally on the islands, it is distilled from crushed vine stems and is a colourless liquid which turns milky when diluted with water. The most popular Greek brandy is Metaxa, which is graded according to strength and quality. Spirits are relatively pricey, but savings can be made by purchasing them in the tax-free Dodecanese islands.

Retsína is an acquired taste. 'White' wine laced with pine-essence, it is usually a rich golden colour and should be drunk well chilled. Many islands produce their own retsina and there are numerous varieties. Often it will not be commercially bottled and on some remote islands, served straight from wooden barrels. *Deméstika* (red or white wine) is available almost everywhere. Certain islands also produce their own wines, including Paros, Rhodes, Crete, Samos and Naxos. Wines from Samos are amongst the best known. Although Greek wine generally does not approach the sophistication of its French and Italian counterparts, there is a sufficiently wide variety to suit most tastes. Local beers, really lagers, are light and refreshing when properly chilled. 'Fix' is probably the most common brand.

Greek mineral waters are highly recommended. A large chilled glass of water is always served with Greek coffee as a matter of course. Greek coffee, similar to Turkish coffee, is thick, dark and syrupy; it comes either *glykó* (sweet), *métrio* (medium) or *skéto* (no sugar). Espresso and cappuchino are increasingly offered as an alternative on the popular holiday islands, otherwise it's instant coffee, known everywhere as 'nes'

Traditional Greek dishes

Avgolémono	Chicken broth with rice, lemon and eggs
Baklavá	Thin layers of pastry (*fíllo*) filled with nuts and spices; soaked in honey
Dolmádes	Vine leaves stuffed with mince and/or rice. *Dolmadákia* (small *dolmádes*) are served as a snack
Kataífi	Shredded wheat pastry, soaked in honey
Keftédes	Meatballs made from spiced mince
Moussaka	Alternating layers of mince and sliced aubergine with white sauce and cheese
Pastítsia	Pie of cheese, macaroni, mince and tomatoes
Souvláki	Meat grilled on a skewer, sometimes with vegetables. Served as a snack with *pita* (unleven bread)
Taramosaláta	Pink-coloured purée of grey mullet roe, breadcrumbs, olive oil and lemon juice
Tsatsíki	Yoghurt with cucumber and garlic
Yemitsés	Vegetables stuffed with mince and/or rice. Usually the name of the vegetable will be given too, eg *piperiés yemitsés* (stuffed peppers)

Nightlife

Although one of the most enjoyable ways to spend an evening is strolling by the sea in the moonlight, or sitting in one of the numerous waterside cafés, the islands do provide other forms of entertainment. There are casinos on some of the larger islands such as Corfu and Rhodes, frequented mainly by tourists. Another form of entertainment becoming increasingly popular on the islands with both locals and tourists alike are the open-air cinemas, though there are indoor ones as well. Films tend to be in various languages, but with Greek sub-titles.

Most nightlife, however, centres around music and dancing. Traditional live bouzouki music is played in the tavernas and hotels, but the best bouzouki music is found in bouzoukias – large nightclubs often located out of town. Plate-smashing still takes place here when the police are elsewhere. Mykonos is *the* island for discos, but Corfu, Rhodes, Ios, Crete and many of the smaller islands also have their fair share.

Shopping

On larger, developed islands the choice of goods available is similar to that in Athens, with additional local specialities – colourful embroidery in Crete, gold jewellery on Mykonos. Rhodes is known for its furs and tax-free shops, Corfu for its woollen sweaters and Kalymnos for its sponges. On very tiny islands, the choice may be limited to locally produced wines and spirits; food products including nuts, herbs, olives and the thick, unrefined green olive oil are also good buys. Many islands sell quantities of copper and leather goods, as well as textiles, hand-woven rugs and embroidery. Shops catering for tourists can usually arrange for purchases to be sent by post. The customer pays extra for this service, but items are well packed and promptly dispatched. Greek banks add a 7% charge to credit card transactions, so it is cheaper to shop with cash.

Island shops are open from *08.00–14.00 Mon–Sat*. They also tend to reopen after siesta, but to be on the safe side, do any essential shopping in the morning and save the evenings for browsing. Greengrocers and bakers cannot be depended on to reopen, as their produce is fresh daily. Markets are generally excellent places to buy straw bags, throw-away clothing and anything cheap and cheerful. Bargaining is mandatory. It is also worth visiting markets in the morning to buy fresh fruit and salad stuff for picnic lunches.

Kiosks are one of the mainstays of Greek shopping. Situated on street corners or in the middle of village squares, kiosks may remain *open until midnight*, selling everything from cigarettes and stamps to newspapers, shampoo and suntan lotion. Although stock varies, kiosks can also be good places to buy local maps, postcards, sweets and souvenir worry beads. It is worth noting that worry beads (*kombolóia*) are up to 30% cheaper in kiosks than in the tourist shops.

Anything hand-made tends to be a good buy, as labour is cheap and materials often of high quality. However, it is important to check prospective purchases thoroughly. Many islands produce local pottery including colourful hand-painted ceramic tiles and vases. Kebab skewers, copper coffee pots and saucepans are everywhere, but candlesticks and heavy brass trays can also be found. Leather goods are durable rather than stylish – undyed and unadorned sandals, belts and shoulder bags – check the stitching and clasps. Woollen flokati rugs are priced by the kilo, and come both machine- and hand-woven. Heavy woollen sweaters, preferably oiled to keep out the chilly winds, are also a popular buy for tourists now.

Luxury items include jewellery and furs. The gold prices on Mykonos are inflated specially for the hapless cruiseship passengers; nearby Paros is cheaper, with distinctive bracelets, brooches and necklaces hand-crafted in silver or gold. Fur farms in the north of Greece breed mink, fox, beaver and muskrat to provide the island shops with sophisticated fur coats. Never buy a fur on impulse – the hot weather helps to dissuade potential customers. Bargaining can be worthwhile.

Due to variations in Greek law, some items such as woollen cloth and spirits are tax-free in the Dodecanese islands but taxable in others. Rhodes, Kos and Patmos have unusually large numbers of off-licences for this reason.

Books & maps

The bookshop in London with the best selection of reading matter related to Greece, including history, classics, maps and guides is the Hellenic Bookshop, 122 Charing Cross Rd WC2 0JR, tel 01-836 7071. *Open 09.00–18.00 Mon–Sat.* The Geographia Bookshop, 63 Fleet St EC4, tel 01-353 2701, *open 09.00–17.15 Mon–Fri only,* also stocks a good selection of maps and guides. It is a good idea to buy maps beforehand, as many of the tourist maps available on individual islands can be very sketchy and inaccurate.

In Athens, bookshops selling publications in English include Librairie Cacoulides at 25–29 Panepistimou, tel 01-3231703 and Eleftheroudakis, 4 Nikis St. Also two bookshops on Amerikis St, numbers 11 and 23. The best large-scale island maps are published by Toubis, available both in Greece and the UK. Toubis also produce guidebooks to some individual islands.

On the popular islands, kiosks tend to stock English newspapers and international bestsellers. On the larger, tourist islands, there is generally one quality bookshop where more serious literature can be purchased. 'Young' islands such as Paros and Ios, have secondhand shops where water-logged paperbacks can be traded in for others in a similar state of disrepair. Most of the islands tend to sell out of maps and guides in English by mid-September.

Athens

The sights and ancient ruins of Athens are amongst the finest in the world, but the sprawling modern city which surrounds them is noisy, dirty and rowdy – chaotic in the extreme. The frighteningly heavy traffic pollutes the atmosphere with fumes, and the roar of the engines adds to the general cacophony of sound which typifies Athens today. No one talks – they shout! After a first visit, many people vow never to return; others learn to love the city for its vibrancy and charm. For island-hoppers it is almost inescapable. Apart from package tours, all international flights arrive and depart from here. Anyone staying a week or more will want to buy a guidebook dealing specifically with Athens. The following is a short guide for those spending a few days in the capital en route to and from the islands.

Only a small part of the city will interest the casual visitor. This area forms a triangle between the Acropolis and the two main squares, Syntagma and Omonia. Syntagma is broad and elegant, lined with open-air cafés. Omonia, with its gardens and fountain is pleasant but dowdy, frequented more by locals. The parallel avenues of Stadiou and Panepistimiou (Venizelou) link the two squares and take about 20 minutes to walk. Everything the visitor wants can be found in this area – hotels, restaurants and shops, and all the most popular tourist attractions are within easy walking distance. This is the heart of Athens.

Plaka is the name given to the maze of streets huddled below the Acropolis. It is the oldest part of the city, and the most picturesque. For years visitors have enjoyed its tavernas, tiny specialist shops and gay atmosphere; at night Plaka is as crowded and lively as Syntagma Square is by day. Recently the area has been smartened up and its somewhat tawdry reputation improved. To dine outdoors in Plaka, then stroll towards the Acropolis in the heavily-scented moonlight is to capture the essence of Athens. An area less discovered by tourists is the fashionable district of Kolonaki. A 10-minute walk north-east of Syntagma Square, there are high-class restaurants and stylish boutiques here.

Arriving in Athens

By air
Athens Airport has two separate and very distinct terminals: the East Terminal and the West, or National, Terminal. There is a free shuttle service between the two *every hour from 08.00–20.00.*

East Terminal
Serves all international flights except Olympic Airways. Facilities include an NTOG office, hotel-reservations counter, car-hire agencies, snack bar, and newsagents. Duty-free shop. The currency exchange office is *open 24-hours a day, throughout the year.* The taxi rank is just outside. It is approximately a 25-minute ride into central Athens.

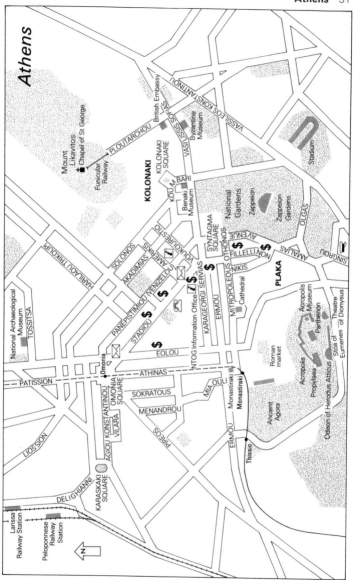

Athens

Between Syntagma and Omonia Squares are countless middle-price A and B class hotels, centrally located and close to most amenities. Cheaper accommodation can be found in the numerous C, D and E class hotels tucked away in the backstreets. There are also rooms to let in private houses and hotels with dormitory-style bedrooms. Those seeking accommodation with character and charm will want to stay in or around Plaka. Guest-houses here are elegant old mansions, often family-run, and offering a more personal service than in the large modern hotels. Amenities, however, may be more basic. Certain hotels of all classes around Syntagma Square and Plaka have roof gardens boasting views of the Acropolis. This is Athens at its romantic best. It is worth keeping an eye out for these hotels on the first trip to Athens, then booking a room for the next visit.

Anyone catching an early morning flight might prefer to stay in one of the numerous hotels in the environs of the airport. Known as Glifadi, this area is a series of streets given over entirely to purpose-built hotels. Glifadi is good for anyone travelling with children, as it is close to the airport, and Athens' nearest beach with full resort facilities is within walking distance. The distance between central Athens and the airport is not great. Tourists staying in Glifadi will find it easy to get into the city for sightseeing or to sample the nightlife.

If arriving without a reservation apply to the Greek Chamber of Hotels, 6 Aristidou St, tel 3236641. The GCOH also have desks at both terminals of Athens airport. Bookings can also be made from the NTOG office, 2 Karageorgi Servias St, right on Syntagma Square. Tel 3237193. *Open until 21.00 May–Sep (closes earlier out of season).*

Eating & drinking

Lunch is generally served from *12.00 noon until 15.00*, dinner from *20.00–23.00*. Breakfast is continental, eaten either in the hotel or in one of the city's numerous cafés. Large hotels serve international cuisine in dining rooms often open to the public. Most tavernas and restaurants offer Greek food only; menus, usually of similar price and selection are in Greek, English and German. However, the choice of food is much wider than on the islands, and Athens has a number of French, Italian and Chinese restaurants.

The best restaurants in Athens are to be found in the Plaka/Syntagma/Omonia area and around the American embassy. The casual visitor should have no trouble finding a place to eat here, as very often waiters touting for custom will approach you in the street. Some tavernas have live bouzouki music; if this is the case, the waiter will let you know. Expect the evening to be a late one.

Plaka is the most popular place for dinner, with several restaurants offering moonlit views of the Acropolis, linen tablecloths and fresh flowers. However, this atmosphere does not come cheap. The charcoal-grilled meat served in the restaurants around Omonia Square is excellent and good value for money. Plaka also provides a good range of snack bars and stalls selling souvlaki or pizzas. The area around the Mitropolis Cathedral, just west of Syntagma Square, has several elegant brasseries. As it is common practice to eat the main meal in a restaurant and move to a café for coffee and dessert, one of the pleasures of a stay in Athens is to end the evening in Syntagma Square, eating ice cream, sipping coffee and watching the world go by.

Tourist information

Useful telephone numbers

Tourist Police 171
Police 100
Chemist (late-night roster) 107
Ambulance 150
Dentist (emergency) 6430001
Lost property 7705711
Property lost on public transport
    5230111

Doctor (emergency) 166
Doctor (late-night roster) 105
Information on bus services 142
Information on rail services 145
Directory enquiries Athens 131
Directory enquiries outside Athens
    132

Tourist Police

The Tourist Police offer a 24-hour service (tel 171) for dealing with complaints and giving information. Headquarters at 7 Syngrou St, tel 9239224.

National Tourist Organisation of Greece

Head office, Room 514, 2 Amerikis St. Tel 3223111/9. *Open 09.00–14.00 Mon–Fri. Occasional Sats.* An NTOG office is located inside the National Bank of Greece at 1 Karageorgi Servias St, tel 3222545. *Open 08.00–20.00 Mon–Fri; 08.00–14.00 Sat.* There is also an office at East Terminal, Eliniko Airport, tel 9799500. *Open 09.00–20.00 Mon–Sat.*

The NTOG publish a weekly booklet *The Week in Athens* listing a selection of events, theatres, cinemas, art galleries, shops, restaurants, nightclubs and hotels. Available free from NTOG offices.

Changing money

Banks are open *08.30–13.30 Mon–Fri.* On weekday evenings in the high season one bank may be open in the Syntagma Square area. There is a 24-hour exchange bureau at the East Terminal, Athens airport. In addition to the main Greek banks, the Commercial Bank of Greece and the National Bank of Greece, the following foreign banks and tourist agencies also offer exchange facilities:

American Express Tourist & Travel Office, 2 Ermou St. Tel 3602196
Bank of America, 39 Panepistimiou. Tel 3251900
Barclays Bank International Ltd, 15 Voukourestiou. Tel 3602196
Chase Manhattan, 87 Akti Miaouli. Tel 4527483
National Westminster Bank plc, 137–139 Filonos (cnr Fillellinon St). Tel 4528330
Williams & Glyn's International, 61 Akti Miaouli. Tel 4527483
Thomas Cook Ltd, 2 Karageorgi Servias St. Tel 3242281

The main post office in Syntagma Square is open *07.00–22.00 Mon–Sat; 09.00–20.00 Sun*. Standing counters are provided for writing and wrapping.
The OTE office, 15 Standiou St is open *09.00–22.00 Mon–Sat; 09.00–20.00 Sun*. Pay on completion of the call.

Shopping

For the discerning consumer, shopping in Athens can be an enjoyable and satisfying experience. Shops are generally open from *09.00–13.00, 16.30–20.00 Tue, Thur & Fri; 09.00–14.00 Mon, Wed & Sat*. Very confusing for anyone staying only a short time. Department stores and some smaller shops operate a complicated system of purchase requiring the services of up to three sales assistants. Domestic items can be purchased in the shops lining Ermou Street, west of Syntagma Square. The kiosks in the Syntagma/Omonia/Plaka area sell books in English, but the largest quality bookshop is Librairie Cacoulides, 25–29 Panepistimou Street, opposite the National Library. Stadiou has the widest variety of shops; Lambropoulos is the largest department store.
   Hand-made items make good souvenirs and are reasonably inexpensive in Greece. Anyone interested in buying embroidery, lace or textiles should first pay a visit to the Museum of Greek Popular Art, 17 Odos Kidathineon, tel 3213018. *Open 09.00–13.00 Tue–Sun. Closed Mon*. Everything on display is authentic and a standard can be set. The Monastiraki flea market is the best place to buy leather goods, kebab skewers, copper and brassware, antiques and secondhand items. There is a large market on *Sunday mornings*. Be prepared to bargain – it's expected!
   A wide selection of luxury goods can also be purchased in Athens. The best jewellery shops are along Venizelou and Voukourestiou. Gold and silver items are sold by weight with a small additional charge for craftsmanship. The fashion shops around Karageorgi Servias sell designer clothes at lower prices than in London, Paris or New York. Furs can be bought from numerous establishments in the Syntagma area. Check the quality of the stitching as well as the pelts; prudent shopping can result in the purchase of a lifetime.

Sights

The sights of Athens should not be missed, but are often very crowded. To avoid the crush, go early in the morning or late in the afternoon. Unfortunately, it is no longer possible to watch the sunset from the Acropolis as it closes at *19.00*.

Acropolis
Athens' most famous monument, the Parthenon, is located on a plateau at the top of this craggy limestone hill. Inhabited since Neolithic times, all earlier phases of building were destroyed by the Persians in 480BC.

The four main buildings now visible all date from the 5thC BC. Entrance to the Acropolis is via the Beulé Gate.

The six Doric columns of the Propylaea mark the entrance to the sacred site. The smaller temple to the right is dedicated to the Athena Nike. Built between 432 and 421BC, it has four Ionic columns at each end. The Parthenon, dedicated to the virgin-goddess Athena, was built between 447 and 438BC. The sculptures of the marble pediment were completed in 432BC. There are 46 columns in the outer colonnade and the remains of a Doric frieze. The Parthenon is a fantastic architectural achievement; not a single straight line was followed in its construction. The interior with its curving floor is now closed to visitors. The Erechtheion on the northern side was built over a 15-year period from 421BC, and is the site of a legendary contest between Poseidon and Athena. The roof of the south porch is supported by the famous Caryatids. *Open 08.00–19.00 Mon–Sat; 09.00–19.00 Sun. Closed Tue.*

Acropolis Museum

On the eastern side of the Acropolis, this museum exhibits finds from the area and contains one of the finest collections of Archaic and Classical sculpture. *Open 08.00–19.00 Mon–Sat; 09.00–19.00 Sun. Closed Tue.* Charge.

Ancient Agora

Situated under the northern wall of the Acropolis, the Agora, or market-place, was the centre of civic and commercial life in Athens. It was here in 399BC that the Athenian philosopher Socrates was tried and sentenced to death by the forcible drinking of hemlock. Many of the early buildings were destroyed by the Persians in 480BC, but considerable rebuilding took place. In AD267, much of the Agora was once again devastated by the Barbarians. The huge gallery known as the Stoa of Attalos was constructed in the 2ndC AD. It has been restored and converted into a museum to house the finds from the Agora excavations. Exhibits include marble sculptures, pottery and coins. Also on display are *ostraka*, sherds of pottery used in secret ballots, which bear the names of men who the Athenians wanted to exile. *Museum and site open 08.00–19.00 Mon–Sat; 09.00–19.00 Sun & hols. Closed Tue.* Charge.

Benaki Museum

Vasilissis Sofias St/Koumbari St. Tel 3611617. 10 mins' walk E of Syntagma Sq. Based on the private collection of Antonios Benakis, the museum houses a large collection of relics and memorabilia relating to the Greek War of Independence (1821–27) and the people who fought in it. Other exhibits include native costumes and some fine icons; one by the Cretan-born artist El Greco, who later lived in Spain, is believed to be a very early example of his work. There is a café on the roof. *Open 08.00–14.30 Tue–Sat. Closed Sun.* Charge.

Byzantine Museum

22 Vasilissis Sofias St. Tel 7211027. 20 mins' walk E of Syntagma Sq. The only museum in the world devoted exclusively to Byzantine art is housed in the 19thC Villa Ilissia built for the French Duchess de Plaisance. In three

of the rooms on the ground floor, the interiors of different styles of Byzantine church have been recreated, with frescos, sculptures, icons and iconostases. *Open 08.00–19.00 Tue–Sat; 09.00–19.00 Sun & hols. Closed Mon.* Charge.

Monastiraki Square

There is a colourful flea market held in the square on *Sunday mornings* with people selling all manner of second-hand items and handicrafts. Worth visiting at other times for souvenir hunting as the area abounds in good quality antique and specialist shops selling icons, jewellery and copperware. Goods bought in these shops will be of a higher standard than those available at the market. On the south side of the square is the former Turkish mosque. Built in 1759, it now houses the ceramic collection of the Museum of Greek Folk Art.

Mount Likavitos/Lykabettus

Take a number 23 bus from Kolonaki Sq. It is possible to walk to the summit, 250m above, but the funicular railway runs *until midnight*. This prominent hill on the Plain of Attica offers splendid views of Athens and the Acropolis. At the top is the attractive multi-domed 19thC Chapel of St George, with its whitewashed walls. There is also a pastry shop and a restaurant. An ideal setting for a romantic evening.

National Archaeological Museum

Tossitsa St/Patission St. Tel 8217717. This excellent museum contains treasures collected from all over Greece, spanning a period of some 6,000 years. The most precious finds from many of the island excavations have been sent here, including those from Delos, Santorini, Rhodes and Samos. If time allows it is a good idea to visit the museum twice, once before leaving for the islands and once on the return trip. *Open 08.00–19.00 Tue–Sat; 09.00–19.00 Sun. Closed Mon.* Charge.

National Gardens/Ethnikos Kipos

Just to the south-east of Syntagma Square, these lovely gardens are the perfect spot for a picnic or a tranquil hour away from the teeming streets of Athens. There are peacocks, a small lake and lots of swans. Until recent years the only public park in Athens, it is meticulously maintained. Open-air exhibitions of sculpture are often held here. The Zappeion Gardens are just south of the Zappeion, a semi-circular hall. Built in 1874, it serves as an exhibition centre and a backdrop for open-air plays.

Theatre of Dionysus

Located on the southern slopes of the Acropolis. This impressive theatre dedicated to the god Dionysus dates from c325BC and was designed to hold some 17,000 people on 64 tiers of seats. The original building phases date from the 6thC BC and utilised a natural hollow on the slopes. The 2ndC BC Stoa of Eumenes with its two-storey Doric colonnade links the Theatre of Dionysus with the Odeon of Herodus Atticus. Money for the construction of the Odeon was donated by a Roman consul in AD161 in memory of his wife. Smaller than the Theatre of Dionysus, the original seating capacity was between 5,000 and 6,000. Today concerts and plays are performed here during the summer.

Piraeus

Remarkably close to Athens, Piraeus is only 7km from the capital, a 25-minute journey by taxi or metro. A noisy, dirty town, for most people it is simply a place to catch the ferry and is almost unavoidable for most island-hoppers – a little touch of hell before entering paradise. Itinerant island-hoppers should linger on one of the 'cross-road' islands such as Paros or Syros, rather than returning to Piraeus, even if it means waiting an extra day or two for the relevant ferry to arrive. Nothing distorts the pleasant memories of an island holiday like a midnight arrival in Piraeus! It is also advisable to return to Athens to find a hotel, even if catching a ferry early in the morning. The airport is even nearer for those who wish to depart immediately.

It is easy to get lost amidst the cacophony and confusion which surrounds this, the largest port in Greece. Traffic roars past at a furious rate, signposts are virtually non-existent and there are few places to sit down. The streets are packed with ticket agencies and stalls selling cheap souvenirs. Piraeus has three main harbours, the Great Harbour, Zea Marina and Mikro Limano. Although the latter two are more attractive, particularly Mikro Limano, only the Great Harbour concerns the ferry traveller. For clarification, the Great Harbour is divided into the North, Middle and South harbours.

Getting there

From the airport
By bus

Greek buses rarely run to schedule. A taxi is the best bet if you are in a hurry to get to the port.

East Terminal No 101 every *20 mins 05.00–22.45*. Arrives Klissovis St, Possidonos Av. No 19 *every hour 08.00–20.00*. Arrives Akti Tselepi.

West Terminal Nos 107 and 109 run to Klissovis St, Possidonos Av.

From central Athens
By bus

Green Bus No 040 *every 10 mins* from Fillellinon St. *24-hour service*.

By metro

From Omonia or Monastiraki stations. Ask for a ticket to Piraeus – it is the last stop. The journey takes approx 25 minutes and is very efficient. However, the station in Piraeus is at the northern end of the harbour, and it can be a long walk to some of the ferries. Service operates from *05.00–23.00*.

By taxi

Taxi is the most efficient way to reach Piraeus and is quite inexpensive, especially if sharing. The driver will probably pick up other passengers, and unless otherwise instructed will drop you off at the north end of the harbour.

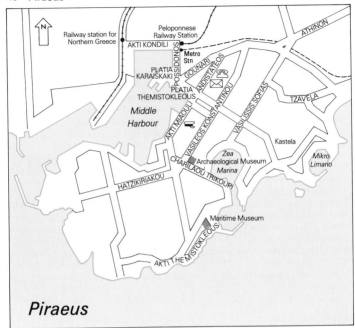

Piraeus

The ferry terminal

Buying tickets

Weekly ferry schedules can be obtained from the NTOG office inside the National Bank of Greece in Syntagma Square, Athens. These should be studied carefully. Most ships leave early in the morning, except those to Crete, which sail in the early evening.

Ticket agencies pack the streets of Piraeus. Blackboards on the pavement announce boats and destinations. Most agents employ the 'hard sell' method, accosting the unsuspecting tourist in the street. Do not be coerced into buying. Ticket prices are set by law, so there is little to choose between one agent and another. However, it is worth shopping around to find the boat offering the most direct route to your destination. Ticket agents are notorious – the boats they handle are always 'the biggest, the best, the fastest, and the only boat to sail on the day you require'. This is not necessarily the case. Agents sell tickets for certain shipping lines only; if there is another boat on a different line sailing the same day, the agent will not tell you. Read the schedule carefully, resist the fast

patter and check with several agencies, noting the departure time and
the name of the boat with each.

An alternative is to avoid the ticket agents altogether. Instead, select a
boat from the schedule and go directly to its berth half an hour before it is
due to sail. As ferries are grouped according to destination, there will often
be another boat there, taking the same route and departing at roughly
the same time. Enquire from the crew how long the journey will take; it
can vary by as much as three hours on longer voyages. Choose a ferry
accordingly, then buy a ticket on board. Buying tickets on board is a perfectly acceptable thing to do, though many officials and agents will deny it.

Finding the ferry/hydrofoil

Allow at least an hour to find and board the ferry/hydrofoil, longer if buying
tickets. The distance from the metro station to the departure point of the
Dodecanese ferries, for instance, is almost 1km. Even at the best of times
it is a hot, confusing walk; particularly unpleasant if carrying heavy
suitcases. The walk to Zea Marina, from which the hydrofoils to the Saronic
islands depart, is south-east of the Great Harbour, and even further from
the metro. Allowing enough time to walk at a comfortable pace is
imperative.

All departure times are clearly marked on blackboards posted in front of
each ship. Unfortunately the docks themselves are not signposted, and the
only way to find a particular ferry is to search for it by name. As ferries
are generally grouped according to destination, this should make the task
slightly easier. However, it is worth remembering that everything to do
with the ferries can be subject to change without notice.

A good tip when searching for a ferry is to be sure to walk on the inside
of the harbour fence rather than on the pavement just outside it. Although
the pavement is less congested and seems the quicker route, there are
very few gates in the fence. Even though you may be directly in front of
your ship, it might take another 25 minutes to reach it if there is not a
convenient opening nearby.

Waiting for the ferry

Piraeus is not a particularly pleasant place in which to kill time, especially
for women travelling alone at night. There are few public benches, and
cafés tend to be unwelcoming. There is a tourist information bureau in Zea
Marina (tel 4135716), *open mornings only*, but no tourist office in the main
port. If waiting for several hours it is a good idea to explore the town.

The streets behind the harbour, especially at the northern end, are
primarily given over to food shops. Buy large wedges of cheese, hunks
of salami and pastries to supplement the poor-quality food available on the
ferries. Other useful items such as torches and corkscrews can also be
found in the area. Nuts, figs and other dried fruits are sold from stalls on
the quay, close to the ferries.

Platia Themistokleous is the largest square in Piraeus, located next to
the Middle Harbour. Platia Karaiskaki, at the north end of the harbour, is

fairly seedy but does have some benches on which to rest. Behind Aktimiaouli Street are several small, shady squares which serve as a refuge from the midday sun.

Anyone interested in ships will be intrigued by the comings and goings of the large container and general cargo vessels in the Great Harbour. The sleek hydrofoils which run to the Saronic islands are moored in Zea Marina. The attractive crescent-shaped harbour of Mikro Limano, also known as Tourkoliamano, provides a marina for yachts and sailing craft which seem to have come from all over the world. There are some excellent seafood restaurants and plenty of waterside cafés here. Both Zea Marina and Mikro Limano are a considerable distance from the Great Harbour. It is easier to reach them by taking the inland road, rather than following the coast.

Sights

Archaeological Museum

Charilaou Trikoupi. Tel 4521598. A wide range of exhibits from the Classical, Hellenistic and Roman periods, including a fine statue, 'Hermes of Kifissia'. *Open 09.00–15.00 Mon–Sat; 09.00–14.00 Sun. Closed Tue.* Charge.

Maritime Museum

Akti Themistokleous. Tel 4516822. Also known as the Shipping Museum. Located on Zea Marina, it displays many interesting items relating to the turbulent naval history of Greece, including models and photographs. *Open 09.00–12.00 Tue–Sat; 10.00–12.00 Sun. Closed Mon.* Charge.

Crete

Crete

General character

Crete is the most southerly Greek island and very popular with tourists. It is the only island many visitors see, and blessed as it is with long hours of sunshine, good beaches, scenic variety and impressive archaeological sites, the choice is a good one. It is, however, no undiscovered paradise. In the past few years tour operators have moved in by the hundred and high-rise hotels are much in evidence.

To enjoy Crete to the full, two things are necessary – plenty of time and independent transport. Fly/drive holiday schemes are a good idea, as car rental, although readily available, can be expensive. Package tours, too, make

sense, as many of the villas and hotels offered are in prime locations. Two weeks should allow enough time for exploring. Anyone in search of privacy and a bit of independence should visit major attractions during off-peak hours only, (late afternoon is ideal) or visit Crete out of season, when the crowds have left and even the most popular beaches are wonderfully deserted. Crete's fine weather ensures swimming is possible through to early October; maybe even later on the sheltered southern coast. January and February are excellent months for sightseeing, but bathing then is only for the hardy.

As with most of the popular islands, tourist facilities are well developed. Several buses daily connect the major

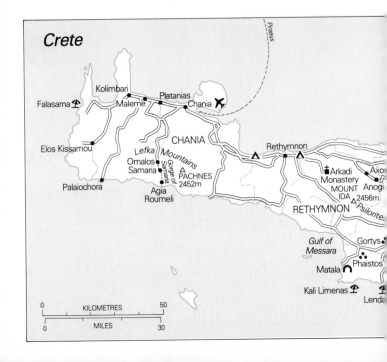

Alternative names   Kriti
Population   502,165
Area   8,312sq km
Area tel codes   Heraklion 081,
Chania 0821, Agios Nikolaos 0841,
Rethymnon 0831
Tourist Police   Heraklion, tel
238100; Chania, tel 24477
NTOG offices: Heraklion (tel
222487/8), 1 Xanthoudidou St.
*Open May–Oct 07.30–19.30
Mon–Sat; 07.30–14.00 Sun & hols.
Nov–Apr 08.00–14.00.* Chania (tel
26426), 6 Akti Tombazi. *Opening
hours similar to Heraklion.*
Harbour Police   Heraklion, tel
282529; Chania, tel 25037
Distance from Piraeus   174
nautical miles/12 hours (direct
service). Up to 22 hours if via other
islands

Travel information

By air
International airports at Heraklion &
Chania serving Europe & the
Middle East. Heraklion: 6–7 flights
daily to/from Athens. Chania: 4–5
flights daily to/from Athens. 4 flights
weekly to Mykonos & Santorini to/
from Heraklion, also daily flight to/
from Rhodes.

By ferry
1–2 daily between Piraeus and
Heraklion & Chania. Frequent
services from Agios Nikolaos to
Rhodes via Karpathos & Kassos. 1
weekly to/from Santorini, Milos,
Sifnos, Serifos, Kythnos. Also
frequent cruiseships.

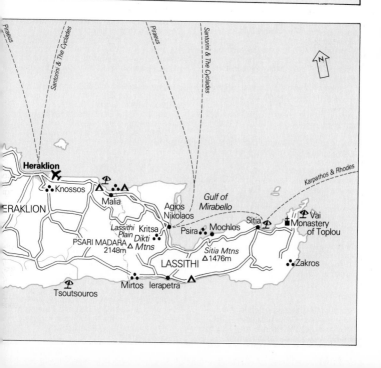

towns along the northern coast, and roads are in good repair. Food is of a high standard, with shellfish often imported from smaller islands, and reasonably priced. Tours, excursions, and watersports facilities are abundant, and most resorts cater very adequately for children. Many of the beaches at these resorts shelve gently and are therefore suitable for toddlers.

Regional features

The largest of the Greek islands, Crete is 257km long and 58km wide. Divided into four main regions, the prefectures of Chania, Rethymnon, Heraklion and Lassithi, each of which has its own capital town. The interior is dominated by four mountain groups. In the east, the Sitia Mountains rise to a height of 1,476m. The highest peak of the Dikti Mountains in Lassithi province is Psari Madara, 2,148m. High in the Dikti Mountains and completely surrounded by them is the Lassithi Plain. Covering an area of some 80sq km, this fertile plateau dotted with windmills and trees is an unexpected sight. In the centre of the island, Mount Ida, the highest peak of the Psilorites, rises to a height of 2,456m. The Lefka Mountains in the west occupy much of the southern part of Chania province. Steep and rugged, the impressive Gorge of Samaria cuts through to the sea. The valleys surrounding the coast are highly cultivated, producing citrus fruit, melons, peaches and grapes. It is said Crete produces 90% of Greece's currants, as well as substantial quantities of wine and olive oil.

Attractive seaside resorts on Crete include Kolimbari, Maleme and Platanias just west of Chania, and Paliochora on the southern coast (227km SW of Heraklion). Interesting inland villages include Elos Kissamou in Chania prefecture (107km SW of Heraklion). Set amongst plane and chestnut trees, the village is the site of an October Chestnut Fair. The mountain villages of Anogia and Axos near Rethymnon retain their traditional flavour.

History

The first inhabitants settled in the eastern part of Crete around 6000BC. The coming of the Bronze Age around 2600BC saw the development of the Early Minoan culture, characterised by its distinctive pottery and the use of copper tools. Towns, palaces, temples and workshops were constructed during the Middle Minoan period from c1900BC, but an earthquake in 1700BC resulted in almost total destruction. The period from 1650–1400BC saw the flowering of the Minoan culture. Links were established with Asia Minor, Africa and the rest of Greece. The palaces were reconstructed and lavishly decorated, and Cretans were held in high esteem for their knowledge and seafaring skills. With the eruption of a volcano on Santorini around 1450BC the palaces were again destroyed, and only Knossos was rebuilt. By the end of the millenium, the Minoan empire was of little consequence.

A series of invasions then began which were to last until the 20thC. First came the Dorians, then the Romans, who in 67BC established a capital at Gortys. In AD961 the island was recaptured from the Saracens by the Byzantine leader, Nikephoros Phokas. In the 13thC the Genoese sold the island to the Venetians who remained here for over 400 years. This was a time of prosperity, when the great Venetian fortresses and public buildings were constructed. Art and literature flourished. The Turks invaded Heraklion in 1669, and were to rule for the next 200 years until the island became part of Greece in 1913. Captured by the Germans in 1941, Crete was eventually reunited with the rest of Greece at the conclusion of World War II.

Ports & towns

Heraklion/Iraklion

Although ferries also call at Chania, Heraklion, with its international airport and close proximity to Crete's most famous landmark, Knossos, is the first stop for most visitors. A noisy, modern city, the largest on Crete, there is little temptation to linger. Nightlife is good, as is the variety of restaurants, but after visiting Knossos and the excellent Archaeological Museum, the majority of tourists leave for more attractive spots. Heraklion's fine Venetian remains are obscured by tourist shops and hotels; the fortress itself is surrounded by modern buildings of a particularly graceless style.

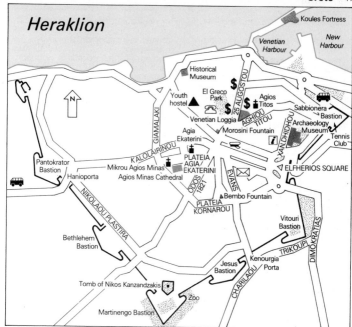

Heraklion

Koules Fortress

New Harbour

Venetian Harbour

Historical Museum

El Greco Park

Youth hostel

Agios Titos

Venetian Loggia

Morosini Fountain

Sabbionera Bastion

Archaeology Museum

Tennis Club

ELFHERIOS SQUARE

Agia Ekaterini

GIAMALAKI

KALOLAIRINOU

Mikrou Agios Minas

PLATEIA AGIA/ EKATERINI

AGHIOU TITOU

VANDHIDHOU

Pantokrator Bastion

Hanioporta

Agios Minas Cathedral

ODOS 1821

EVANS

Bembo Fountain

PLATEIA KORNAROU

Vitouri Bastion

NIKOLAOU PLASTIRA

Bethlehem Bastion

Jesus Bastion

Kenourgia Porta

TRIKOUPI

DIMOKRATIAS

Tomb of Nikos Kanzandzakis

CHARILAOU

Zoo

Martinengo Bastion

Activity centres around Elefherios Square (just south of the NTOG office and the Archaeological Museum) and the Morosini Fountain. Constructed in 1628 and encircled by outdoor cafés and restaurants, it is also known as the Lion Fountain – its 14thC lions were taken from an earlier monument. On a hot summer's evening it is almost obscured by the crowds of young people and tourists strolling happily around the tiny square.

Sights

Archaeology Museum

Xanthou Dhidhou. Tel 282305. Second in importance only to the Athens Museum, this museum houses a superb collection of Minoan items. It is best to visit the museum before going to any of the Minoan sites as it clarifies and illuminates the period. Exhibits include some fine frescos from Knossos, jewellery, ceramics and stone work gathered from all the Minoan palaces. The famous 16thC BC statuette of the snake goddess is also displayed here.

Open 08.00–19.00 Tue–Sat, 09.00–19.00 Sun; 08.00–11.00 Mon. Charge.

Greek Orthodox churches

The church of Agia Ekaterini (St Catherine), in the square of the same name, was built in 1555 and altered in the 17thC. In the Basilica are six icons by the 16thC Cretan artist Mikalis Damaskinos. Basilica open *10.00–13.00, 17.00–19.00.* Charge. The large 19thC cathedral of Agios Minas is also in the Plateia Agia Ekaterini together with its attractive chapel Mikrou Agios Minas. The church of Agios Titos in Plateia Agios Titos was originally founded in the Byzantine era, but subsequently destroyed by an earthquake. The present church built in 1872, was originally a mosque. Today it houses the head of St Titos, the island's patron saint.

Historical Museum

The interior of a traditional Cretan home has been recreated in this museum. Folk art exhibits include traditional local fabrics and costumes, beautiful embroidery and wood carvings. Also relics from the island's Byzantine, Venetian and Turkish periods. *Open 09.00–13.00, 15.00–17.30 Mon–Sat. Closed Sun.* Charge.

Koules Fortress

Known by its Turkish name Koules, only a shell of this 16thC Venetian castle now remains. It affords a commanding view of the city. *Open 07.30–18.30 Mon–Sat; 09.00–14.00 Sun.* Charge.

Venetian buildings

The Loggia, on Augostou St, is a reconstruction of the original 16thC building destroyed during the last war. It stands opposite the bus stop for Knossos. The Martinengo Bastion encloses the tomb of the Greek author Nikos Kazandzakis who died in 1957. There is a good view of the town from here. The 13thC Basilica of St Mark has been converted into a hall used for concerts and lectures.

Venetian walls

Massive and imposing, the walls which surround the city are up to 29m thick in some places. Along the walls are 12 small bastions and three gateways, the main city entrances being at Hanioporta and Kenourgia Porta.

Agios Nikolaos

69km SE of Heraklion. Capital of the Lassithi prefecture, Agios Nikolaos is the prettiest town on Crete, popular with visitors throughout the year. Built on the western shore of Mirabello Bay, the most interesting feature is the lake in the centre of the town. Lake Voulismeni, 60m deep, is connected to the sea by a narrow man-made channel. Discos and tavernas line the quayside and the town is especially known for its watersports facilities.

Sights

Archaeological Museum

Off Paleologou St. Tel 22462. The museum contains some fine terracottas and many finds from the excavations at Kritsa, Mirtos and Mochlos nearby. *Open 08.30–19.00 Mon–Sat; 09.00–14.00 Sun. Closed Tue.* Charge.

Chania/Hania

150 km NW of Heraklion. Crete's second largest town is a blend of traditional and modern architecture. Several Venetian and Ottoman buildings cluster near the port, with modern suburbs spreading out behind. Good air and sea connections with the mainland make Chania a popular tourist town. It is also the commercial centre of western Crete and the island's capital. The large cruciform marketplace, unique in Greece, bustles with activity. Stalls overflow with the fresh fruit which grows so abundantly further south. Several distinct districts make up the old town. The Topanas Quarter to the left of the harbour, is characterised by its lovely old mansions and a maze of criss-crossing streets. The Kastelli is the site of the Venetian citadel. Parts of the original 14thC walls can still be seen. Recent excavations in this area have revealed remains of Kydonia, a Late Minoan site. There is a small zoo in the attractive public gardens. Designed in 1870, they are located in the south-eastern part of town. Along the waterfront, which was much featured in the film 'Zorba the Greek', are the Customs House, the Port Police and the Tourist Information office.

Sights

Archaeological Museum

Halidon St. Tel 24418. The museum is housed in the largest Venetian church on Crete, St Francis. Displays finds from several excavations in western Crete including Kydonia. Neolithic and Early Minoan pottery, coins, weapons and ornaments. *Open 09.30–16.00 Mon–Sat; 10.00–15.00 Sun & hols. Closed Tue.* Charge.

Greek Orthodox churches

The cathedral of Trimartiri (Three Martyrs) in the Evraiki Quarter was built in 1860. The church of Agii Anargiri in the Splazania Quarter contains Byzantine frescos. Nearby is the large church of Agios Nikolaos built by the Venetians.

Halepa Quarter

On the eastern side of the town. The house of the Greek statesman Elefherios Venizelos stands in the Halepa Quarter. A statue of this famous Cretan is in a nearby park. The 19thC church of St Magdalene, built in Russo-Byzantine style, is also located in this district.

Naval Museum

On the western side of the Venetian harbour. Exhibits many items commemorating Greek seafaring history including models and photographs. *Open daily 10.00–12.00, 17.00–20.00.* Charge.

Ottoman buildings

The Mosque of the Janissaries, built next to the Venetian harbour in 1645, now

Chania

Lighthouse

Venetian Harbour

N

Naval Museum

Mosque of the Janissaries

TOPANAS

AKTI TOMBAZI

KASTELLI

Kydonia

San Rocco Church

Agios Nikolaos

Agii Anargiri

Archaeological Museum

EVIRAIKI

Cathedral of Trimatiri

HALEPA

Market

VENIZELOU

HALIDON

GIANARI

$

$

SKALIDI

KISSAMOU

KIDONIAS

APOKORONOU

Public gardens

Zoo

houses the Chania Branch of the National Tourist Organisation of Greece. The lighthouse which stands at the entrance to the harbour was also built by the Turks.

Venetian buildings

The church of St Francis was built by the Venetians in the 16thC; the little church of St Rocco in the 17thC. The outer ramparts of the city were completed in 1590. Construction of the harbour and breakwater also dates back to the Venetian occupation.

Rethymnon/Rethimno

78km W of Heraklion. Lying slightly off the tourist track, Rethymnon receives fewer visitors than Crete's larger towns and is more pleasant as a result. High-rise hotels are concentrated to the right of the harbour along the broad sandy beach, leaving the old town remarkably unspoilt. Numerous waterside cafés twinkle with candlelight at night. The lanes below the fortress are narrow and

gloomy. A good place to buy hand-made sandals, local Cretan embroidery and other souvenirs, but easy to get lost in the maze. Expect a long walk from the port to the bus station; if carrying heavy suitcases, hail a taxi from the square near the public gardens.

Sights

Archaeology Museum

Housed in the early 17thC Venetian Loggia. The museum displays a large collection of coins. Also pottery, weapons and jewellery from local excavations. *Open 09.00–15.30 Mon–Sat, 10.00–15.00 Sun. Closed Tue.* Charge.

Arimondi Fountain

At the foot of the main street, this fountain was erected by the Venetians in 1629. The water trickles from the mouths of four beasts separated by four Classical pillars.

Fortezza

The Great Gate leads to this impressive Venetian fortress. Built in 1574, it is sited on a promontory in the northern part of the town. *Open 07.30–20.00 Tue–Fri; 09.00–16.30 Sat–Mon*. Charge.

Nerantzes Mosque

Formerly a Franciscan church, this mosque with its attractive minaret is located in the centre of Rethymnon.

Public park

Dimitrakaki St. The park, once a Turkish cemetery, contains an aviary and a small zoo. It is also the location of an annual Cretan wine festival *15–30 July*. The plane trees provide welcome shade.

Accommodation & eating

Crete has a phenomenal number of hotels and guest-houses; mostly modern and with good facilities. Occasionally, as in Rethymnon, old Venetian mansions have been converted into pensions. Probably less comfortable than the modern purpose-built hotels, they are full of character and charm. Four hotels in Heraklion – the first stop for most visitors – include the A class **Astoria** (tel 286462), the B class **Kastro** (tel 284185), the C class **El Greco** (tel 281071) and the C class **Ivi** (tel 289039). Three hotels in Chania are the A class **Kydon** (tel 26190), the B class **Porto Veneziano** (tel 29311) and the C class **Kriti** (tel 21881). In Agios Nikolaos accommodation ranges from the Luxury class **Mirabello Village** (tel 28400) to the C class **Pergola** (tel 28152). In Rethymnon try the B class **Brascos** (tel 23721), the C class **Valari** (tel 22236) or the D class **Acropole** (tel 29774).

Restaurants and tavernas are equally plentiful, in all price ranges and qualities. For possibly the best seafood in Greece, walk into one of the waterside tavernas in the resort of Reythmnon, where the visitor can watch caiques unloading the main course while choosing a starter from the menu.

Sights

Arkadi Monastery

97km SW of Heraklion. Accessible from Rethymnon (23km SE). Surrounded by olive groves on the lower slopes of Mount Ida, the monastery was founded in the 11thC. The present building dates mainly from the 17thC, but the fine west front, combining elements of Baroque and Classical architecture, was completed in 1587. The monastery has become a symbol of national independence, following an event in November 1866. The abbott of the monastery resisted the Turkish invasion, and instead of surrendering, took the decision to blow up part of the building. Nearly 1,000 people died. An annual festival commemorates the event every *9 November*.

Gorge of Samaria

SW of Heraklion. Cutting deeply through the Levka Mountains. The longest gorge in Europe, this narrow ravine with its small winding stream runs for 18km through some beautiful, wild country. It extends south from the village of Omalos (37km S of Chania) to Agia Roumeli on the coast and must be explored on foot. The walk takes 7–8 hours, but shorter tours are arranged by several tourist agencies in Chania and Heraklion. It is a fascinating, solitary place, the only region where the *kri-kri* (wild goat) is still found in its natural habitat on Crete. Patrols are stationed at four key points along the route to advise independent walkers.

Gortys/Gortyn

45km S of Heraklion. In Roman times the capital of Crete and the North African province of Cyrenaica. Excavations have revealed an extensive archaeological site. Outstanding remains include the 2ndC AD Praetorium, the residence of the Roman governor and a Nymphaeum, or shrine of the Nymphs, also dating from the 2ndC AD. One of the most remarkable finds is the Code of Gortyn Law. Inscribed on stone tablets in Dorian dialect in the 5thC BC, these were later incorporated into the Roman Odeon built in AD100. To the north, across the stream, are the remains of a theatre and the ancient Acropolis. *Open 08.00–19.00 Mon–Sat, 09.00–19.00 Sun*.

Knossos

5km S of Heraklion. The capital of the Minoan kingdom, Knossos is one of the most famous archaeological sites in Greece. A 20-minute bus ride from Heraklion, the bus stop is outside the Venetian Loggia. A guide book and map of the site are essential as it is always crowded and the ruins are extensive.

The site was first occupied in Neolithic times around 6000BC. The first palace was constructed around 1950BC during the Middle Minoan period, and was subsequently destroyed by a great disaster around 1700BC. The palace was rebuilt at the time which saw the flowering of the Minoan culture. It is the remains from this period which are seen at the site today. Three storeys high and built on a low hill, the palace must have been an impressive sight, with its splendid architecture, monumental staircases and beautiful, coloured frescos decorating the walls of most of the main rooms. In the throne room, the alabaster throne is flanked by griffins, painted in deep ochre and terracotta. As well as the maze of royal apartments, workshops and stores have also been discovered. Many of the stores containing the large earthenware *pithoi*, used for storing oil. The palace is entered via the west porch. *Open 08.00–19.00 Mon–Sat, 09.00–19.00 Sun.* Charge.

Malia
34km E of Heraklion. Provincial Minoan palace, larger than that at Phaistos, but not as grand. As at Knossos, the original palace dates from the Middle Minoan period, around 1900BC. It was, however, subsequently destroyed and rebuilt over the centuries. Grand apartments and domestic quarters were constructed around a large central court. There are also numerous granaries and store-rooms. A 15-minute walk north-east from the palace leads to the cemetery of Chryssolakkos. The famous gold bee pendant, now in the Archaeological Museum in Heraklion was found here.

Matala
70km SW of Heraklion. The cliffs here are honeycombed with caves which found fame in the 1960s when hippies set up residence in them. Overlooking a sandy bay, the area is still popular with young people and the tourists who come to photograph them, though most people now sleep on the beach.

Monastery of Toplou
130km E of Heraklion. On the north-eastern tip of the island, halfway between the towns of Sitia and Zakros, where a Minoan palace is currently under excavation. A rough track leads to this splendidly sited 14thC monastery, which also lets rooms to visitors. Founded in 1365, the monastery houses the famous icon 'Lord, Thou Art Great' painted by the Cretan master Ioannis Kornaros in 1770.

Phaistos/Festos
62km SW of Heraklion. Beyond Gortys, overlooking the Gulf of Messara on the south-west coast of the island. The site of Crete's second major Minoan palace.

As on the other sites, the remains of two distinct palaces can be identified in successive phases. The first from 1900–1700BC the second from 1650–1450BC when it was destroyed in the Late Minoan period. The West Court and Theatral area, with its rows of tiered seats, are part of the old palace. The monumental entrance with its grand stairway facing the West Court, belong to the more recent palace which was built around a central, paved court. *Open 08.00–19.00 Mon–Sat, 09.00–19.00 Sun.* Charge.

Beaches

Crete is ringed by sandy beaches which are amongst the finest in Greece. Although it is said the southern and eastern coasts are warm enough for bathing all year round, this is for the adventurous only. Miles of open sand stretch east and west from Heraklion. The other major towns of Agios Nikolaos, Chania and Rethymnon all have sandy beaches nearby. Falasarna (197km W of Heraklion) on the island's western tip is excellent. Sandy coves on the southern shore, including Kali Limenes, Lendas and Tsoutsouros, can be reached on foot or by jeep, but are more easily accessible by boat. Vai, the most photographed beach on Crete (179km E of Heraklion) is a beautiful crescent of sand backed by palm trees on the eastern tip of the island.

Sports

Fishing
No licence is required to fish from the shores of Crete, which are particularly suited to this sport. Motorboats and equipment can be hired from most resorts. Deepsea excursions are, however, rare.

Mountain climbing
The Greek Alpine Club has established mountain bases at Lefka Ori Kalergi (altitude 1,680m) where there is a ski lift, and Lefka Ori Volikas (altitude 1,480m), tel (0821) 24647. Also at Psiloritis Prinos (altitude 1,100m), tel (081) 287110.

Snorkelling
Masks, flippers and equipment can be bought in most large towns. Spear fishing is legal, but it is illegal to take underwater pictures. This law is particularly enforced around the fascinating submerged ruins off the island of Psira in the Gulf of Mirabello, near to Mochlos.

Waterskiing
Most resorts provide equipment for this popular sport; para-gliding facilities may also be available. In Chania contact the Chania Maritime Club, tel 24387.

Tennis
Many resorts and large hotels have tennis courts. Two clubs on Crete are the Heraklion Tennis Club, Beaufort Av, tel 283015 and the Chania Tennis Club, Dimokratis Av, tel 21293.

Specialities

Wines & spirits
Red wines from Crete include Castello, Saint Antonio, and Mantiko which is dry. Minos Palace is a dry rosé. Vilana is a medium white, Regalo a dry white. There are white and rosé varieties of Logado, and Minos has a large selection of reds and whites of varying qualities, also brandy and ouzo. Rakee (raki) is a lethal-looking clear spirit made on Crete. Sip it slowly.

The Cyclades

Amorgos

General character

An isolated, brooding fortress of an island, Amorgos was used in Roman times to house exiled prisoners. A surprise, then, to sail into the lovely port of Katapola; a picturesque town built in true Cycladian style. Tiny, domed chapels guard each promontory while houses and churches nestle cosily around the curving bay.

The walk from Katapola to the ancient capital of Chora Amorgos is hot and dusty and should not be attempted in the midday sun. A battered school bus makes the journey twice a day, but no one seems to know exactly when or where from. A call to book a taxi might lead to a ride in a pick-up, a shambling estate car already full of other people and their animals, or occasionally, a private journey in the Dodge school bus itself.

Amorgos is a delightful place, snug and secret from most visitors, who stick safely to the neighbouring islands of Paros and Naxos. Little English is spoken and concessions to tourism are minimal. This lack of popular appeal is indeed its greatest asset. Although in July and August, Germans, Scandinavians and vacationing Greeks crowd into the island, outside this time the ambience is distinctly native.

A friendly, outgoing population and an ancient capital of outstanding beauty make a stay on Amorgos something to remember.

Regional features

The most easterly of the Cyclades, this rocky, mountainous island snakes through the Aegean like a grey serpent. The large car ferries take one hour to connect the main port of Katapola in the south with the secondary port of Egiali further north; when winds are high, communications are often non-existent. Overland, a path running along a high mountain ridge connects the two ports; it is said a bus occasionally attempts the journey, but no local could confirm this.

Amorgos abounds in local wildlife; lizards are everywhere, and snakes should be kept watch for. If well equipped (with sturdy shoes, food and water) the island is ideal walking country,

Island chain	Cyclades
Population	1,720
Area	121sq km
Area tel code	0285
Tourist Police	tel 71210
Harbour Police	tel 71259
Distance from Piraeus	12 hours

Travel information

By ferry
1–2 weekly from Piraeus in summer; 3 weekly in winter. 1 weekly to Astipalea, Kalymnos, Kos, Nissiros, Tilos, Symi, Rhodes; 2–3 weekly to Naxos & Paros. In high season possible day excursions from Naxos; 1–3 weekly to Donoussa, Iraklia, Koudonissi, Schinoussa.

though the rugged terrain and lack of good beaches make it less suitable for those with children.

Ports & towns

Katapola

Charming harbour tucked between two promontories, appearing to be three separate hamlets linked by a pine-shaded promenade. The town's commercial centre is located in the area around the quay. Most tavernas, food shops and bars are here, there is also a yacht supply station. Facing squarely out to sea is a handsome, silver-domed church. From here a lazy track fringed with palms and flowers begins the ascent to Chora Amorgos on the hill. On the far side of the harbour is a residential area with attractive pensions straddling the hillside. The town beach is near here.

Chora Amorgos

8km E of Katapola. A pretty, white labyrinthine town, perched on a high plateau. To one side, terraced slopes lead down to the sea; on the other, an unbroken line of perfectly formed windmills dominate the landscape. Each turn of the narrow, cobbled streets, empty of cars, reveals a small chapel or a house with richly painted doors. There are very few shops – a couple of stores sell basic items. The tiny main square consists of a bank, a chapel and a sophisticated café. The OTE office, a post office and a small archaeological museum containing neo-Classical remains are located nearby. Enquire in the café for the man with the key and expect a long wait.

Egiali/Aegiali
18km NE of Katapola. Tranquil harbour tucked under the cliffs. The ferry docks at a rocky wharf and would seem to provide the main activity; there is little nightlife. Houses are attractive, with brightly painted balconies and there is a sheltered sandy beach.

Accommodation & eating

Chora Amorgos as yet has no hotels (though one is under construction) and only a few rooms to let. Egiali has the only listed hotel: **Mike's** (tel 71247) C class; there are also rooms to let in the town. The accommodation in Katapola's guest-houses and pensions is very good value for money. Most of them are clean and spacious, with pretty decorative

detail. Eating is best in Katapola, although more than half the bars and tavernas are only open from mid-July to the end of August. The only proper café in Chora Amorgos is run by a journalist from Athens. It serves tasty toasted sandwiches and filter coffee to the accompaniment of soaring classical music.

Sights

Hozovoitissa Monastery
9km E of Katapola. Lying just below Chora Amorgos (but still a 20-minute walk down the cliff path) is this breath-taking monastery, founded in 1088. The white buildings cascade down the cliff like buttermilk poured from a pitcher. Inside, the rooms are long, narrow and very dark. The miraculous icon of the Virgin is housed here, together with scrolls, parchments and sacred relics.

Minoa
1.5km SW of Katapola. On the hill above the port is the site of the ancient city of Minoa. Remains preserved include a gymnasium and a temple of Apollo.

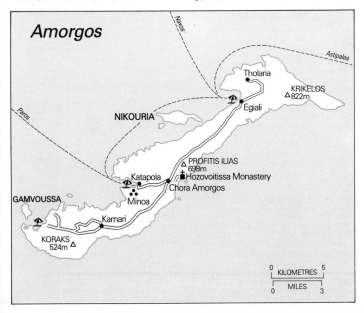

AntiParos

General character

Although many consider AntiParos
merely a satellite of Paros, its larger
neighbour, this pretty sweet-smelling
island has a solid personality of its own.
As Paros itself becomes more and more
popular some visitors are heading
straight to AntiParos for its uncrowded
beaches and an air of tranquillity which
Paros often lacks. Even on this more
remote isle, however, tourism is
increasing and life is lived to a disco beat.
AntiParos is young, vibrant, and with
cheap rooms and an excellent campsite,
likely to stay that way. Tranquillity
comes in the form of long walks and
good beaches, all within easy reach of
the main town.

The 40-minute boat ride from Paros is
a surprisingly choppy one. Caiques call
first at the attractive port of AntiParos
Town, then continue on to Spileon. A
day excursion allows ample time to
explore both, but leaves little time for
swimming. Bathing is a major attraction
on AntiParos.

Regional features

Separated from Paros by a narrow
channel, the two islands were joined
together in prehistoric times. Most of the
beaches on AntiParos are blessed with
fine golden sand; if one does not appeal,
try another – the west coast is less
explored than the east. The island's only
road runs along the east coast from the
town to Spileon, the stalactite cave on
the slopes of Mount Aghios Ilias.
Suitable only for pedestrians and
motorcycles (although there are plans to
tarmac it) the road is hot and dusty so
take water along.

Ports & towns

AntiParos Town

Pine trees line the harbour of this pretty
port, the only settlement on the island.
A windmill (now a disco), a whitewashed chapel and a roofless arched
building of local stone make up the
skyline. The harbour's crystal-clear
waters reveal hundreds of tiny fish
swimming just below the surface. Most
of the village rambles along a main street

Island chain   Cyclades
Population   635
Area   35sq km
Area tel code   0284
Tourist Police   tel 61202
Harbour Police   tel 21240 (Paros)

Travel information

Not accessible directly from
Piraeus.
By ferry
Caique service 1–3 times daily
during summer from Parikia on the
island of Paros, journey time approx
40 mins. Occasional caique service
from Pounta on Paros in the high
season. In winter, negotiate with
local fishermen.

which ends in a central square dominated by a large church. To one side of
the square is a post office and a bank.
The bank is open *Mon, Wed & Fri
08.00–12.00.* Further along are the ruins
of an ancient fortress. No cars are
allowed on the island, although in July
and August motorcycles can be hired
from the house behind the windmill.

Accommodation & eating

AntiParos Town has three listed hotels
plus rooms to rent. Hotels are the C class
Chrissi Akti (tel 61206), the **Mantallena**
(tel 61220) and the **Anargyos** (tel
61204), both D class. Due to the island's
increasing popularity, it is best to book
in advance if arriving in July and August.
A good, shaded campsite is situated
only a few hundred metres from
AntiParos' nudist beach. Most of the
island's young population seem more
interested in drinking; bars equal if not
exceed the number of tavernas.

Sights

Spileon

SW of AntiParos Town. Approx 2 hours'
walk or a short caique journey. Situated
on the slopes of Mount Aghios Ilias,
which rises to 229m, the cave is a hot
20-minute climb uphill. Teams of mules
meet most caiques and visitors are

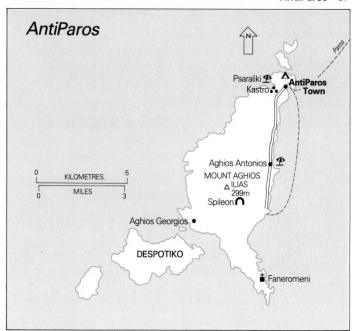

AntiParos

Psaraliki
Kastro
AntiParos Town

Aghios Antonios
MOUNT AGHIOS
ILIAS
299m
Spileon

Aghios Georgios

DESPOTIKO

Faneromeni

Paros

0 — KILOMETRES — 5
0 — MILES — 3

advised to take advantage of this service, even though it is a bit pricey (be warned – tour operators in Paros mention neither the mules or the steep price). At the entrance to the cave is a simple whitewashed chapel. Descent is by narrow steps to a depth of 70m, though the cave is actually much deeper.

Inside, all is gloomy and spooky. Impressive 3m long stalactites look like gigantic icicles, and the central chamber is arched and vaulted like a cathedral. Graffiti, both modern and old, covers the walls; Lord Byron is said to have left his mark here. Bring rubber-soled shoes and a torch. The trek back down the hill offers stunning views of neighbouring isles, with a welcoming taverna and rocky beach at the bottom. Cave *open most mornings*. Charge.

Beaches

There are half a dozen good beaches within easy walking distance of AntiParos Town. As well as the town

beach, the east coast provides three sandy coves all in a row. At Psaraliki Beach there are windsurfers, pedal boats, canoes and motorbikes for hire. The northern 'hook' of AntiParos, where the campsite is situated, has more good beaches, including a wonderful sandy dune-backed strip where nudists congregate. At the south-western end of the island, overlooking the islet of Despotiko is a beach with a taverna.

Satellite islands

Despotiko
SW of AntiParos. A windswept islet just 1km from Aghios Georgios on AntiParos, provides the best fishing the area offers. Snapper and mullet are the prime catches. Hire fishing boats from Scopas Travel Agency in Paros (tel 0284 22300) or enquire at Captain Yanni's office by the square in AntiParos.

Delos

General character

Excursion boats leave Mykonos daily for
Delos. The sea is often rough and the
wind chilly. Travellers are advised to take
along a sweater. This sacred island is a
charming place to visit. The impressive
site extends for over 1,200m and in
spring is covered with brightly coloured
wild flowers. In summer, the grassy
spaces between the ruins look like a
patchwork in various shades of yellow
and green, leading all the way to Mount
Kynthos. For the amateur, four hours is
sufficient to touch upon everything of
interest, but a map is essential for
clarification. Those who wish to study
Delos in more detail will have to return
again, for there is almost no
accommodation and the boat leaves
promptly. In the high season the crowds
can be enormous; if this is the case,
begin touring at one of the outlying sites
such as the Gymnasium in the north-
western corner, and then work
backwards. The museum,
unfortunately, is often closed due to theft
and damage. Site open *09.30–16.00
Mon–Sat; 10.00–15.00 Sun & hols.*
Charge.

Regional features

Delos is only 5.5km long and just over
1km wide. The only feature of interest
is the archaeological site. Delos' resident
population of 16 is primarily composed
of catering staff, and archaeologists from
the French School. Mount Kynthos rises
behind to a height of 112m.

History

This tiny island was once amongst the
most important religious and political
centres of ancient Greece. In mythology,
the birthplace of Artemis, goddess of
hunting and childbirth, and of her twin
brother Apollo, the god of light – children
of Leto and Zeus. It has now been
established there were inhabitants on
Delos as early as the 3rd millennium BC.
By the 7thC BC, Delos was of such
importance it became the headquarters
of the Amphictyonic League of the
Ionians, an influential maritime
confederation. The economic and

Island chain   Cyclades
Alternative names   Dilos
Population   16
Area   3sq km
Area tel code   0289

Travel information

By caique
Daily from Mykonos harbour at
09.00, returning at 12.30. In winter
Tue & Thur only. Journey time
approx 45 mins. Have exact change
for fare. Guided tours from Mykonos
at 10.15 Tue & Thur during summer
months. Occasional excursion boats
from Paros during the high season.

political importance of Delos caused
great rivalry with the Athenians, and in
543BC a purge of the island was ordered
following the 'discovery' of an oracle. All
the tombs were removed to the
neighbouring island of Rinia.

In 478BC the Delian Alliance was
formed, putting Delos under the
protection of Athens. The treasury of the
Alliance was founded on Delos, but later
moved to the Acropolis in Athens in
454BC. In 426BC a second purification
was ordered, this time forbidding both
births and deaths on Delos, and
resulting in further weakening of the
island's political and economic position.
It was to be almost 200 years before
Delos, with the help of Macedonia,
regained its former status. The island
became a flourishing port for all the
Mediterranean, entering into a second
age of prosperity around 250BC.
Invading troops and raiding pirates
contributed to the gradual downfall of
Delos, which by the 3rdC AD was so
complete, the island was deemed
worthless when put up for sale by the
Athenians. No buyer came forward. In
1872 major excavations were begun by
the French School of Archaeology and
these continue today.

Accommodation & eating

There is only one hotel on Delos, the B
Class **Xenia** (tel 22259). Its four
bedrooms (seven beds) are often booked

up years in advance. Camping is sometimes allowed in fields behind the site; check with the Tourist Police in Mykonos and be sure to bring provisions. The Tourist Pavilion has a snack bar serving expensive, unappetizing food. A far better idea is to buy snacks from one of the excellent bakeries in Mykonos and picnic in the fields.

Sights

House of the Masks
At the southern end of the site, this house is best known for its fine mosaic floors. It is thought that the house might have served as an inn for performers from the nearby theatre. One mosaic depicts the twin dramatic masks of comedy and tragedy.

Monument of the Bulls
A long, narrow Hellenistic building dating from the 3rdC BC. Named after the bull-headed capitals on the columns, it was probably dedicated to a naval victory.

Mount Kynthos
On the summit of this sacred mountain are the remains of a 3rdC BC temple dedicated to Athena and the Kynthian Zeus. There was probably a temple on this site from as early as the 7thC BC. The cave on the lower slopes was once a shrine to Hercules, containing a Hellenistic marble altar and a statue.

Museum
Tel 22259. This museum has unfortunately had a turbulent history. It opened to house most of the finds from the excavations, including statues, figures and vases, then closed again. Several of the best examples were subsequently shipped to Athens. A few years ago it reopened, but at the time of going to press it was once again closed. Enquire with the Tourist Police for current information.

Sacred Lake
Filled in since 1926, there is now a palm tree, planted in the centre of the depression. This is to commemorate the sacred palm which Leto is said to have clung to when giving birth to Apollo. His sacred swans and geese were once kept here.

Sanctuary of the Foreign Gods
A long, low, terraced building. The southern section was reserved for Egyptian gods, the northern section for the Syrian gods. This extremely large temple had a paved courtyard, its own theatre designed to hold 450 worshippers, and an avenue lined with miniature sphinxes and grand altars.

The Three Temples of Apollo
Very little is now visible on the site of these ancient temples. The earliest, and also the smallest, was built of porous stone and dates from the 6thC BC. The second and largest was begun in 477BC, though not completed until the 3rdC BC, and had a row of 13 columns along each side. The most recent was built by the Athenians after 426BC. It is located between the two older temples.

Terrace of the Lions
This avenue more than any other has become the landmark of Delos. Leading north and overlooking the Sacred Lake, nine lions in marble brought from Naxos stand guarding the site. Built in the 7thC BC, five are still intact – lean, hungry and remarkably evocative.

Theatre
Built around 300BC, the auditorium was divided into three sections and designed to hold 5,500 spectators. Much of this ancient theatre is now in ruins, but the orchestra portion has been restored.

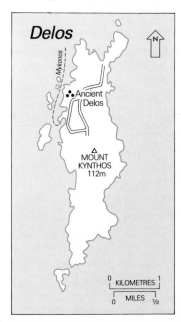

Delos

Donoussa

General character

Donoussa is a remote island, both in character and geographically. Only a smattering of English is spoken, and there is little in the way of tourist amenities. Boats call in occasionally, bringing much-needed supplies, but anyone planning a visit to Donoussa or its satellite isles should be prepared to rough it a bit. When seas are rough, the island is cut off completely and the main port is so underdeveloped that a small boat must steam out to pick up cargo and passengers from the larger ferries. Donoussa is an excellent island for those seeking peace and tranquillity, although the lack of facilities may inhibit the less adventurous.

Regional features

One ring road connects the main port with the tiny settlements of Haravgi, Mersini and Kalotaritissa. Vineyards dot the landscape as far as the eye can see. The north-east and north-west coasts

Island chain   Cyclades
Population   116
Area   13sq km
Distance from Piraeus   108
nautical miles/13 hours

Travel information

By ferry
1–2 weekly from Piraeus; occasional day excursions from Paros; occasional caique service to/from Santorini & Naxos. In the high season the SS Marianna sails to/from Amorgos 1–3 times weekly.

end in low, rocky, uninhabited peninsulas; the mountain in the centre of the island is 383m high.

Ports & towns

Donoussa Town

The island's only town rises up the hillside, a narrow paved track bordered by stones leads to the top. There can be no more than 40 buildings altogether, mostly just one-storey with flat roofs, and whitewashed to a dazzling brightness.

A blue-domed chapel stands next to the town beach; a larger, double-domed church stands guard over the harbour. When the sea is particularly rough, the local fishing boats are drawn up onto the beach for protection. There are the remains of a prehistoric settlement some distance from Donoussa Town.

Accommodation & eating

There are only a few rooms to let in private houses; enquire locally if no one approaches with an offer on the quay. Donoussa Town's three cafés serve simple, basic food, but all have shady verandahs with bamboo roofs.

Beaches

The town beach provides reasonable bathing, but even better is a sandy cove approx 3km east. Reached from Haravgi, it is a stiff walk, but anchorage facilities are available for small craft.

Satellite islands

Iraklia

With an area of over 17sq km, Iraklia is the largest of the group but has a population of just 95. There is a taverna in the main port of Aghios Georgios, and a huge cave on the northern slopes of Mount Papas.

Keros

The most easterly of the group, Keros has a mountain peak rising to 432m and the ruins of a medieval castle to the north.

Koufonissi

The collective name given to a chain of tiny islets. Kato Koufonissi has just five full-time inhabitants; North Koufonissi is larger, with a couple of tavernas along its southern coast and beaches on its eastern shore.

Schinoussa

There is a hotel in the port, and a town on the hill above with a medieval fortress, a church and a taverna. There is a beach near the village of Mesaria.

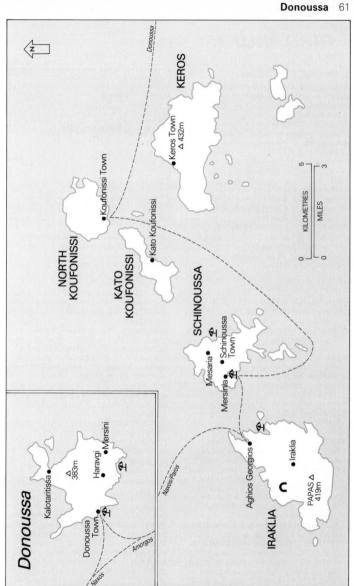

Folegandros

General character

Folegandros is a romantic, desolate place
only recently discovered by tourists. In
consequence they are welcome and well
received. Plumbing and electricity are
relatively new to the island and still
present problems – most of the
pensions lack running water and
electricity cables spark and hiss at night.

Folegandros is an ideal island for
walkers – public transport is at best
limited, and the hills, of grey stone and
vivid orange earth, hold many surprises.
There are scattered outlying settlements,
whose gracious and hospitable
residents will offer water and probably
food as well, so amazed will they be at
meeting a foreigner. Chora on the hill,
approx one hour's hike from the port, is
populated with such folk and is
outstandingly pretty.

Regional features

Folegandros is one of the smallest
Cycladian islands to have a permanent
population. One road, recently paved,
leads from the port to the capital above.
Along the road are tiny white shrines on
pedestals where votive offerings are
made. The interior, mountainous and
desolate with mile upon mile of dry-
stone walling, is populated by black
goats with pointed horns and wild,
devilish faces.

Ports & towns

Karavostasis/Orme

A little harbour nestled in the folds of
steep hills. Stone terraces slope down
to the sea on one side; a rocky wharf on
the other provides shelter, making the
water in the bay calm and clear. There
are a few pensions and three tavernas,
but no real shops – all is quiet until a bus
or a boat arrives, providing the day's
activity.

A little chapel with a bell tower stands
at the end of the wharf, and behind it the
OTE office is bedecked with flowers. A
well in front of the church provides fresh
drinking water. Bus timetables in Greek
are pinned to a prominent telegraph
pole; one bus leaves for Chora at 07.30
and another in the early afternoon. It is

| Island chain   Cyclades |
| Population   570 |
| Area   32sq km |
| Area tel code   0286 |

Travel information

By ferry
1–3 weekly to/from Piraeus. 1–3
weekly to/from Santorini & Sikinos.
1–2 weekly to/from Ios & Paros. 1–2
weekly to/from Kimolos, Kythnos,
Milos, Naxos, Serifos, Sifnos &
Syros. Summer caique service to/
from Ios & Sikinos.

claimed the bus turns into a taxi after
dark, but don't count on it.

Chora/Folegandros

4km NW of Karavostasis. Charming
village almost 300m above sea level.
Streets end abruptly to display a stunning
view of the sea and miles of zig-zagging
stone walls. Cars must be parked at the
entrance to the town next to one of the
innumerable domed churches. Village
squares are actually flower-filled
crescents around which are shops, cafés
and tavernas. The first approached
encloses a circular garden, filled with
vines and blossom trees; the butcher's
shop has pride of place. The post office
and the ticket agent are off to one side;
a medieval quarter is obscured by more
modern buildings. There is no bank.

Livadi

3.5km SW of Karavostasis. This hamlet
located above Katergo Bay has an
official campsite, three tavernas and a
good beach with trees providing
welcome shade.

Accommodation & eating

There are only a couple of rooms to let
in the harbour, so it is best to take the
bus to Chora directly after disembarking
from the ferry. Chora itself has only one
hotel, the attractive D class **Hotel
Danassi** (tel 41230), and a limited
number of rooms. Many private houses
have flat roofs and generous owners, so
those caught without accommodation
might be able to sleep under the stars
with a borrowed blanket. For the less

adventurous, however, there is an official campsite at Livadi.

The **Remezzo** taverna in the port is one of only three; request crab in any of them but be prepared to wait for the fishermen to return – worthwhile for some of the best seafood in Greece. **Niko's Restaurant** in the Chora serves breakfast in the garden.

Sights

Chrisispilio

5km NW of Karavostasis. Just to the north of Chora lies this huge cavern with stalactites and stalagmites. Getting there is difficult, so enquire in Chora about hiring a guide.

Panayia Church

5km NW of Karavostasis. 19thC church just north of Chora, built on the side of a hill, overlooking the sea. Graced with a multitude of white domes, this attractive building is the largest on the island. Nearby are the ruins of a Venetian fortress.

Beaches

The beach at Livadi is sandy, and there are places to eat nearby. However, the island's best beach, Katergo, can be reached from Livadi after a walk across the hills. It boasts a lovely sandy strip and an islet in the bay, and can also be

Satellite islands

Sikinos

Ferries to Folegandros call first at Sikinos, a greener, more fertile island with a port and an old capital – Chora – on the hill above, but very few amenities. The trip to Chora must be made on foot; once there it is a rather pretty place, with very few foreigners and some basic tavernas. A ruined monastery, Zoodochos Pigi, looms from the rock above. Most visitors prefer to stay in the port, which has a sandy beach nearby. The harbour has no pier, so tiny blue and white motorboats meet each ferry to take passengers ashore. At Episkopi, a 1½-hour walk SW of Chora is a Heroon, or shrine, dating from the 3rd century AD. It was converted four centuries later into a church.

reached by occasional boats from Karavostasis. The beaches on the north coast are accessible only by boat.

Specialities

Pottery

Flowered pottery with decorative handles, made by artists living in the hills. Sold at Atlantida, the attractive shop in Chora.

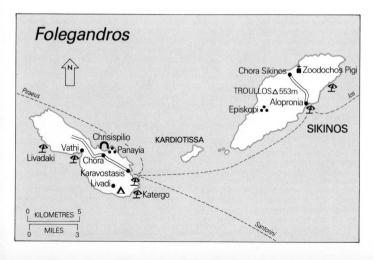

Folegandros

Ios

General character

Ios is ideal for backpackers, sun-worshippers, and anyone under the age of 25. Ever since this bare brown island with its attractive capital joined the main ferry route it has been the haunt of the young. Rowdy and restless, its miles of golden beaches are covered from end-to-end in the high season, with near-naked golden bodies. Although camping and nudism are permitted only on official sites, tolerance is the key-note, both by the authorities and by the young people who pour into the island by the ferryload. More than a dozen discos line the streets of the main town; sunset at the Ios Club, when classical music is played, is a long-standing tradition.

More foreigners than Greeks man the tills in the boutiques, bookstalls and cheap eating places. These come to life late in the day and stay open equally late in the evening. Ios is not for everyone. Violence and theft are more common than on perhaps any other Greek island (although still minimal by most standards), and late in the season the remnants of the young at play are scattered throughout the popular areas – broken bottles, abandoned knapsacks and discarded clothing. For some, a stay on Ios is a 24-hour party, to be remembered and recollected throughout the winter months. For others it can be hell on earth, the furthest from a tranquil Greek island it is possible to imagine. However, most of the people who visit Ios confine their explorations to the two main towns and the principal beaches; for those who do strike out on their own, especially towards the isolated east coast, the beaches are deserted and the locals friendly.

Regional features

Ios is a bare, rocky island with only one proper road. A good bus service connects Gialos the port with Ios Town, then makes the descent to Milopotamos beach. Unfortunately this is the total extent of public transport and towards the eastern coast the road peters out into little more than a dusty track. Archaeologically, the island offers little, but more than 400 churches and monasteries are scattered through the hills. Water is quite scarce, and this can present sanitation problems in the high season.

Island chain   Cyclades
Population   1,450
Area   108sq km
Area tel code   0286
Tourist Police   tel 91222
Harbour Police   tel 91264
Distance from Piraeus   111 nautical miles/11 hours

Travel information

By ferry
Daily from Piraeus in summer, 2–3 weekly from Piraeus in winter. Daily connections in summer to Paros & Santorini; less often in winter. Frequent connections to Folegandros & Sikinos.

Ports & towns

Gialos
Gialos is connected to Ios Town by a cobbled donkey path which winds up the hill. At night it is unlit, and should not be attempted without a torch. A jumble of cafés, hire shops and hotels, Gialos is the first port of call for the hundreds of daily new arrivals. The Acteon Tourist Office, on the main square, has left-luggage facilities. There is a yacht supply station.

Ios Town
2km E of Gialos. A lovely town with perfectly formed white Cycladic buildings and an impressive row of 12 windmills. The narrow streets throb to the sound of jazz, disco and rock music and there are many bars and tavernas. The bus stop is on the edge of the town, near the OTE and post offices.

Accommodation & eating

Local people with guest-houses and rooms to let greet each ferry, although in the high season 'roughing it' may be required. The D class **Nissos Ios Hotel** (tel 91306) is right on Milopotamos beach. The D class **Acteon** (tel 91207) in Gialos is on the main square, next to the harbour where the ferry docks. The two campsites are good value for money, offering showers, washing facilities and eating places. Pay one price if sleeping in a tent, even less for a sleeping bag only. Fish is rather expensive on the island, and most people stick to *souvlaki* stalls or pizzerias.

Sights

Homer's Tomb

Plakotos. N of Gialos. 2–3 hours by donkey or on foot. It is said that Homer's mother was a native of Ios, and it was to Ios that the poet returned to die and was subsequently buried. Little remains of the structure reputed to be Homer's Tomb, in the north-east of the island. On the slopes of Mount Erimitis overlooking Plakotos Bay, the site is difficult to find and a local guide may be necessary; enquire at the office of the Tourist Police.

Plakotos itself was an ancient city destroyed by an earthquake; only a tower now remains.

Beaches

There are many coves and bays around the island, accessible only on foot or by hiring a boat. The more inaccessible the beaches, the more secluded the bathing will be. Two of the island's more popular beaches are listed below.

Milopotamos

5km SE of Gialos. A long crescent of sand overlooked by a whitewashed chapel. There are tavernas and rooms to let; a windsurfing school operates during the summer months. Very crowded as public transport is good.

Manganari

SE of Gialos. A caique leaves Gialos every morning for Manganari Bay on the southern tip of the island. There are two tavernas, one at either end of this vast beach.

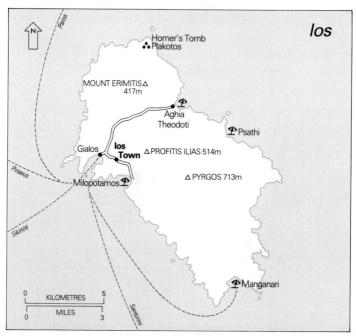

Kea

General character

Lying just three hours' travelling time
from Athens, Kea is an excellent
alternative for anyone seeking an island
just a short distance from the mainland.
Unlike the equally close, but over-visited
Saronic islands, Kea is unused to foreign
visitors, and anyone arriving on this
green, wooded isle will be treated with
courtesy and warmth. A popular spot
with discerning Greek holiday-makers,
(therefore best to book accommodation
if arriving in July and August), there is a
native sophistication about Kea which is
most appealing.

The hill-top town of Ioulis, built on a
mountainside and crowned by an
ancient citadel, is nicely shabby, and
unaffected by the tourist trade. Clothes,
shops and food are above average in
standard, and although there is little in
the way of discos and nightlife, the walks
are interesting and the bathing quite
good.

Regional features

Although from the ferry Kea appears a
barren island, it is actually one of the
most agriculturally rich of all the

Island chain   Cyclades
Alternative names   Tzia
Population   1,650
Area   131sq km
Area tel code   0288
Tourist Police   tel 22100
Harbour Police   tel 31344
Distance from Athens   approx 3
hours by bus & ferry

Travel information

By bus & ferry
1½ hours by bus from Athens to
port of Lavrion; 1½ hours by ferry to
Kea. Daily boat from Lavrion in
winter; 2–3 boats daily in summer.
Tel 0292 25249 for further
information.

Cyclades. Cattle farming is the main
source of income, providing Kea with
island luxuries like beef, milk and dairy
produce. Nuts and vegetables are locally
grown, and honey is produced in
abundance. The highest mountain,
Profitis Ilias, rises to 568m and there are
fertile valleys at Milopotamos and Pisses
in the west.

Ports & towns

Korissia
Genial harbour lined with ticket agencies,
tavernas and bars. Buildings with red-
tiled roofs cluster around a sand and rock
beach; further along, the buildings give
way to trees leading up to a windmill on
the horizon. Rising to the left of the
beach (when facing the sea) is a small
church with a red dome and blue
windows. What little nightlife the island
offers is centred around Korissia, and
there are motor scooters and bicycles for
hire.

Ioulis/Chora
5km SE of Korissia. Ioulis is built on the
side of a mountain, its tiers of houses
connected by cobbled paths or steps.
From the ancient fortress at the top the
town appears as little white specks of
stucco crowned by red roofs and
domes. At night the view is equally
impressive, the closely-strung lights
below mirroring the stars above. The

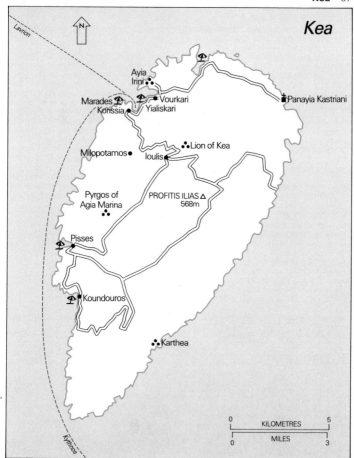

Kea

Lavrion

Ayia Irini

Marades
Korissia
Vourkari
Yialiskari

Panayia Kastriani

Lion of Kea

Milopotamos

Ioulis

Pyrgos of Agia Marina

PROFITIS ILIAS △
568m

Pisses

Koundouros

Karthea

Kythnos

| 0 | | | | | 5 |
KILOMETRES

| 0 | | | 3 |
MILES

town hall is situated on a slight plateau, a pink Venetian mansion with four statues guarding its upper balcony. Nearby is the Archaeological Museum, *open most mornings*, containing the most important finds from the excavations at Ayia Irini.
Vourkari
2.5km N of Korissia. Picturesque fishing village where it is possible to buy fresh fish straight from the boats. Near the village is the sandy beach of Yialiskari.

Accommodation & eating

Accommodation on Kea is limited. Rooms to let are scarce and there are only four hotels on the entire island. Two C class hotels in Korissia are the **Karthaea** (tel 31222) and the **Tzia Mas** (tel 31305). Spectacularly sited is the D class **Ioulis** (tel 22177), in the town of the same name. Open all year, its rooms are slightly bare, but the view, especially at sunset, is superb. The 200-room B class **Kea Beach Hotel** (tel 21544) is open during the summer months only, but offers modern amenities including a swimming pool, watersports and a disco. Most of these hotels have restaurants open to the public; the fishing village of Vourkari is the best place to eat fresh fish.

Sights

Ayia Irini

2.5km N of Korissia. Near the village of Vourkari is a prehistoric site dating from 3000BC. Best preserved are walls and buildings thought to have been constructed during the Middle Bronze Age, around 2000BC. A temple erected during this period survived an earthquake in 1450BC, and continued as a place of worship during subsequent occupations.

Karthaea Ancient City

SE of Korissia. Located on the south-eastern coast of the island and accessible only on foot or by motorcycle. Of the four ancient cities established on Kea, Karthaea was the most important. The remains of temples, statues, grand buildings and an acoustically excellent theatre, can be seen today. By comparison, little is visible of the other ancient cities of the island, buried now beneath the modern towns of Ioulis, Korissia and Pisses.

Lion of Kea

6.5km SE of Korissia. Easily accessible from the town of Ioulis, this stone lion dating from the 6thC BC, is the object of many local myths and legends. Carved out of the rock it is 6m long and stands 3m high, with a faint smile on its face.

Monastery of Panayia Kastriani

11km E of Korissia. Located on the north-eastern coast of the island, this dramatically sited monastery is known as the Madonna of the Castle. Built on the top of a hill overlooking the sea, it consists of two churches – the first constructed in 1708, the second and larger one in 1910. The Icon of the Madonna, which gave the monastery its name, is housed in the smaller chapel. It is said that local shepherds found the icon on top of the hill and built the church to honour it.

Pyrgos of Agia Marina

12km S of Korissia. Impressive Hellenic tower approx 100m in height. The interior staircase has been partly destroyed.

Beaches

Rock and sand beach near Korissia, sandy beaches just to the north at Yialiskari and to the west at Marades. Also a sandy bay at Pisses, south-west of Korissia.

Kythnos

General character

Kythnos is a rugged little island which offers, as its chief attraction, warm and welcoming hospitality. Located in the north-west of the Cyclades group, Kythnos has remained off the main tourist track. With little in the way of holiday amenities, archaeological sites or architectural splendours, it is likely to stay as such. What Kythnos does offer is a chance to observe the three main towns and two taxis ply the route. Expect to share them with families carrying groceries or even live chickens, and do not be

Island chain	Cyclades
Alternative names	Kithnos
Population	1,500
Area	99sq km
Area tel code	0281
Tourist Police	tel 31201
Harbour Police	tel 31290
Distance from Piraeus	52 nautical miles/4 hours

Travel information

By ferry
6 weekly to Piraeus in summer; 2 in winter. 5 weekly to/from Lavrion in summer; 2–3 in winter. 1 weekly to Kea; occasional services to Kimolos, Milos, Santorini, Serifos & Sifnos.

surprised if the taxi driver runs errands in neighbouring towns in your time, if not at your expense. Four buses daily trundle from the main port of Merihas to the spa town of Loutra. However, the last one returns in the afternoon and it is easy to get stranded. There is little accommodation and many visitors sleep on the beach; though the spirit of friendship is such that the local people may offer a bed for the night free of charge.

Regional features

The island's bare brown hills are interspersed with fertile valleys. In the dry season, the riverbeds sport bright pink flowers, vivid against the brown earth. Beehives producing excellent honey dot the landscape. Also once known as Thermia, there are hot springs on the island at Loutra, believed to have healing properties. Despite this, fresh water can be a problem towards the end

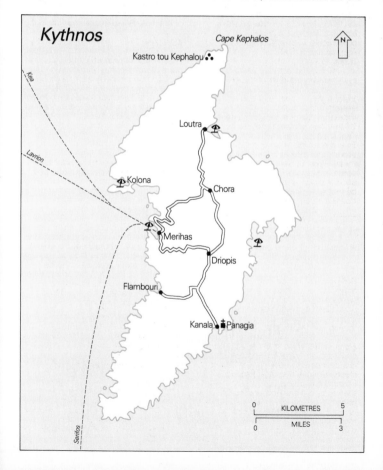

Kythnos

Cape Kephalos

Kastro tou Kephalou

Kea

Lavrion

Loutra

Kolona

Chora

Merihas

Driopis

Flambouri

Kanala · ■Panagia

Serifos

| 0 | KILOMETRES | 5 |

| 0 | MILES | 3 |

N

of the summer and hot tap water is a
real treat at any time of year.

Ports & towns

Merihas
The island's principal port is a line of
white buildings along a wide sandy bay.
Many have red-tiled roofs in the
Venetian, rather than Cycladian manner.
There are only a few tavernas. The beach
is fringed by thick fir trees hung with
lights which are lit late at night. These
cast a rather eerie glow over the sea
and the narrow street curving along
behind. Merihas is a genial, low-key
town; locals and tourists mingle in
pleasant harmony.

Chora
6km NE of Merihas. Flat, white, capital
town housing the post office and
service industries but little else of
interest.

Loutra
1km NE of Merihas. Loutra has been
known since ancient times for its
thermal baths. The town itself extends
along the length of a sandy bay. In the
centre of town, just behind the beach is
a small park. To the right, on a low bluff,
stands a miniature castle, the private
summer home of a local resident. The
thermal springs run underneath St
Anastia church which is situated next to
the baths. Adjoining the baths is the
bungalow-style Hotel Xenia. Twin
streams of water, only 20m apart, course
either side of the hotel – the
temperature of one is precisely 48°C, the
other is a constant 78°C.

Accommodation & eating

Chora has no hotels or rooms to let;
Loutra and Merihas only a few. In
Loutra, the C class **Xenia** (tel 31217) is
only open from June to October. In
Merihas try the C class **Possidonion** (tel
31244) or the **Hotel Kythnos** (tel 31247)
with its verandah overlooking the harbour.
Food is distinctly Greek – fresh and well
cooked; bakeries sell excellent cheese
pies, fresh daily. The **Restaurant
Catarina** in Loutra is one of the few
tavernas to sell the respected local wine
of Kythnos, available only from the barrel.

Sights

Kastro tou Kephalou
18km NE of Merihas. Located on Cape
Kephalos on the north-east tip of the
island approx one hour's walk from
Loutra. The ruins of this castle, built by
the French pirate Bonné also mark the
site of the island's medieval citadel
abandoned in the 17thC.

Beaches

Within walking distance of Merihas are a
series of sandy coves backed by pine
trees; check them out first by taking the
bus to Chora. Boats for fishing
expeditions can be hired in Merihas. Taxi
boats also leave from Merihas for
several other beaches; enquire locally for
details. Best for bathing is Kolona Beach
north of Merihas, where, it is said, the
sea stays warm throughout the year. It
is a lovely spot for watching sunsets.
There is another good beach close to
the hamlet of Kanala in the south, where
there are a few rooms to let and a
secluded monastery nearby. Buses
occasionally run to Kanala.

Mykonos

General character

Two decades ago Mykonos was known primarily to Greeks, and archaeologists on their way to Delos. Now, this small picturesque island is known all over the world; its dazzling cube-shaped houses, lovely port and row of windmills typify for many the ultimate Greek island. Its charms are indeed considerable, but due to its small size and massive popularity, Mykonos has suffered more than many from the ravages of tourism. Every other shop in the capital's maze of streets seems to sell furs or gold jewellery; prices are inflated for bartering with the cruise passengers who arrive twice a day. The air-traveller's first glimpse of Mykonos – a windmill perched on a plateau – now sports an advertisement for Olympic Airways. The nightclubs, a legacy from the late sixties when the island became the haunt of the jet-setters, also strike an incongruous note.

For disco dancers and sun-worshippers Mykonos is ideal and many young people vow never to leave. For those who want to enjoy the island at a less frantic pace, it is best to go out of season and stay out of town. The island's interior is a delight, with over 400 churches sprinkled like salt through the bare brown hills. Mykonos is an island for everyone – the food is excellent, the scenery magical and the Tourist Police cordial and helpful.

Regional features

Mykonos is the least undulating of all the Cyclades; rocky and barren, producing only a little wine, barley and figs. Its beaches are sandy, although often crowded. The local architecture is the island's most interesting feature; it is claimed the distinguished architect and planner Edward Le Corbusier, upon visiting Mykonos, exclaimed 'What-ever architecture had to say it is said here'.

All the houses are neatly cubic, many with external staircases leading to honeysuckle-laden balconies. Several in the countryside have crenellated chimneys or decorative designs carved

---

Island chain   Cyclades
Alternative names   Miconos
Population   5,500
Area   85sq km
Area tel code   0289
Tourist Police   tel 22482
Harbour Police   tel 22218
Taxi rank   tel 22400
Distance from Piraeus   94 nautical miles/8 hours

Travel information

By air
International airport with flights from Europe. Up to six flights daily from Athens (planes very small), 1–2 daily to Santorini; 4 weekly to Crete, Kos & Rhodes. Less frequent in winter.
By ferry
Up to 3 daily to/from Piraeus; daily to Ios, Paros, Syros, Tinos. 5 weekly to Naxos, 1 weekly to Santorini. Daily caique to Delos. Less frequent in winter.

---

into the whitewash. Chapels and churches seemingly outnumber houses; chapels are often located in back gardens – tiny one-room buildings with coloured cupolas or domed roofs painted red or the palest blue.

Ports & towns

Mykonos Town/Khora
This sparkling capital is featured on hundreds of postcards distributed throughout Greece; the crescent-shaped harbour with a blue-domed church on the jetty and the windmills, sails intact, high on a hill above. Of these windmills, only one still works and demonstrations are occasionally given. The town's maze of backstreets was built as a foil for pirates, and getting lost in Mykonos Town is part of a visitor's agenda. In the last few years town maps have been published, but they do little to alleviate the enjoyable confusion. Tucked away in these streets are above average bakeries, and shops where goods are reasonably sophisticated, if pricey. Above the town stands the

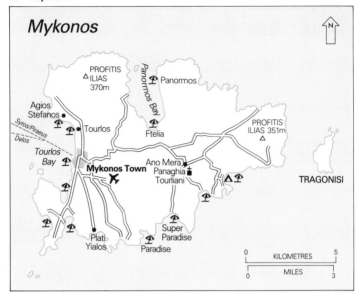

Mykonos

PROFITIS
△ILIAS
370m

Panormos

Panormos Bay

PROFITIS
ILIAS 351m
△

Agios
Stefanos

Tourlos

Syros/Piraeus

Delos

Ftelia

Tourlos
Bay

Mykonos Town

Ano Mera
Panaghia
Tourliani

TRAGONISI

Plati
Yialos

Super
Paradise

Paradise

0					5
		KILOMETRES			
0		MILES			3

Mykonos branch of the School of Fine Art – well worth visiting.

The area known as Little Venice is one of the more attractive quarters of the port. The pastel-coloured buildings sport trellised balconies overhanging the sea. The waterfront area centres around a small square with its statue of Manto Mavrogenous, a local heroine from the War of Independence in 1821. Taxis and buses to the beaches leave from here. To the left of the harbour, (when facing the sea) are the headquarters of the Tourist Police, a public toilet and the quay for boats to Delos. Petros the pelican patrols with diligence. This tame bird (or one of his ancestors) has been the mascot of Mykonos for over a decade, and is the object of an inter-island dispute over his ownership. The island as a whole can be very windy; the capital, with its closely packed white buildings trapping the heat, is often very, very hot.

Ano Mera

9km E of Mykonos Town. The only other established settlement on Mykonos, of interest chiefly for the monastery of Panaghia Tourliani just to the north of the village.

Accommodation & eating

Both are above average in quality, although accommodation is often booked up by visitors from the previous season or by package tours. For hotels near to beaches try the C class **Korfos** (tel 22850), the C class **Paralos Beach Hotel** (tel 22600) or the D class **Platys Yalos Hotel** (tel 22343). In the capital, or near it, are the A class **Leto Hotel** (tel 22207) and the C class **Zannis** (tel 22481). There are also private rooms to let. Most of the beaches have snack bars or tavernas nearby, and Khora itself abounds in places serving good food; there are several seafood restaurants in and around Little Venice. The bar next to the ferry landing stage is open 24 hours a day during the summer months.

Sights

Archaeology Museum

Mykonos Town. Situated to the far right of the harbour (when facing the sea). This museum contains relics, not only from Mykonos, but also from the great mass burial sites on Rinia, the isle to which residents of Delos were exiled when approaching death. *Open 09.00–15.00 Mon–Sat; 10.00–14.00 Sun. Closed Tue.* Charge.

Folklore Museum

Mykonos Town. On the other side of the harbour, this attractive museum features hand-woven textiles, a noteworthy collection of wall plates, plus furniture and photographs. *Erratic opening hours*, check with the Tourist Police. Charge.

Monastery of Panaghia Tourliani

9km E of Mykonos Town near Ano Mera. The monastery has an attractive 15thC carved open-work campanile. The museum is open to the public and contains embroidery, church vessels and other ecclesiastical exhibits.

Beaches

Paradise beach and Plati Yialos beach are the most popular, and are easily accessible by bus from Mykonos Town. Super Paradise, further along, is an unofficial nudist beach and well-known in gay circles. Panormos Bay and Ftelia are less crowded, as are the sandy coves between Paradise and Plati Yialos.

Specialities

Nightlife

Mykonos comes to life after dark. With probably the highest percentage of nightclubs per capita of any of the islands. Visitors can take their pick of jazz clubs, rock clubs, Greek clubs or cabaret. Some of the best-known nightclubs on Mykonos include the Windmill Disco, Nine Muses, Remezzo's and Pierros. Energetic young things might take in several in one evening, and for those determined to dance the night away, 1984 saw the publication of a map with all hot spots clearly labelled. Available from souvenir stalls.

Naxos

General character

Naxos is the largest of the Cyclades, and many consider it the most beautiful. On his first trip to Greece, Lord Byron fell in love with it, and so inspired was the composer Richard Strauss with the myth of Theseus deserting Ariadne on this green, fertile island he wrote the opera 'Ariadne auf Naxos'. The landscape is one of crumbling mansions, towers and far-off ruins illuminated by sunsets. Valleys are lush and well-watered, the beaches can be excellent, and over 40 picturesque villages are dotted around its coasts and hills. Buses from the capital connect with several villages, but progress tends to be slow. Cars and jeeps can be rented in Naxos Town, but the best way to travel on the island is by motorscooter. It is cooler and pleasanter, the breeze rushing past is ladened with the scents which are typical of the island – citrus, fig and the slightly musty smell of fern.

Visitors returning to Naxos after a break of several years will be disappointed. Hotels and tourist complexes have sprung up and package

Island chain   Cyclades
Population   14,100
Area   428sq km
Area tel code   0285
Tourist Police   tel 22100
Harbour Police   tel 22300
Distance from Piraeus   103 nautical miles/8 hours

Travel information

By air
Airport due for completion in 1986.
By ferry
5–7 weekly to/from Piraeus; 5–7 weekly to Paros, 1 weekly to Ios, Santorini & Crete. Frequent caiques to Amorgos, Delos & Mykonos during summer.

tours from a variety of countries are on the increase. But Naxos is a large island and its mystery is strong; first-time visitors arriving in May or September should still find it as evocative as Byron did.

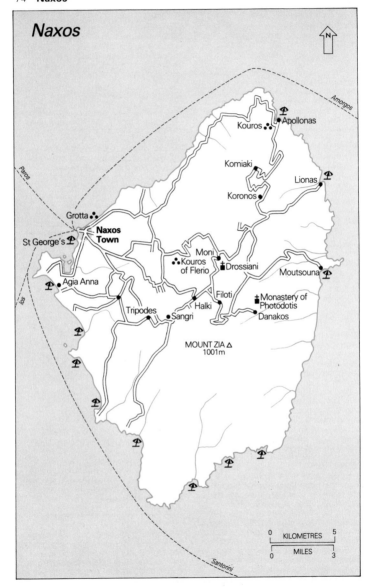

Naxos

N

Amorgos

Kouros • Apollonas

Komiaki

Lionas

Koronos

Paros

Grotta

Naxos Town

St George's

Moni
• Kouros
of Flerio

Drossiani

Moutsouna

Agia Anna

Filoti

Monastery of
Photodotis

Tripodes

Halki

Sangri

Danakos

MOUNT ZIA △
1001m

| 0 | KILOMETRES | 5 |
| 0 | MILES | 3 |

Santorini

Regional features

The island is 29km long and 19.5km wide, bisected by a mountain range which includes the highest summit in the Cyclades, Mount Zia, rising to over 1,000m. Various fruits are cultivated in the valleys, including lemons, oranges, figs and olives. Emery is produced in abundance and Naxian marble was used for many of the statues on the sacred island of Delos.

Civilisation on Naxos spans 5,000 years; as well as the crumbling Venetian and Turkish façades the remains of more ancient cultures can be found in the interior, from Mycenean vessels – now in the museum – to Roman fortifications.

Ports & towns

Naxos Town/Chora
The initial view of Naxos Town is enchanting. The ferry doors swing wide to reveal, perfectly framed, the ruins of the ancient Temple of Apollo. Built on the islet of Palatia, which is connected to the town by a causeway, the temple, thought to date from 530BC, was never completed.

Naxos Town, which rises into the hills like a citadel, is crowned by a Venetian fortress. More of a city than most Cycladian ports, it is industrious and rather unwelcoming. The residents are private and somewhat aloof, forcing foreigners to create their own jolly community, centred around St George's beach.

Inside the buildings, ceilings are high and interiors often gloomy; some however, are superb. Small shops, like the pharmacy with its shining mahogany shelves, or the Venetian mansions of notable families with coats of arms above the doors are buildings of great character. The birthplace of the Naxian saint Nikodimos is called the House of the Kallivrousi and though more modest, is well worth a visit. Also of interest is the Old Market, a warren of tiny lanes and dark, claustrophobic tunnels.

The remains of a Mycenean settlement have been found at Grotta, just to the north of the town; to the south is St George's beach, around which the modern hotels cluster. From this narrow coarse-sand beach there is a splendid view of the tiny church of Myrtidiotissa on its private islet; a perfect spot for sunsets. There is a yacht supply station in the town.

Apollonas
51km NE of Naxos Town. Surrounded by green hills, the village of Apollonas is located in an attractive bay. There are many sandy beaches in the area and several disused marble quarries. One of the island's most fascinating antiquities, an unfinished marble statue of Apollo fully 10.5m in height, lies nearby. Rapidly developing as a tourist centre, there are daily buses from Naxos Town in the high season.

Agia Anna
9km S of Naxos Town. Ideal swimming resort for those with children. The broad, extensive sandy beach has many facilities. A boat leaves daily from Naxos Town in the high season, returning in the afternoon.

Danakos
23.5km SE of Naxos Town. A small village, prettily sited, containing numerous waterwheels. Just above Danakos is the Byzantine Monastery of Photodotis. In the nearby village of Moni is the Byzantine church of Drossiani dating from the 8thC AD. It was once decorated with frescos, but these have been taken to Athens for restoration, hopefully to return.

Halki/Khalki/Chalkio
17km SE of Naxos Town. A collective name given to a number of scattered hamlets interspersed with olive groves. The surrounding area abounds in monuments of all periods, from megaliths to Venetian castles. Some of the small Byzantine churches have fine frescos decorating the walls.

Sangri
12km SE of Naxos Town. Sangri is the collective name for three hamlets in a region ringed by windmills, castles, Byzantine and Venetian ruins. A distinctive place, with cobbled streets and tiny courtyards. Although mentioned on all the tourist maps, Sangri is bewildered by foreigners, and reacts with wonder and delight. There are no eating places, so take a picnic.

Tripodes
9km SE of Naxos Town. A large, attractive village with flagstoned streets and fine buildings. Wine is produced here, and the parish church, formerly a monastery, contains some valuable icons. On the outskirts are the ruins of Paliopyrgos – a lovely tower dating from the Pelasgian era.

Accommodation & eating

There are large tourist complexes at
several of the beaches, and rooms to let
in many villages. Of the hotels in Naxos
Town there is the B class **Ariadne** (tel
22452) commanding a good view of the
harbour, the C class **Renetta** (tel 22952)
and the D class **Anixis** (tel 22112).

Ten minutes' walk left from the
harbour (when facing the sea) is St
George's beach, where at least 50 hotels
cluster in the streets behind its shores.
All are modern and clean, and anyone
booking a package tour will probably be
housed here very comfortably. Bring a
torch and be sure to memorise the
turnings from Naxos Town as the route
can be confusing after dark. The C class
Hotel Maroulis (tel 22036) offers some
privacy, as it is screened from the road
with bamboo; the C class **Nissaki** (tel
22876) has a chapel within its grounds.
The simple E class **St George** (tel 23162)
has a roof terrace overlooking the sea.

The harbour area of Naxos Town is
lined with tavernas and cafés serving
delicious pastries. There are several
clubs along the beach where live music
is played.

Sights

Archaeological Museum

Naxos Town. Of principal interest are
small Classical torsos, a Roman mosaic
and several Cycladic idols. *Open
08.00–11.00, 15.00–18.00 Mon–Sat.
Closed Tue.* Charge.

Cathedral of Zoodochos Pigi

Naxos Town. Greek Orthodox cathedral
built around 1785. Its treasures include
a fine marble iconostasis, with icons
painted by Dimitrios Valvis of the Cretan
school; a pulpit and a bishop's throne,
also of marble. Materials from earlier
buildings were used in its construction.

Kouros of Flerio

10km E of Naxos Town. Massive Archaic
marble statue dating from the 7thC BC.
Lying near the site of an ancient marble
quarry, the *kouros*, broken and
unfinished, measures 6.4m in length.
Another *kouros* near the village of
Apollonas (51km NE of Naxos Town) is
an impressive 10.5m in length.

Specialities

Local wines

Red, rosé or white Promponas, or the
superior quality Ariadne wine.

Kitrou

A liqueur, made from an extract of the
leaves of lemon trees grown on the
island. It is available in four varieties:
white, green, white super special (more
alcohol, less sugar) and yellow super
special (very sweet). Buy it from the
large shop on the waterfront in Naxos
Town which gives free tastings and
smells of lemons.

Paros

General character

Genial, light-hearted island with good beaches, good food and a pleasing, gentle landscape. Paros has become very popular in the last five years; if arriving in the high season without accommodation booked, be prepared to sleep outdoors. A favourite with almost everyone – island-hoppers, young sophisticates, families. Unobtrusive hotel building on the outskirts of the port of Parikia just manages to contain the hordes. Organised and efficient; helpful service industries, a reasonable bus network and lots of organised excursions around the island all go towards making a stay on Paros enjoyable. Perhaps too noisy for those seeking real solitude, but for others in many ways the most pleasant island in the Cyclades.

Regional features

Oval in shape, a mountainous interior rising to over 700m gives way to soft fertile plains. Paros abounds with fruit trees, primarily fig, olive and cherry; pistachios, flowers and grapes are also plentiful. Only one danger: a short, black snake known as the horned viper – usually found amongst rocks.

Ports & towns

Parikia/Paroikia

A chain of white, bright buildings encircling Mount Profitis Elias like a necklace. Busy and bustling, Parikia throbs to the sound of disco music, but also provides quiet, sweet-smelling corners as well. Boutiques and craft shops are amongst the best in Greece and, despite the hordes, Parians actually enjoy visitors.

The narrow streets and attractive squares can be confusing initially; Parikia sprawls unexpectedly and the town's main commercial district is tucked down a side alley. The best way to recognise this street – called Lochagou Kortianou – is by the two banks flanking its entrance: the Commercial Bank on the right; the National Bank on the left. Two good bookshops sell publications in

Island chain   Cyclades Population   7,880 Area   195sq km Area tel code   0284 Tourist Police   tel 21673 s.o. Harbour Police   tel 21240 Distance from Piraeus   90 nautical miles/8–9 hours

Travel information

By air
2–5 flights daily from Athens in Jul & Aug. 2 flights most days in other months.
By ferry
1–3 daily from Piraeus May–Sep; 5 weekly from Piraeus in winter. Jul & Aug boats from Paros to Samos, Ikaria 2–3 weekly; Sifnos, Naxos, Ios 2 daily; Santorini 1–2 daily; Syros 5 weekly; Tinos 4 weekly; Amorgos, Serifos 2 weekly; Folegandros, Sikinos, Kos, Rhodes 1 weekly. Plus day excursions to Mykonos, Delos, AntiParos; occasional boats to Schinoussa, Donoussa, Koufonissi and Iraklia.

English, and everything needed for the beach tumbles from baskets outside the shops.

Central reference point is the harbourside windmill, around which amenities and restaurants fan in four principal thoroughfares. From June to September the windmill is the Tourist Information Office, and can help with accommodation. The bus station is approx 1km to the right (when facing the sea), near the Harbour Police station. Close to the bus station is a left-luggage office, rare for Greece. The OTE office is just to the left of the windmill, on a promenade packed with tavernas and ticket agencies. Jeeps and motorcycles can be hired here.

The waterfront stretches for almost 3km; at the far western edge, overlooking the town, lies Aghia Anna Hill, where there are more windmills and a few hotels. This is a good place to watch the sun go down. Although better beaches lie outside Parikia, the town

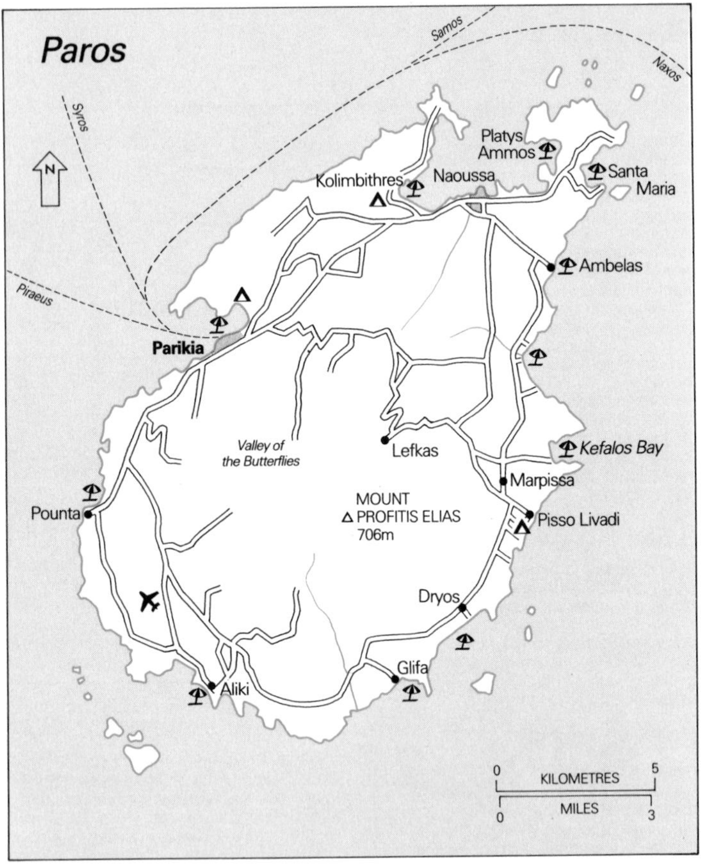

Paros

Samos

Naxos

Syros

Platys
Ammos

Kolimbithres Naoussa ⚓Santa
Maria

Piraeus

⚓Ambelas

⚓Parikia

Valley of
the Butterflies

Lefkas

⚓*Kefalos Bay*

Marpissa

⚓Pounta

MOUNT
△ PROFITIS ELIAS
706m

⚓Pisso Livadi

Dryos⚓

⚓Glifa

⚓Aliki

| 0 | | KILOMETRES | | 5 |
| 0 | | MILES | | 3 |

beach at the foot of the hill is narrow,
sandy and reasonably clean.

Naoussa
12km NE of Parikia. Attractive fishing
port on the north coast. Day excursions
leave from here, as do morning buses to
many of the best beaches. Popular with
young people but suffering from tourism,
the best time to visit is in the evening
when calm resumes; no cars are allowed
in the central square. A good place to
eat and to buy tasteful souvenirs; the
Kanhmera shop creates witty, well-
crafted dolls, and copper jewellery

abounds. Cathy and Kostas Gavalas,
who run the Nissiotissa Tourist Agency
in the main square (tel 51480), spent 20
years in New Jersey, USA and speak
fluent English. There is a bank and two-
booth OTE office.

Lefkas
11km SE of Parikia. Picturesque, quiet
village in the middle of the island.
Nearby are the quarries from which
came the famous translucent Parian
marble, used for the 'Venus de Milo' and
in the construction of Napoleon's Tomb.
Pottery is made in Lefkas now.

Accommodation & eating

Pensions, rooms to let, bungalows and hotels of all classes are scattered throughout the island. Particularly attractive is the B class **Xenia Hotel** (tel 21394), with a windmill close by and its stunning views of Parikia and the sea. Naoussa can be pricey. There is a campsite in Parikia (tel 22082), one in Pisso Livadi (tel 41749), and one near Kolimbithres beach (tel 51595).

The variety of food on Paros is uncommonly good. As well as traditional dishes and seafood there are cafés selling Italian-style pastries and strong filter coffee, plus lots of fast-food places of varying quality. Parikia boasts a Chinese restaurant, a hamburger bar and three crêperies. The **Balcony Crêperie** (tel 22074) is especially nice – located in the former mayor's home and run by a girl from London; strong cocktails too.

Sights

Archaeological Museum
Parikia. Three-room museum of local artefacts, housed in a building next to the high school (walk up the street to the right of Ekatontapyliani Church). Most prized possession is a 1m section of the Parian Chronicle dating from c265BC – an account of Greek history carved in Parian marble and detailing local events and cultural activities. Another part of this Chronicle is on display in the Ashmolean Museum in Oxford. *Open 08.30–12.30, 16.00–18.00 Mon–Sat; 09.00–15.00 Sun. Closed Tue.*

Ekatontapyliani Church
Parikia. Also known as the 'Church of One Hundred Doors'. This is one of the oldest and most important churches in Greece; commissioned by the Byzantine Emperor Justinian in the 6thC AD. After an earthquake 400 years later major reconstruction took place using 'new' materials from other buildings. The tomb containing the remains of the Parian saint, Aghia Theoktisti, lies in the north transept.

Valley of the Butterflies
6km SW of Parikia. Descend by coach or by donkey; early morning is the best time to go. The valley is cool and refreshing, the butterflies abundantly beautiful. Although the valley is open all summer, the butterflies live through July and August only. Touristy but fun. Charge.

Beaches

There are nine beaches within a half-hour's walk of Parikia (the one near the campsite has shallow water suitable for children). Naoussa has several fine swimming areas, three of which are Santa Maria, Platys Ammos and Kolimbithres. Kolimbithres has a taverna. The waters all around Paros are excellent for both snorkelling and fishing.

Specialities

Local wines
Lagari – red, white and rosé (white is best) and the more expensive Kavarnis – red, white and rosé.

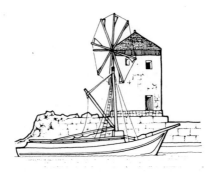

Santorini

General character

The most dramatic of all the Greek islands, Santorini is justifiably popular. The beautiful capital, Fira, stands 200m above the sea at the top of the steep, burnt-orange cliffs. White domes stand out starkly against the dark volcanic rock. Mules used to be the only form of uphill transport from the port, but now a funicular railway operates, easing the burden on the animals.

Santorini is on every island-hopper's list. As well as its outstanding scenic beauty, the ancient ruins are particularly interesting. However, these dual attractions are threatening the island's character. Cruise ships, excursion boats, private yachts and car ferries descend on Santorini in ever increasing numbers. The stone steps rising to the capital have been worn smooth by the continuous tread of tourists' feet. Taxis, mules, meals and hotels are noticeably more expensive than on other islands, and even out of season, accommodation can be difficult to find. If arriving without accommodation booked, a good tip is to reserve a room on the spot, then explore some of the nearby Cycladic islands, returning to Santorini when the room becomes available. A worthwhile exercise, as Santorini should be savoured, especially at sunset when the sea turns pink in contrast to the black volcanic rock.

Regional features

This crescent-shaped island is in fact what remains of an enormous volcano. According to some scholars, it was the eruption of this volcano some 3,500 years ago which devastated the great Minoan cities of Crete. The centre of the volcano disappeared during the eruption, producing what is considered to be the largest caldera in the world. When the caldera filled with sea water this area became what is now the bay of Egeon Pelagos. In the middle of the bay lie the Kaimeni islands, still actively volcanic. The cliffs on the western side of the island, forming the rim of the crater, rise to a height of over 300m. Much of the land is covered with pumice and lava, accounting for Santorini's

Island chain	Cyclades
Alternative names	Thera/Thira
Population	7,100
Area	76sq km
Area tel code	0286
Tourist Police	tel 22649
Harbour Police	tel 22239
Distance from Piraeus	130 nautical miles/12 hours

Travel information
By air
International airport serving Europe. 2–3 flights daily to/from Athens, 4 flights weekly to/from Heraklion, Crete during summer; 3–4 flights weekly to/from Mykonos during summer; 3 flights weekly to/from Rhodes during summer.
By ferry
1–2 daily to/from Piraeus; 1–2 daily to/from Ios & Paros in summer, less often in winter. Frequent connections with Crete & Naxos. Frequent excursion boats & cruises from neighbouring islands and the mainland throughout the summer.

famous black beaches. Vines, fruit and tomatoes are grown in this soil.

Ports & towns

Fira/Thira/Phira

Lovely town, strung precariously around the rim of the crater, now the edge of the sea cliff. A series of 587 steps zigzag their way up the cliff to Fira from its port of Skala down below. The churches seemingly stacked on top of each other, offer spectacular views of the caldera. Most island activity centres around Fira, with the best restaurants, shops and tour operators based here. Tickets for excursions to the major sites can be bought from a number of agencies, as can maps and books. As well as an archaeological museum Fira has several fine churches, including both Greek Orthodox and Roman Catholic cathedrals. Inside the Orthodox cathedral is a Byzantine museum displaying ecclesiastical relics. *Open most mornings.*

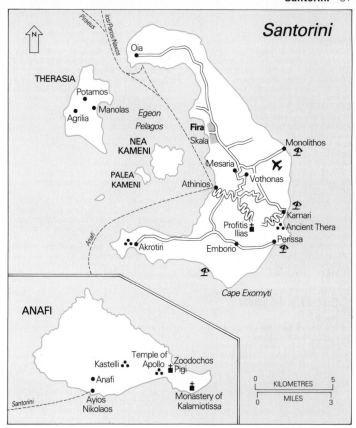

Ormos Athinios

7km S of Fira. The western port at which most car ferries dock. Buses and taxis connect this uninteresting town to the island's capital, Fira.

Accommodation & eating

Although the island has numerous hotels, pensions and rooms, the demand is even greater, so book as far ahead as possible. Several hotels have a spectacular view of the caldera; one of these is the A class **Atlantis** (tel 22232). Other hotels include the C class

Panorama (tel 22481) and the D class **Tataki** (tel 22389). Guest-houses in traditional island homes can be rented in the village of Oia/Ia, on the north-west tip of the island. Organised by the NTOG, tel 71234 for further information. There is a youth hostel on the north side of Fira offering inexpensive accommodation; usually full, but mattresses can be taken out onto the flat roof. Fira abounds in cafés and cocktail bars with splendid views of the volcano. Meals in its numerous restaurants are pricey by Greek standards but on the whole above average in quality.

Sights

Akrotiri

15km SW of Fira. Set in a small ravine,
this archaeological site has attracted
considerable attention since Professor
Marinatos began excavations in 1967.
The professor has since died and is
buried on the site. Although not as
impressive as Knossos in Crete, the
houses and streets date from the same
late-Minoan period. Many fine frescos
were unearthed from the thick layers of
volcanic rock, most notably a springtime
scene of lilies and birds covering three
walls. At the moment the frescos are in
Athens, but will hopefully be returned
to Santorini in the near future. *Open
09.30–16.00 Mon–Sat; 10.00–15.00
Sun.* Charge. The village of Akrotiri, 1km
to the north has a medieval castle.

Ancient Thera

12km SE of Fira. A settlement existed at
Thera before the 9thC BC, although
most of the ruins seen date from
300–145BC. The central street leads to
an Agora 110m long, which was
bordered on the northern side by a row
of shops; to the south is the double-
aisled Royal Stoa (or Stoa Basilike)
which has columns along one wall and a
Doric colonnade. Many of the nearby
houses had fine decorative mosaics and
advanced plumbing systems. The
impressive Terrace of the Festivals and
the 6thC BC Temple of Apollo Karneios
was once the scene of Dorian cult
worship. Erotic graffiti carved on the
rocks dates from the 7thC BC. At the
southern end of the city is the
Gymnasium of the Ephebos. *Open
09.30–16.00 Mon–Sat; 10.00–15.00
Sun.* Charge.

Archaeology Museum

Fira. In the north part of the town near
the Roman Catholic cathedral. This
museum exhibits vases and jars from the
excavations at Akrotiri and Thira, 6thC
BC pottery, and Hellenistic and Roman
sculpture. *Open 09.30–16.00 Mon–Sat;
10.00–13.00 Sun. Closed Tue.* Charge.

Monastery of Profitis Ilias

12km SE of Fira. Situated on the highest
peak of the island, it is claimed that
Crete can be seen from here. The
monastery, dating from 1711, is

Satellite islands

Anafi

30km E of Santorini. Accessible by
occasional ferry from Piraeus or by
boat from Santorini, this island is
well off the beaten track and
perfect for those seeking solitude.
Locals speak little English and are
slightly wary of tourists, although
rooms in private houses can be
found.

There is only one port, Ayios
Nikolaos, and one village a 15-
minute walk away. A sandy beach
lies near the port, but as with most
things on Anafi, is lacking in
amenities. Fresh water and food
are scarce, but traditional island life
is very much intact. At the
monastery of Kalamiotissa a
celebration is held every autumn
with much feasting and dancing.
There is a partly ruined medieval
castle to the north and to the east
the remains of a Temple to Apollo.

Kameni Isles

W of Santorini. There are frequent
excursions from Fira to these small,
volcanically active isles in the bay of
Egeon Pelagos. Private boats can
also be hired in Fira. If planning an
excursion to these 'burnt' islands,
take sturdy shoes, sunglasses and
a sunhat.

Nea Kameni is a 20-minute boat
ride from Skala. It takes 30 minutes
to climb to the top, 125m above.
Pungent sulphurous fumes rise up
from the King George I crater. The
landscape is a harsh one; volcanic
ash and lava, interspersed with
ravines, fissures and fumaroles.

Therasia/Thirassia

W of Santorini. 20-minute boat ride
from the port of Oia. The steep
cliffs along the east coast of
Therasia are part of the western rim
of the caldera. The population of 245
is supported mostly by fishing. It is
possible to find food and a room in
the port of Manolas. Therasia's
main appeal is as a refuge from the
crowds on Santorini, there is little
to do except lie on one of the
island's two beaches. On the
southern coast are the ruins of a
middle Cycladic settlement,
thought to pre-date Akrotiri.

distinguished by its fine icons. A Folklore Museum is devoted to old monastic crafts such as like leatherworking and winemaking. The museum is open 08.00–13.00, 14.30–18.00 Mon–Sat. Linger afterwards to observe the stunning sunsets from this vantage point.

Beaches

Santorini's beaches of dark volcanic sand are extraordinary. They get blazing hot in the sun, so it is a good idea to wear sandals and take a mat or thick towel to sit on. The two main beaches are Kamari (10km SE of Fira), on the east coast, and

Perissa (15km SE of Fira) further south. Both are served by buses and have cafés or tavernas nearby. Monolithos (7km E of Fira) also on the east coast, is less crowded, but has fewer facilities. A lonely walk over the southern foothills will lead to Cape Exomyti and another sandy strip. It is said the remains of an ancient harbour can be seen underwater.

Specialities

Local wines
Nichteri is white and very dry, Visanto, also white, is strong and sweet.

Serifos

General character

A quiet, low-key island, Serifos is really only popular with Greek tourists, Germans and a few stray Americans. Its white capital on the hill, Hora, cascades down the mountainside in traditional Cycladian fashion, and although interesting for a day trip, can feel unwelcoming. Only the port of Livadi is geared up for tourism, and most visitors stay in its hotels and guest-houses. At night, the lights of Hora mingle with the stars overhead casting a warm, romantic glow over Livadi's bars and tavernas which are surprising in their sophistication. Many visitors to Serifos rarely leave the vicinity of the port, as public transport is minimal and taxis rare. A couple of rickety buses run the Livadi/Hora route, but they are infrequent and the journey, punctuated with hairpin bends, is a heart-stopping experience. As an alternative, bicycles can be rented from the 100 Pipers Disco Bar along this road.

Regional features

Serifos, together with its neighbour Sifnos, is a barren island – predominantly brown rock. There is, however, plenty of fresh water from the numerous streams running off the mountains. Fruit and vegetables are grown in the fertile plains around Livadi. The contrast can best be seen from the

Island chain   Cyclades
Alternative names   Seriphos
Population   1,135
Area   73sq km
Area tel code   0281
Tourist Police   tel 51300
Harbour Police   tel 51470
Distance from Piraeus   73 nautical miles/5 hours

Travel information
By ferry
4–7 weekly to/from Piraeus, 4–7 weekly to Kimolos, Milos & Sifnos; 1–2 weekly to Paros Jun–Aug only. Occasional boats to Kythnos & Syros.

Livadi/Hora road – miles and miles of brown earth, with vivid splashes of emerald green which, close up, reveal orchids and blossoming flowers. The mountain peak of Troulos in the centre of the island rises to a height of 585m. Serifos has several fine sandy beaches, three of which are within easy walking distance of the port of Livadi.

Ports & towns

Livadi
Lively, genial port on a horse-shoe shaped bay. Despite the lack of obvious tourist facilities, amenities are quite

good. One shop sells very attractive jewellery and hand-made artefacts; next door is a neon-lit snack bar dispensing terrific Italian-style ice cream. On a hill just outside town a lovely open-air disco provides dancing under the stars, and the seafood in the tavernas is always fresh. Bathing on Livadi beach is pleasant enough, but an even better beach is reached by scrambling down the path in front of the chapel to the right of the harbour (when facing the sea). Camping and discreet nudism are tolerated here. The OTE office, the Tourist Police and a good bakery are located in the town itself.

Hora/Serifos

3km NW of Livadi. Hora is a fine example of a Cycladian capital, notable for its size and position. The main square, where the bus stops, consists of the post office, two ouzeris and two kafeneíons. The simple Taverna Stavros, up the hill

on the left, offers a stunning view over dark brown plains to a turquoise sea. Expect little English to be spoken, at Stavros' or, indeed, anywhere else in Hora. It is an aloof, industrious town, and although rooms to let are available they must be sought out. Forty marble steps lead from the square to a plateau housing a pretty church and a Town Hall of stately proportions. Wrought-iron balconies sporting pagan-looking winged swans overhang flagstoned alleys. The Town Hall itself is painted in garish colours. Steps spiralling upwards lead, eventually, to the Kastro – a crumbling Venetian fortress which once offered refuge for the island's entire population. From the top the view is stunning, but take a sweater as the wind can be chilly. During the ascent, it is interesting to notice that several cube-shaped houses have been built into the walls of the old fortress.

Accommodation & eating

Hotels and pensions are filled with Greek tourists in July and August, so during those months it is best to book in advance. Three pensions in Livadi are the B class **Perseus** (tel 51273), the C class **Mai Strali** (tel 51381), and the E class **Cyclades** (no tel). The main hotel is the C class **Serifos Beach** (tel 51209). Three campsites are currently under construction and should be completed soon. For the moment camping is tolerated on a few beaches. Food is above average in quality, and as well as the excellent ice cream parlour there is a pizzeria in the backstreets of Livardi.

Sights

Caves

Two interesting caves can be reached on foot from Livadi, though it is easier and quicker to go by boat.

Cave of the Cyclops
SW of Livadi. On the far south-western tip of the island near the village of Mesa Akrothira, the cave has some fine stalactites.

Koutalas Cave
20km SW of Livadi. Near the village of Koutalas on the south coast of the island this cave was once occupied by the early inhabitants of Serifos. Considerable remains have been unearthed.

Church of Panayia
11km NW of Livadi. Located in Panayia, the largest inland village on Serifos. This Byzantine church, built in the 10thC, is the oldest on the island. Sadly most of its fine frescos are now gone.

Monastery Taxiarchos
16km N of Livadi. Near the village of Galani, this fortified monastery was built in 1600. Now attractively whitewashed with its red dome and red-roofed chapel it contains Byzantine manuscripts; an icon and some fine 18thC frescos.

Beaches

There are three beaches located within easy walking distance of Livadi; sandy and backed by trees. Roads run to the beaches of Mega Livadi on the west coast (21km W of Livadi) and Koutalas on the south coast (22km SW of Livadi), though infrequent buses make going by caique easier. Other beaches accessible by caique are Sikania (19km NW of Livadi) and Plati Gialos (N of Livadi), both on the north coast.

Specialities

Local wines
Marko, a rich golden retsina.

Sifnos

General character

Sifnos is green and brown, a mountainous fortress of an island, with several enchanting inland villages and over 300 domed churches. Secluded sandy coves and tiny ports cling to its rugged shores. Sifnos is for walkers, with a network of easy mule tracks covering much of the island. Scattered throughout the rocky hills are the remains of some 40 round towers dating from the Classical period, also scores of decorative and highly distinctive two-storey dovecotes.

From mid-July until the end of August, Sifnos is enormously popular. Recently, boats from Paros have added numerous visitors to Sifnos; this route between the central and western Cyclades is the

Island chain   Cyclades
Alternative names   Siphnos
Population   2,100
Area   73sq km
Area tel code   0284
Tourist Police   tel 31210 s.o.
Harbour Police   tel 31617
Distance from Piraeus   76 nautical miles/6 hours

Travel information

By ferry
4–7 weekly to/from Piraeus, 4–7 weekly to Kimolos, Milos & Serifos; 1–2 weekly to/from Paros Jun–Aug only. Occasional service to Kythnos & Syros.

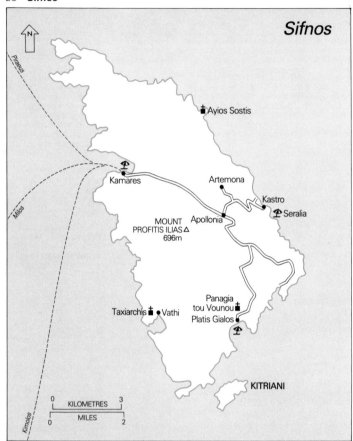

Sifnos

only one which directly connects the two island groups and is a much-needed link. Those seeking peace and seclusion in the high season should head for one of the other western Cyclades. Out of season, however, the predominant sounds are the peeling of church bells and the cooing of doves.

Regional features

Unlike many islands, Sifnos has an abundance of fresh water; even in the dry season, red and pink flowers bloom in profusion along the course of the narrow riverbeds. In spring the southern part of the island is a virtual garden of wild flowers, in contrast to the rocky northern region which remains barren. The terraced fields along the eastern coast yield fine grapes and olives; to the west Mount Profitis Ilias rises to a height of 696m.

In antiquity, Sifnos was much celebrated for its silver and gold mines. However, according to legend, the islanders offended the oracle at Delphi and Apollo destroyed the mines. All that now remains of the island's former wealth is a mine near the church of Ayios Sostis on the north-eastern coast.

Ports & towns

Kamares
6km NW of Apollonia. Until fairly recently, this port was the territory of potters and fishermen, with the potters' worksheds along the northern shore of the narrow gulf and the fishing boats to the south. However, due to the island's increasing popularity with tourists, most of the worksheds are gone, or have been turned into bars and discos. Kamares is a friendly place, but other villages on Sifnos are more interesting.

Apollonia
Only 20 minutes' bus ride from the port, Apollonia is a high, sprawling inland town built on the terraced slopes of three hills. On the summit of each hill stands a tiny hamlet; a picturesque view from the bars and cafes of this island capital is practically guaranteed. It is a town of beautifully restored streets, alleys and churches, with a friendly local population. The town centre is located down a narrow alleyway to the left of the Square of Heroes (when looking out from the post office); if in doubt, follow the signs reading 'Hotel Sifnos' – this pretty inn is surrounded by quality shops and restaurants. Apollonia is the place to get buses to the neighbouring villages, all startlingly different from each other.

Artemona
2km N of Apollonia. Named after Artemis, the goddess of nature and hunting, Artemona is an elegant village, filled with fine *Archintaspitia* (grand Venetian mansions), charming Cycladian dwellings and churches of distinction. The best is the church of Panagia ta Gournia, richly decorated with elaborate paintings and icons hanging on a particularly fine iconostasis.

Kastro
3km E of Apollonia. Until the early 19thC, this medieval town was the island's capital, and had a population of some 2,000 people; today there are only 100 residents, whose houses cluster below the ruins of the ancient fortress. It is a charming village, steps and bridges lead to tiny streets on the upper levels, lined with medieval dwellings. These houses often sport doorways only 1m high, which lead to secret courtyards or cool interiors; dovecotes are much in

evidence. The Archaeological Museum is attractively sited and displays some interesting artefacts. Below the town is the small port of Seralia which has a pebble beach.

Platis Gialos/Platy Yalos
10km S of Apollonia. Positioned on a sandy bay, Platis Gialos is the island's main beach resort, with pensions and bars in abundance. It was once so full of working potters, that the beach was used to store the huge crates of ceramics waiting to be picked up by ship. In summer, the beach and the pensions become quite crowded, so it is best to book in advance.

Vathi/Vathy
S of Kamares. Accessible only by boat from Kamares or Platis Gialos, or by mule track from Apollonia (a three-hour trek). Vathi is a small and secluded settlement located on the west coast of the island and ringed by five hills. The village feels cut off from the world; it has only a couple of shops and the white church of Taxiarchis, a former monastery which now rents rooms out to visitors.

Accommodation & eating

Both are very good on Sifnos and much in demand in the high season; Siphniote chefs are said to be some of the best in Greece. For accommodation, try the C class **Hotel Stavros** (tel 31641) in Kamares or the C class **Hotel Sifnos**

(tel 31624) in Apollonia. Two monasteries offer quiet rooms, **Taxiarchis** in Vathi and the former convent of **Panagia tou Vounou** near Platis Gialos. **Zorba's Tavern** in Kastro has a wonderful view and serves local cheese (very crumbly). Kamares has a proper Italian restaurant and lots of take-aways.

Sights

Museum of Folk Art

Apollonia. The museum houses excellent examples of the island's traditional crafts, including ceramics, textiles and furniture. *Open 09.30–13.00,*

17.00–19.00 Mon–Sat. Closed Tue & Sun.

Specialities

Pottery

The tradition of pottery-making on Sifnos is thought to date from the 3rdC BC, but is sadly now a dying art. In the 1930s there were around 500 potters working on the island; today there are less than a dozen. One of the best working kilns can be seen near the beach of Platis Gialos, where the local potter uses conifer branches for fuel and keeps large tanks of water and clay in front of the workshop.

Syros

General character

In the 19thC Syros was an important industrial, shipping and commercial centre. The island's prominent position in the Aegean prompted the building of not only Greece's first shipyard, but also the largest harbour in the Mediterranean, earning Syros the sobriquet 'the Manchester of Greece'. Prosperous Syriots ordered the construction of great mansions, warehouses, schools and mills which commemorate a period of great wealth and cultural development.

Sadly, the coming of the railway network and the rise of Piraeus, much closer to Athens, brought about a decline in the island's importance. Today most visitors to Greece by-pass Syros entirely, which is a pity. It has excellent inter-island ferry links and is a pleasant place for a one- or two-day stop-over, allowing island-hoppers to avoid entirely the nightmare of Piraeus. Bicycles and scooters for trips to other villages can be hired from the main port of Ermoupolis. Most places provide reasonable accommodation and food. Beaches are sandy and serviceable, with facilities for watersports.

Regional features

Syros is a fairly dry island and water shortages are possible in the high season. Although there are few high

Island chain	Cyclades
Alternative names	Siros/Syra
Population	19,700
Area	84sq km
Area tel code	0281
Tourist Police	tel 22630
Harbour Police	tel 22690
Distance from Piraeus	83 nautical miles/5 hours

Travel information

By ferry
3–5 daily to/from Piraeus; daily to/from Rafina on the mainland; daily to Mykonos & Tinos; 6 weekly to Andros; 1 weekly to Milos, Serifos & Sifnos; 2 weekly to Samos, Ikaria & Patmos in summer.

mountains much of the terrain is hilly; for those who find cycling too strenuous the bus system is a good one. There is little natural vegetation, apart from in the area around Posidonia in the south. Vines, almonds, olives and figs are grown.

Ports & towns

Ermoupolis

Ermoupolis is the capital, not only of Syros, but of all the Cycladic islands. A solid working town, lacking the

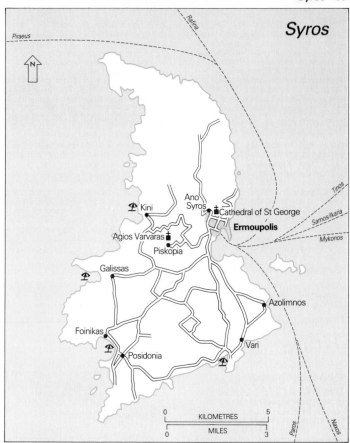

Syros

Piraeus

Rafina

N

Kini

Ano Syros

Cathedral of St George

Ermoupolis

Tinos

Samos/Ikaria

Mykonos

Agios Varvaras

Piskopia

Galissas

Azolimnos

Foinikas

Vari

Posidonia

| 0 | KILOMETRES | 5 |
| 0 | MILES | 3 |

Paros

Naxos

picturesque whiteness of most Cycladian capitals. Its grey harbour and industrious air is not immediately appealing when compared with more glamourous neighbours such as Paros and Mykonos. The waterfront shops are functional and utilitarian. On the far side of the harbour are fruit warehouses, and huge cranes used to unload cargo from the ships which steam in daily. Ermoupolis is prettiest when viewed from one of the streets rising up the hill to the village of Ano Syros.

A stroll around the area known as 'Ta Vaporia' reveals elegant 19thC mansions. The attractive sidestreets, cobbled and overhung with wrought-iron balconies, offer the type of services most useful to island-hoppers: pharmacies, dry cleaners and hair dressers. Directly behind the harbour is Plateia Miaoulis, an impressive square lined with fine neo-Classical buildings. The OTE office is here, along with the post office and the Town Hall.

Ano Syros

2km N of Ermoupolis. High above the sea and crowned by the Catholic cathedral of St George. Ano Syros is a medieval Venetian village with twisting streets and numerous flights of steps. There are several fine churches, and the Convent of St Joan founded in 1635 by King Louis XIII of France.

Foinikas/Finix/Phoenikas
12km SW of Ermoupolis. The remains of a Roman wall can still be seen in this resort town on the west coast.

Accommodation & eating

Most of the villages near the sea offer rooms to let. Hotels in Foinikas include the C class **Olympia** (tel 42212) and the E class **Cyclades** (tel 42255). Ermoupolis offers several hotels including the A class **Ypatia** (tel 23575), but it can be more fun to stay in the cheap, unlisted pensions – often crumbling neo-Classical mansions. Eating is in tavernas and cafés; the sophisticated **Chez Michel** in Plateia Miaoulis, Ermoupolis, is a taverna-cum-French bistro.

Sights

Apollon Theatre
Ermoupolis. This sadly neglected building just behind the Town Hall is a relic from the island's prosperous past. It was constructed as a miniature version of La Scala in Milan, and until the beginning of this century, presented a season of Italian opera each year.

Archaeological Museum
Ermoupolis. Located up a flight of steps next to the Town Hall. This three-room museum exhibits finds from Syros, Amorgos and Paros. *Open Mon–Sat 09.00–15.30, Sun 10.00–14.00. Closed Tue.*

Churches
Syros abounds in churches, one of the most notable being the 15thC Ayios Nikolaos in Ermoupolis with its monument to the Unknown Soldier by the Greek sculptor Vitalis. On Vrontathi Hill, above the capital, is the church of Anastasis; the Catholic cathedral of St George is on the twin summit of Ano Syros. The oldest Byzantine church on Syros is located in the fragrant hills near Piskopio.

Specialities

Loukoumia
A type of sweet, also known as Turkish Delight. Made on Syros and sold throughout Greece.

Tinos

General character

Tinos is known as the 'Lourdes of Greece' with thousands of pilgrims coming each year to pay homage to the miraculous icon of the Virgin Mary. A serene, low-key island, popular with Greek holiday-makers, though even in the high season accommodation is likely Little in the way of tourist amenities, there is, however, a cinema, a bank, a post office, a doctor and a dentist.

Regional features

The landscape of Tinos is dotted with over 600 medieval dovecotes. These attractive white structures, together with some 1,200 family chapels give the island its distinctive appearance. No fewer than 64 villages are scattered about, perched high on mountain ridges or set low in cultivated

Island chain   Cyclades
Population   7,730
Area   194sq km
Area tel code   0283
Tourist Police   tel 22255 s.o.
Harbour Police   tel 22348
Distance from Piraeus   86 nautical miles/6 hours

Travel information

By ferry
Daily from Piraeus in summer; 10–15 weekly from Rafina in summer; 3–4 weekly from Rafina in winter. Boats most days to Andros & Syros; in summer to Paros & Naxos. Occasional day excursions in Jul & Aug to Mykonos, Delos, Paros & Naxos.

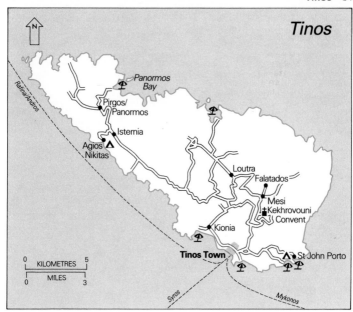

valleys; a few are accessible only by rough paths. Little private transport hire, but a reasonable bus service runs approx three times daily. The noisy, crowded buses are invariably jammed with locals, not to mention local produce; to hire a taxi tel 22470.

Ports & towns

Tinos Town
A clean, pleasant town, lying on the south-west tip of the island. Many two- and three-storey buildings topped by red-tiled roofs. All the important shops are here, as well as several hotels and restaurants on the waterfront. A broad avenue leads from the quayside to the church of the Evangelistria, reposing on a hill overlooking town and harbour. The town has no less then eight museums and art galleries.

Isternia
28km NW of Tinos Town. Situated above the tiny port of Agios Nikitas on a picturesque bay. Surrounded by hills, this is a particularly green and fertile part of the island. The dome of the church is attractively decorated – inlaid with a mosaic of pottery tiles.

Loutra
13km NW of Tinos Town. Up in the hills, this is one of the island's most attractive villages, with its Venetian houses and fountains. The carpentry school in the 17thC monastery is open to the public.

Pirgos/Panormos
33km NW of Tinos Town. One of the largest villages on Tinos, with a sleepy main square shaded by plane trees. Green marble, much prized by sculptors, is quarried in the surrounding hills and a School of Fine Arts has been established here. Completed works are exhibited in the local museum.

Accommodation & eating

Tinos has over a thousand hotel beds, plus lots of rooms to let. There are two campsites on the coast, one at Agios Nikitas (30km NW of Tinos Town) and one near St John Porto (6km E of Tinos Town). Avoid the weeks either side of 25 March and 15 August, the two main feast days, when the island is packed

with pilgrims visiting the Church of
Evangelistria. The A class **Tinos Beach
Hotel** at Kionia, just up the coast from
Tinos Town has good facilities for ·
families with a main building and
bungalows. In the main port, try the B
class **Favie Souzane** pension (tel
22693). Tinos Town is also the best
place to eat, with tavernas and cafés all
around the harbour.

Sights

Archaeological Museum
Tinos Town. Just below the church, this
relatively modern building has been built
in the style of the island's dovecotes.
The upper floors contain numerous
pottery vases. Amongst the most
interesting exhibits are those from the
excavation of the Sanctuary of Poseidon
and Amphitrite (4km NW of Tinos Town)
near Kionia. Poseidon is said to have rid
the island of its plague of snakes by
sending storks to eat them. *Open
09.00–14.00, 16.00–18.00 Mon–Sat;
10.00–14.00 Sun. Closed Tue.* Charge.

Evangelistria Church
Tinos Town. Built of white marble from
the islands of Paros and Tinos, this
church is dedicated to Our Lady of Good
Tidings and houses the famous icon of
the Virgin Mary, discovered in 1822. This
miraculous icon is believed to have
healing properties, and numerous
pilgrims visit the church each year to
seek cures. The icon itself dominates the
interior of the church; jewel-studded
and lavishly adorned with gold and silver
votive offerings, it is normally
surrounded by candles. There is a small
museum connected with the church.
Open daily 08.30–20.30.

Kekhrovouni Convent
12km NE of Tinos Town. Built in the
12thC, the nuns of this large convent
make lovely lacework and are pleased to
receive visitors. The convent's museum
contains several fine post-Byzantine
icons.

Beaches

Reasonable, but not stunning. Best are
at St John Porto (6km E of Tinos Town),
Kionia (3km NW of Tinos Town) and
Panormos Bay (36km NW of Tinos
Town). All have tavernas within walking
distance.

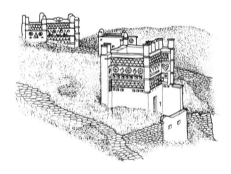

The Dodecanese

Astipalea

General character

Although technically one of the Dodecanese, Astipalea is more like a Cycladian island. White cube-shaped buildings tumble down from a fortress high above, unfortunately though, it lacks Cycladian grace. On a clear day it is possible to see the islands of Amorgos and Santorini.

In Astipalea Town, the main port, two large causeways and a telephone tower obscure the view, and recent construction throughout the island is unsightly evidence of a new drive towards tourism. Residents are extremely friendly, however, and the women still wear traditional dress in some villages.

Island chain   Dodecanese
Alternative names   Astypalea
Population   1,030
Area   97sq km
Area tel code   0242
Tourist Police   tel 61207
Harbour Police   tel 61208
Distance from Piraeus   165
nautical miles/8–10 hours

Travel information

By ferry

1–2 weekly to/from Piraeus, Paros, Kalymnos, Kos, Nissiros, Tilos, Symi, Rhodes.

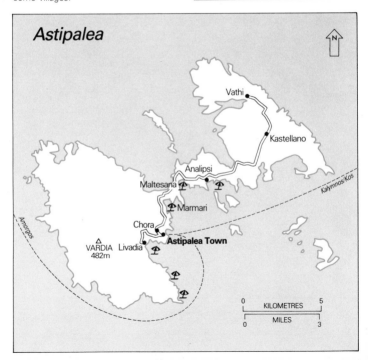

Regional features

Astipalea is mountainous and arid, although to the west of Astipalea Town there is a valley of pine trees. The island is shaped like a moth, with bays and sandy coves around the edges of its wings. One road connects the village of Livadia with its outlying neighbour Vathi, but the best way to travel is by hiring a boat in Astipalea Town.

Ports & towns

Astipalea Town/Skala

The island's main port and the hub of all activity. Most tavernas and hotels are located around the wide harbour, and there is a sandy town beach. Hire taxis here, or catch the little blue bus which greets each ferry as it docks. There is a bank, a doctor, and an OTE office. The hotels under construction to the left of the harbour (when facing the sea) will boast a lovely view, but offer little in the way of aesthetic appeal.

Chora

1km up the hill from Astipalea Town. The Venetian capital of the island, the village is dominated by the castle, built around 1230 by the Quirini family who ruled Astipalea from the 13th to the 16thC. From a distance, the twin domes of the church of Evangelistria tou Kastro (Madonna of the Castle) seem to be part of the fortress; in fact the chapel lies just above. A row of windmills lines the ridge between Chora and Astipalea Town.

Livadia

2km SW of Astipalea Town. Nestling in a fertile valley, Livadia is the nicest place to be on Astipalea. There are rooms to let and one or two tavernas; the beach is sandy, but lots of seaweed is washed ashore.

Vathi

19km NE of Astipalea Town. The island's northernmost village. When the Italians occupied the Dodecanese in 1912, Astipalea was the first island to be invaded. The fortress of Kastellano in Vathi dates from this period.

Accommodation & eating

Three D class pensions are the **Aegeon** (tel 61236); **Astynea** (tel 61209) and **Paradissos** (tel 61224). The best restaurant in Astipalea Town is the **Hotel de Paris** which serves home-made brioche and good ice cream. It is run by a Frenchman who also rents rooms out.

Beaches

There are sandy beaches at Astipalea Town, Livadia and Maltesana (4km NE of Astipalea Town) where the remains of Roman baths and a mosaic are preserved.

Halki

General character

After years of neglect and decay this charming little island is undergoing a revival. The ruined mansions built in Venetian style, known as *Archintaspitia*, are in the process of being renovated. There is now a paved road to the beach; Tarpoon Springs Boulevard, named after a place in Florida, USA by Halkians in America who donated the funds.

Halki is lovely, unspoilt, carrying legend and tradition into the 20th century. However its remoteness does present problems. There is no hot water, and the cold is apt to be laced with salt. Food is expensive, imported from Rhodes, and as a trade-off much of Halki's prime fish is sent to restaurants on the more popular island. There is no bank (although travellers' cheques may be cashed in the OTE office) and anything other than basics should be bought in advance.

Regional features

Clean air, sparkling sea and three windmills silhouetted on the skyline are Halki's distinguishing features. Transport is by donkey or on foot; be sure to wear rubber-soled shoes as the paths can be smooth and slippery.

Island chain   Dodecanese
Alternative names   Chalci/Khalki
Population   335
Area   28sq km
Area tel code   0246
Tourist Police   tel 71273
Distance from Piraeus   302 nautical miles/18–22 hours (depending on the ship)

Travel information

By ferry

4–5 weekly from the port of Kamiros Skala on Rhodes; 1 weekly from Piraeus; *Panormitis* service once a week connecting Halki with the other Dodecanese islands. Seas can be rough and smaller boats cancelled – allow time for being stranded at Kamiros Skala or on Halki itself.

Ports & towns

Niborio

The picturesque island capital and port with its *Archintaspitia* rising on a hill overlooking a harbour busy with fishing boats. Pride of place belongs to the church of Aghios Nikolaos, patron saint

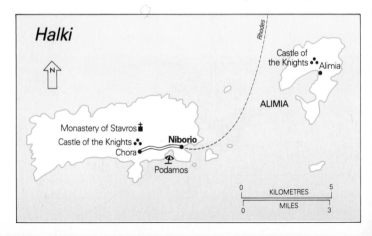

Halki

Castle of the Knights •• Alimia

ALIMIA

Monastery of Stavros ♦
Castle of the Knights ••
Chora   **Niborio**
⚓
Podamos

Rhodes

KILOMETRES 0 ––––––– 5
MILES 0 ––––––– 3

of sailors; its clock tower is now obsolete, but still impressive. One doctor, three policemen, three shops and two public telephones keep the island in order. Old Halki, or Chora, looms on the hill above Niborio but is now largely uninhabited.

Accommodation & eating

Several pensions and rooms to let. **The Captain's House** pension (tel 71201) has air-conditioning and showers. The **Omonia** taverna serves seafood, the establishment with wooden trim next door sells wine from the barrel, and the speciality of the **Houvardas** restaurant is a plate of giant beans cooked in tomato sauce.

Specialities

Traditional ceremonies
Blessing of the Dead On Boxing Day families gather in the small cemetery to pay homage to loved ones by covering the graves with sweet cakes and pastries.
Weddings The bride and groom parade through the streets of Niborio with their

respective families before meeting in the square to be escorted to the church. During the ceremony itself, at a prearranged signal, the bride and groom attempt to step on each other's feet. Whoever manages this first is the 'boss' of the marriage.

Beaches

Podamos Beach is a 10-minute walk up slippery paths through the town. It is long, curving and beautifully sandy. Bungalows near the beach are for hire, but tend to get very hot in high summer; enquire locally for details on rental.

Satellite islands

Alimnia
NE of Halki. Lying between Rhodes and Halki is the islet of Alimnia – two large humps of rock connected by a sand bar. Uninhabited since 1912, its principal point of interest is a ruined castle of the Knights of St John.

Kalymnos

General character

Independently prosperous from the sponge trade, Kalymnos has fewer tourist amenities than many islands of a similar size. Pothia, the main port, bustles with industry and all around are signs of sea-faring and trade – ships, nets, boat repair stations, small cargo lorries. Resort facilities are concentrated around Myrties on the west coast.

Regional features

Kalymnos with its 70km of coastline, is a barren island; high and rocky, striped with bold bands of lush green foliage. The road to Myrties is lined with trees, the route to Vathi dotted with beehives. Windmills are a feature of the skyline, as is the castle in the town of Chora. The northern tip of the island juts,

Island chain Dodecanese
Alternative names Kalimnos
Population 14,300
Area 111sq km
Area tel code 0243
Tourist Police tel 28302
Harbour Police tel 28137
Distance from Piraeus 183
nautical miles/12–14 hours

Travel information

By ferry
4–6 weekly to Piraeus, Kos, Leros & Rhodes. 3 weekly to Patmos, 3 weekly to Pserimos in summer, 2 weekly in winter.

abandoned, into the sea. The road which leads to it peters out into mountain.

Ports & towns

Pothia/Pothea

Large, busy harbour where a carnival
atmosphere prevails when the sponge
boats return. At these times the single
woman traveller should attempt to be
elsewhere; tavernas and bars in Pothia
are designed to cater for the needs of
sailors. At most times, however, Pothia
is a pleasant enough town, with
serviceable shops and facilities, including
a bank, a post office and a bus station.
There is also a hospital and an
archaeological museum.

Chorio

2km NW of Pothia. On the hill above
Pothia, this pretty white village with its
three windmills was once the capital of
Kalymnos. It grew up around the
medieval Castle of the Knights on the hill
nearby.

Myrties

7.5km NW of Pothia. Pretty resort town
overlooking the island of Telendos. The
winding lane which leads to the sea is
bordered by hibiscus and other
flowering shrubs. Tables in the tavernas
are shaded by arbours; palm trees and
pensions are plentiful. The village of

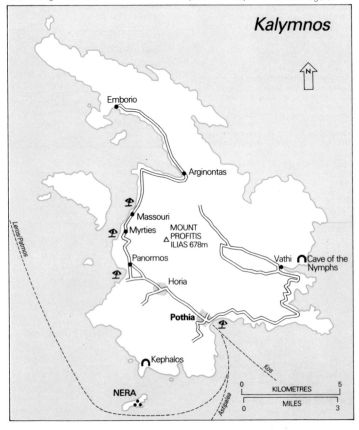

Kalymnos

Massouri 1km up the coast to the north
is a similar resort.

Vathi/Vathis

12km NE of Pothia. Possibly the
sweetest-smelling village in the
Aegean; tangerines and lemons are
exported from here in huge quantities.
Following a twisting journey through a
landscape almost lunar in quality, an
abrupt turn reveals the port far below –
a green, self-contained oasis nestling in
bare brown rock. An arm of turquoise
water leads to the sea, where tiny
picturesque vessels, heavy with cargo,
ply the route from the harbour to the
larger vessels waiting in open water.
Next to the school a bubbling spring
brings fresh water from the mountains.
Two tavernas but no rooms to let.

Accommodation & eating

Several pensions around Myrties are
built on the hillside, offering lovely sea
views of Telendos. Three pensions are
the B class **Themis** (tel 47230), the C
class **Delfini** (tel 47514) and the D class
Myrties (tel 28912). Eating is restricted
to the usual tavernas and cafés. One of
the prettiest is the **Restaurant Myrties**
(tel 28912) in the village of the same
name, where diners on the verandah
can watch the boats coming and going.

Sights

Caves

The irregular, 70km-coastline of
Kalymnos conceals many caves
accessible only by boat.

Cave of the Nymphs

NE of Pothia. On the east coast of the
island beyond Vathi. Known more

recently as the Cave of the Seven
Virgins, taking its name from the legend
of the seven young women who sought
refuge there from invading Turkish
pirates.

Kephalos Cave

SW of Pothia. Located on the southern
tip of the island. It has impressive
stalagmites and stalactites and was
formerly a sanctuary to Zeus. Charge.

Specialities

Sponges

Kalymnos is the 'sponge capital' of the
Greek islands. One of the most
interesting sponge-processing factories
is approx 1km west of Pothia harbour.
In the courtyard, men in wide-brimmed
hats tread barefoot on the black
sponges to release the 'milk'. The
sponges are then dipped in a vat of acid
to bleach them to the familiar – and much
more attractive – yellow colour.
Amateur divers can search for their own
sponges with the help of the Kalymnos
Diving School (tel 28545). Boats and
equipment are supplied.

Satellite islands

Nera

S of Kalymnos. Only 1km from the
southern tip of Kalymnos, this tiny
islet is uninhabited save for a small
monastery. Meals are served in a
restaurant in the cloisters, but be
sure to enquire locally before
setting off. Hire boats in Pothia.

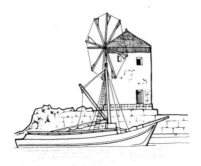

Kos

General character

This ancient and historic island, which abounds in ancient monuments and ruins of rare beauty, is in danger of being spoilt forever. Package tours land in specially chartered flights several times a day in the high season. Kos Town, architecturally graceful in the Turkish style, throbs to the beat of disco music and young people out for a good time. Souvenir shops and restaurants outnumber more domestic facilities; roads out of Kos Town sport new tourist complexes, and the former fishing village of Kardamena has been almost totally engulfed.

If peace and tranquillity appeal, take one of the numerous boat excursions to smaller islands such as Pserimos or Nissiros. Frequent ferries, along with good beaches and good food are some of the pleasures of Kos. A tip: day excursions to neighbouring islands are expensive compared to the normally scheduled ferries, many of which go to the same islands, often at the same hour. Persevere in the Tourist Office for comprehensive information.

Regional features

Kos has over 100km of coastline, much of which is sandy. The Dikeos mountain range covers almost half the southern side of the island. Soil is fertile, irrigated by spring waters, and agricultural produce is abundant. Roads are quite good but public transport patchy; it is best to hire a scooter or bicycle, or rely on taxis. There is no bus to the airport.

History

Kos Town was founded in 366BC and rapidly became one of the maritime powers of the Aegean. The island had been conquered by Alexander the Great 30 years earlier, but eventually fell into the hands of the Romans in 82BC. Kos was subsequently annexed to the Byzantine Empire, and suffered the ravages of Saracen pirates and other invaders until handed over to the Knights of St John in 1315. Like Rhodes,

---

Island chain   Dodecanese
Alternative names   Cos
Population   20,350
Area   290sq km
Area tel code   0242
Tourist office   tel 28227. *Open in summer 08.00–13.00, 18.00–20.00, in winter 08.00–15.15 Mon–Sat.*
Harbour Police   tel 28059
Distance from Piraeus   200 nautical miles/14–16 hours

Travel information

By air
International airport serving Europe. 1–3 flights daily from Athens; 1–2 most days to Rhodes; 4 weekly to Mykonos Jul & Aug.

By ferry
6 weekly to Piraeus, Patmos, Leros, Kalymnos, Rhodes; 2–3 weekly to Nissiros, Tilos, Symi; 2 weekly via *Panormitis* service to other Dodecanese islands; irregular service to Chios, Lesbos, Lemnos, Crete, Santorini, Milos. Excursions in summer months: daily to Patmos, Rhodes, Kalymnos; 5 weekly to Pserimos; 4 weekly to Nissiros; 3 weekly to Leros; 1 weekly to Samos. 'Flying Dolphin' hydrofoils to Rhodes, Patmos, Samos & Leros. Jun–Sept.

---

it fell in 1522 to the Turks who occupied for 390 turbulent years, before surrendering to the Italians in 1912. Kos finally became a part of Greece 35 years later in 1947.

Ports & towns

Kos Town

Built along the north-eastern coast, this is a lovely capital town with palm trees providing ample shade. The narrow entrance to its large, almost circular harbour is guarded by the Castle of the Knights. Like Rhodes Town, the skyline of Kos is dominated by minarets and towers. If the Turkish influence is the most distinctive, the Italian is the most

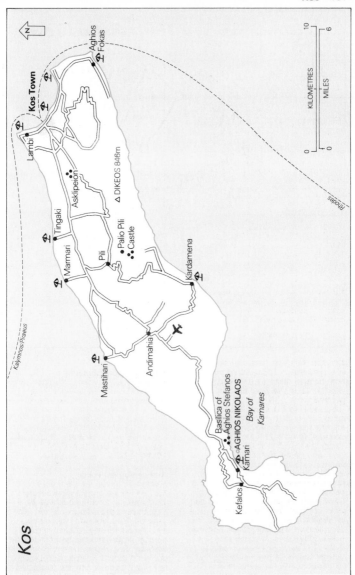

Kos

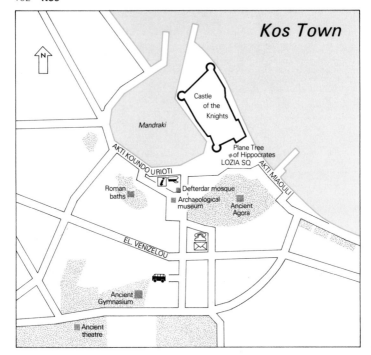

prevalent. Kos was badly damaged by
an earthquake in 1933, and all but the
most durable buildings flattened; the
Italians then set to work erecting a
'planned town'.

A good time to explore the town and
appreciate its harmony is during the
afternoon between 14.00 and 17.00
when a rare tranquillity descends.
Otherwise it sizzles along with its
summer visitors; the sound of
motorbikes is background
accompaniment to the general cacophony
of urban holiday life. The town is good
for eating and shopping; this is the place
to have clothes cleaned, or to buy films,
books and sandals. Drink is cheap, and
although Kos is more expensive than its
lesser-known neighbours, it is possible
to get value for money on a range of
goods. The exchange bureau next to the
Bank of Greece is open evenings and
Saturdays during the summer in addition
to normal opening hours.

Sights

Archaeological Museum

In the Piazza of Eleferia opposite
the 18thC Defterdar mosque, this
attractive museum contains several
rooms of artefacts. Principal amongst
them are mosaics dating from the 3rdC
AD and several fine statues, especially
one of Hermes with a dog at his feet.
*Open 09.30–16.00 Mon–Sat;
10.00–15.00 Sun & hols. Closed Tue.*
Charge.

Archaeological ruins

Scattered throughout the town of
Kos are ruins of outstanding beauty.
The finds are so numerous that the
locals have adopted a casual attitude
towards them. A few to search for
include an ancient Gymnasium and a
portico of five columns dating from the
3rdC BC. Located at the entrance to the
ancient Agora, it was probably brought
here from another site and re-erected at
a later date. Also an amphitheatre, now

well restored, where theatre troupes sometimes perform in the summer.
Castle of the Knights
Built by the Knights of St John in the mid 15thC it was constructed for defence purposes, probably on the site of an older structure. Following an unsuccessful raid by the Turks, a second fortified wall was added and finally completed in 1514. The deep moat is now planted with palm trees which flank the handsome gate. Within the castle are remains from many ancient Classical sites. *Open 09.00–15.30 Mon–Sat; 10.00–15.00 Sun & hols. Closed Tue.* Charge.
Plane tree of Hippocrates
Situated in Lozia Square, which adjoins the Castle of the Knights, this massive, twisted old plane tree now has to be supported with props. Hippocrates was born on Kos around 460BC; this ancient Greek physician, known as the father of modern medicine, is said to have taught his students beneath this tree. Though not actually possible as the tree is not sufficiently old, it is a nice story and emphasises Hippocrates' link with Kos.

Kardamena
25km SW of Kos Town. An attractive fishing village, but definitely for those who enjoy a lively holiday. This resort abounds with hotels, tavernas, discos and people. There is a golden six-mile beach ideally suited to children, and the locals make interesting pottery. There are the remains of a Hellenistic theatre nearby.

Kefalos/Kephalos
43km SW of Kos Town. Built on the hill above, and dominating the view of the Bay of Kamares. Nearby is a ruined Castle of the Knights. The port below is Kamari, where there is a sandy beach, good for swimming. At the northern end of the bay are the remains of the early Christian Basilica of Aghios Stefanos; just offshore is the islet of Aghios Nikolaos with its tiny chapel of the same name.

Pili
17km SW of Kos town. A mountain village right in the centre of the island offering splendid views across the water to Pserimos and Kalymnos. A path leads to Palio Pili (4km to the south) where there are the remains of a Byzantine kastro.

Tingaki
11km W of Kos Town. Peaceful, sparsely populated beach resort with one or two hotels and tavernas serving good food. The beach is broad and sandy, with umbrellas provided as a shield against the forceful north wind.

Accommodation & eating

Much accommodation comes pre-paid with an air ticket. If arriving without a place to stay, Kos Town is the likely venue; hotels and pensions are plentiful. The Tourist Office can provide a list, but shopping around first is advisable – a bit of shade or a large airy room is excellent refuge from the rowdiness outside. Hotels worth trying are the B class **TheoXenia** (tel 22310), and the C class **Acropole** (tel 22244) – no English spoken but a delightfully shabby large house. Just outside town is the A class **Ramira Beach Hotel** (tel 28489). In Tingaki try the B class **Tigaki Toulas Hotel** (tel 29206).

Eating is excellent in Kos Town. Seafood is fresh and tasty, and even reasonable value if sampled in one of the restaurants away from the waterfront. The **Platanos Restaurant** behind the ancient ruins known as the Agora, serves only so-so food, but the view is superb; minarets to the left and a bubbling fountain to the right.

Sights

Asklipeion
4km SW of Kos Town. This temple, dedicated to the worship of health and art, is one of the most important ruins on the island. Dating from the 4thC BC, it comprises three main levels connected by wide, handsome steps. There are also Roman baths with a well-preserved hypocaust dating from the 1stC AD.

Altars and statues grace this pleasant site; the most charming spot is by the fountain of Pan. Until the Roman occupation, a type of Olympic Games was held here every five years. *Open 09.00–16.00 Mon–Sat; 10.00–15.00 Sun & hols.* Charge.

Specialities

Local wines
Glafkos, a medium-dry white wine with a slightly tart aftertaste and Apellis, a medium-dry red table wine. Also retsina bottled by Theokritos.

Leros

General character

Friendly, prosperous and off the beaten track, Leros lacks the dramatic beauty and easy accessibility of many other Dodecanese islands. As a result, visitors are treated with naive curiosity by many of the locals; a pleasing situation likely to change once the new airport is completed. At the moment there is little tourist development and, at first sight little to appeal. It is best known as a naval base and the sight of a World War II battle in 1943. However, those who stay on Leros profess to love it.

Regional features

Leros is a small hilly island with a ragged, indented coastline producing many bays and natural harbours. Ideal for swimming and fishing. The island's commercial centre is formed by three villages so close together as to be almost indistinguishable. Two of these villages, Platanos and Agia Marina are only 500m apart, and together form the capital. The bare brown rocky hills are interspersed

Island chain Dodecanese
Population 8,130
Area 53sq km
Area tel code 0247
Tourist Police tel 22221
Harbour Police tel 22224
Distance from Piraeus 171
nautical miles 10–12 hours

Travel information

By ferry
4–6 weekly to Piraeus, Kalymnos, Kos, Patmos, Rhodes; *Panormitis* service once a week via all the Dodecanese islands; 1–2 weekly to Samos.

with fertile valleys where olives, figs and vines are grown.

Ports & towns

Lakki
Tall palm trees tower above solid grey mansions, huge and echoing, built by the Italians in heavy Mussolini style.

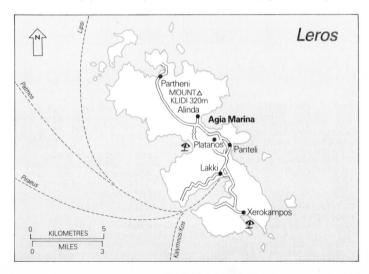

Lakki was once an important harbour, its almost circular basin easily cordoned off in wartime. Much of the town is redundant now, with the Art Deco edifices containing offices devoted to maritime activities. If arriving on the Piraeus/Rhodes midnight ship, Lakki is a glorious sight – grand and ghostly like a deserted 1930s film set. In the daytime there is little point in lingering.

Agia Marina

4km N of Lakki. The prettiest of the three principal villages. Approached by a steep road from Platanos on the hill, which is lined with churches and villas in private grounds. The tiny harbour is pine-fringed, and tavernas are peaceful. Shops sport balconies in faded Venetian style.

Panteli

3km N of Lakki. The centre of nightlife on Leros, this is a rough and ready resort with discos and bouzouki music blaring from every corner. Women feed chickens on a waterfront which offers stupendous views over Asia Minor. Little girls are fascinated by anything foreign which glitters.

Platanos

3.5km N of Lakki. The island capital, on the hill just south of Agia Marina, houses the Town Hall, a museum and all the necessary shops. Most are found around the main square, the hub of activity, day and night. Cobbled,

residential streets wind tortuously up the steep hill to the Kastro at the top. Pastel-coloured villas are hung with vines.

Accommodation & eating

The C class **Hotel Panteli** (tel 22152) and the D class **Hotel Platanos** (tel 22620) are both reasonable. For Art Deco novelty try the **Hotel Leros** (tel 22940) in Lakki. Tavernas are romantic in Agia Marina and rowdy in Panteli.

Sights

Archaeological Museum

Platanos. 3.5km N of Lakki. Located in the main square, this small museum exhibits local artefacts. Of primary interest are the grave goods found on the island. *Open most mornings 10.00–14.00.*

Kastro

Platanos. 3.5km N of Lakki. Built high on the hill above the capital, there is a commanding view from this Byzantine fortress. Renovated by the Knights of St John and the Venetians, it was converted much later into an observatory by the occupying Italians during World War II. Within the Kastro is the church of Kyras Kastro which houses the Icon of the Virgin.

Lipsi

General character

Tiny, industrious, with a gem of a town and very courteous people; on its way up in popularity. No cars (and no bicycle hire), although one taxi is rumoured to run in July and August. Rural, but not tranquil, the silence is broken by the sound of heavy farm equipment and all around this lovely island are signs of the working life.

Regional features

Lipsi has a long, irregular coastline. The only settlement is located in a natural harbour on the south-west coast. Lipsi Town rises from the sea like a mirage. Crowned by a church with three turquoise domes, these shapes and colours are mirrored by small chapels

Island chain Dodecanese
Alternative names Lipsoi/Lipsos
Population 575
Area 16sq km
Area tel code 0247

Travel information

By ferry

Daily caique during the high season from the islands of Patmos & Leros, less often during other months. *Panormitis* offers an irregular weekly service connecting Lipsi with all the Dodecanese islands; enquire locally.

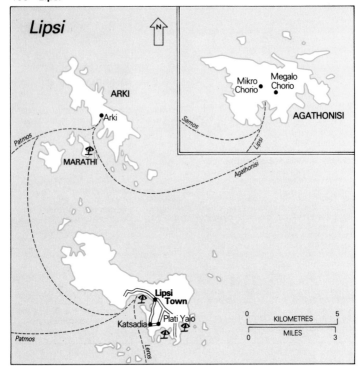

perched on every promontory around the island. There are caves around the far shores, but roads are primitive and boats can be scarce. Behind the town, to the east, is a fertile farming valley.

Ports & towns

Lipsi Town

Predominantly blue and white when viewed from the sea, the town is surprisingly colourful. Residents have painted their cube-shaped houses in bright colours, giving the winding streets a rakish, gypsy feel. The main square, with its simple cafés and shady trees, also houses the post office and a kiosk selling cigarettes and post cards. The village shop, embellished with gargoyles, is painted vivid red and yellow.

Accommodation & eating

The D class **Calypso** (tel 41242) stands right on the quayside and is the only hotel on Lipsi. There are, however, several pensions, **Pension Flisvos** has the best view. If staying in one of the small private houses on the hillside, expect to find goats and cows in the front garden. There is a taverna on the hill, as well as several cafés and eating places along the harbour serving traditional Greek fare.

Beaches

One sandy beach is located just west of the town, further round the bay. The best sandy beach is at Plati Yalo, a 30-minute walk to the south-east, where there is a small taverna and lovely clear water.

Specialities

Hand-woven carpets
In the pale, square building overlooking the harbour, attractive young girls weave carpets to be shipped to Athens. Visitors are welcome to watch the weavers at work.

Satellite islands

Agathonisi
NE of Lipsi. Remote island, to the north of the Dodecanese, supporting a fishing community. Linked once a week with the main Dodecanese islands via the steamer *Panormitis*. There are two villages on the island, Megalo Chorio and Mikro Chorio.

Arki
N of Lipsi. Remote fishing community with a population of around 50. Little has been done to promote tourism; buildings are grey and unlovely. There is no refrigeration and, in fact, no electricity. Supplies, including ice, are imported from Patmos, so food is very basic. Best to take a sleeping bag, as accommodation is also basic, and the few available rooms may be occupied. Also linked once a week via the steamer *Panormitis*, Arki, with its one village and three churches, has its own tiny satellite island just outside the harbour – Marathi.

Marathi
N of Lipsi. Tiny island south-west of Arki, with a sandy beach on the east coast. There is a good taverna open in July and August. Check in Arki before hiring a boat.

Nissiros

General character

A gem of an island, little known to tourists and boasting an impressive, dormant volcano. The picturesque port of Mandraki has fine facilities offering peace and tranquillity (once the excursion boat from Kos departs). Nissiros is perfect for walkers.

Regional features

Nissiros smells of figs and almonds. Nuts were once exported from the island by the ton, but now most of these fragrant trees are left unpicked. The road from Mandraki to the volcano twists through steep terraced fields, offering wonderful views of Turkey on the horizon and the tiny harbour far below.

Ports & towns

Mandraki
Attractive capital and port with a long, rambling promenade. Away from the harbour, the streets are a maze of alleyways so narrow the balconies of

---

Island chain   Dodecanese
Alternative names   Nisyros
Population   916
Area   41sq km
Area tel code   0242
Tourist Police   tel 31201

Travel information

By ferry
1–2 weekly to/from Piraeus, Amorgos, Astipalea, Kalymnos, Kos, Leros, Lipsi, Paros, Patmos, Rhodes. Jun–Sep day excursions from Kos 4 times a week.

---

opposing houses form a natural sunshield. Splashes of dazzling colour relieve the whiteness of the buildings, which include a bank, a post office and a doctor's surgery. Along the flagstone path to the left (when facing the sea) is the early 19thC rock-hewn Monastery of Panaghia tou Spilliani, built out from a cave in the cliff. As well as the usual shops and tavernas there is a charming

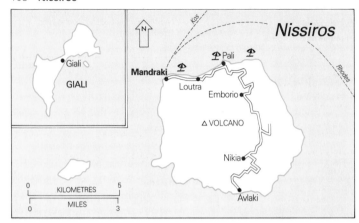

antique shop run by Yoanna Avtgi. During the summer months Yoanna sells ethnological pieces collected from all over Greece, including hand-woven cloth decorated with traditional Cretan designs. The ruins of a medieval Kastro, built in 1315 on the site of the ancient Acropolis, can be seen above the town.

Emborio
8km SE of Mandraki. Perched on the rim of the volcano, opposite its twin hamlet of Nikia. The combined population of the two villages is so small that the school only has seven pupils. Nearby are the ruined walls of an ancient castle.

Nikia
13km SE of Mandraki. The prettier of the two hamlets on the rim of the crater and offering marginally the better view, though from both it is spectacular.

Accommodation & eating

A new hotel is under construction in the spa village of Loutra, where there are thermal baths. Mandraki offers rooms to let in houses, with balconies overlooking the sea. The **Three Brothers Hotel** (tel 31344) has 15 modern, tastefully decorated rooms. The best place to eat is at **Romantzo**, the taverna opposite.

Sights

Volcano
The road from Mandraki to Emborio and Nikia follows the rim of the crater, which is 4km in diameter. Vivid, green and naturally fertile, in spring the slopes are covered in wild flowers; they also support a healthy crop of vines. It is possible to walk down into the crater. Take sturdy shoes and sunglasses as the path is steep and dusty. Bright yellow, sulphurous springs bubble away at the bottom, and the air is thick with sulphurous fumes. Where there is most activity the ground is soft and spongy, and rocks must be used as stepping stones. Some of the springs emit a low deep roar, like Hades calling from below. After this long and dusty climb, visit the café on the outer rim selling cold drinks and almonds.

Specialities

Sumada
A sweet almond cordial found only on Nissiros. Buy a lethal-looking unmarked bottle from the taverna in Mandraki. Non-alcoholic.

Satellite islands

Giali
NW of Nissiros. Only a 15-minute boat ride from Mandraki, this smooth, bare, beige island looks like a giant pumice stone. In fact, pumice is exported all over the world from here, exploited with sophisticated equipment brought in for the purpose. There is a golden sandy beach here.

Patmos

General character

Patmos retains an air of serenity despite the huge numbers of tourists in the high season and the hordes of trippers who invade daily to visit the Monastery of St John the Divine. Although the monastery has receded in political importance, it still exerts a powerful social influence. Patmos is calm and tranquil; even the discos are muted. Monks with black beards and cassocks often vie for taxis with bikini-clad sun-worshippers; something which could happen on no island other than Patmos.

The island attracts a loyal following; many of the same people return year after year, rarely straying onto neighbouring isles even for a day. Conversation is elevated, food is better than average and views on the horizon are exceptional.

Regional features

Patmos is small enough to drive around in approx 40 minutes, but the best way to enjoy the island is to explore on foot. Goat tracks criss-cross the hills and lead even to the most remote beaches. Visible from most points is the Monastery of St John – a grey, fortress-like structure, from which the town of Chora tumbles down. Skala, the principal

Island chain	Dodecanese
Population	2,534
Area	34sq km
Area tel code	0247
Tourist Police	tel 31303
Harbour Police	tel 31231
Distance from Piraeus	163 nautical miles/10 hours

Travel information

By ferry
6 weekly from Piraeus; 6 weekly to/from Leros, Kalymnos, Kos, Rhodes; 3 weekly to/from Samos; 1–2 weekly to/from Ikaria May–Sep; occasional boats to Paros & Syros. The *Panormitis* service connects Patmos with all the Dodecanese islands once a week. Day excursions in summer to Ikaria, Samos and Lipsi; 'Flying Dolphin' hydrofoils Jul & Aug to Kos & Rhodes 3 times weekly; to Leros 2 times weekly.

port, is directly below; a good bus service connects the two. From St John's it is possible to see the islands of Samos, Fourni, Ikaria, Lipsi and Arki, as well as the Turkish coast.

Ports & towns

Skala
The port is best seen at night. On the far side of the harbour sailboats are silhouetted against the dark sky; above, the lights of Chora, high in the hills, twinkle like stars. There is a small cemetery a little way from the harbour. Its immaculate, symmetrical tombstones are lit each evening by individual candles, which throw out an evocative light. By day Skala loses charm but gains in efficiency; most hotels are here, as is a large off-licence doubling as a bank, an OTE office, a post office, and a booking office for boat trips around the island. The Apollon Tourist Agency right on the harbour (tel 31356) is one of the best in the Dodecanese.

Chora
4km S of Skala. Light, white maze of buildings at the foot of the massive

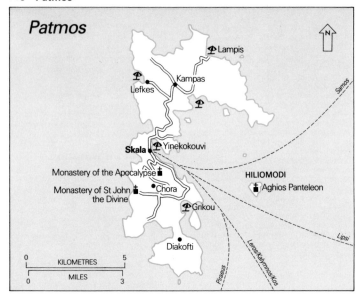

Patmos

Lampis
Kampas
Lefkes
Skala · Yinekokouvi
Monastery of the Apocalypse
Monastery of St John the Divine · Chora
Grikou
Diakofti
HILIOMODI
Aghios Panteleon
Samos
Lipsi
Piraeus
Leros/Kalimnos/Kos

KILOMETRES 0 5
MILES 0 3

Monastery of St John. Only pedestrians are allowed on the twisting streets, and when the monastery is closed Chora is almost devoid of tourists. An elegant, eerie ghost town of deserted mansions with shuttered windows. These houses were built primarily in the 17thC by wealthy shipping magnates; today they are owned mainly by contemporary merchants who use them for only a few weeks of the year. The silent, classical beauty of Chora is not to everyone's liking, but for those seeking solitude it is perfect.

Accommodation & eating

There are two or three rooms to let in Chora but these must be discovered on foot. Most accommodation is in Skala. Three hotels right on the waterfront include the B class **Patmion Hotel** (tel 31313), the C class **Hotel Chris** (tel 31403) and the B class **Skala Hotel** (tel 31343). Attractive apartments can be rented from Victor Gouras, who runs the **Patmian House** restaurant (tel 31180) in Chora, which *Vogue* magazine describes as serving 'some of the best food not only in Greece but anywhere'.

Skala offers a good choice of fish tavernas.

Sights

Monastery of St John the Divine
Chora. 4km S of Skala. Founded in 1088 as a tribute to St John the Theologian, this is one of the oldest and richest religious houses in Greece, earning Patmos the sobriquet 'the sacred isle of the Aegean'. Frescos and wood carvings cover the walls; the Treasury contains many priceless items such as a bishop's crozier of gold and enamel studded with 62 diamonds, and the 11thC mosaic icon of St Nicholas in a silver frame. There are over 2,000 ancient volumes in the library, including a rare edition of the Book of Job. Each year at Eastertime thousands of pilgrims from all over Europe arrive to worship at the monastery. *Open all year 10.00–12.00, 14.00–18.00 Mon–Wed, Sat; 10.00–12.00 Thur & Fri. Closed Sun.* Charge.

Monastery of the Apocalypse
2km S of Skala. Midway between Skala and Chora, this small, multi-chambered shrine encircles the front of the Holy

Grotto. Traditionally it is believed that it was in this cave that St John wrote the Revelation in AD95, while in exile for teaching the word of Jesus Christ. *Open all year 08.00–12.00, 16.00–18.00 Mon–Sat; 10.00–12.00 Sun.*

Beaches

Just outside Skala is the small, pebbly beach of Yinekokouvi. A better choice is Grikou beach in the south. Also pebbly, Grikou has become a low-key resort offering windsurfing, a beach-side restaurant, and accommodation at the B class Xenia Hotel (tel 31219).

Satellite islands

Hiliomodi

E of Patmos. Lying opposite the port of Skala, this tiny, rocky island is shaped like a snail. The only building on Hiliomodi is the church of Aghios Panteleon. On July 27, the church's annual feast day, boatloads of pilgrims arrive from Patmos. On the western shore is a beach of almost black volcanic sand.

Pserimos

General character

Pserimos is an island for swimming and enjoying the sun. The buildings in its one tiny village are too primitive to appeal to those seeking more than privacy and a tranquil way of life. The only entertainment is a wooden forerunner to the pinball machine in one of the village's three tavernas; the only sound at night is the tinkling of goat bells and the wind rustling through pine trees. Locals are charming and hospitable, bemused by the tourists – children will gaze wide-eyed at the sight of a Sony Walkman.

Regional features

Situated midway between Kos and Kalymnos, Pserimos is a bare rocky

Island chain Dodecanese
Population 72
Area 15sq km
Area tel code 0243

Travel information

Not accessible directly from Athens.
By ferry
5 weekly in summer from Kos, less often in winter. 2 weekly from Kalymnos.

island, with tufts of vegetation peeping out from between the rocks. One dusty path leads up past the church and a distinctive house made of bamboo, before petering out into fertile fields.

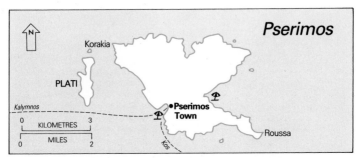

Ports & towns

Pserimos Town

No more than a handful of houses and one shop, the main street is actually a sandy beach which sweeps around the bay before linking with the path behind the harbour. The most distinguished building is the chapel, set in an enclosed courtyard and painted a dazzling blue. A free-standing bell tower of elaborate proportions stands to one side. The interior of the church with its wood carvings and a smiling lady to light a votive candle on the visitor's behalf, is dim and perfumed. Beyond the tower is the cemetery, poignantly simple. Arched glass boxes replace tombstones, and inside each box is a candle, a vase of plastic flowers and an aged, fading photograph of the departed.

Accommodation & eating

Two of the three tavernas offer basic rooms to rent. The owner of the one to the left of the harbour (when facing the sea), is a former seaman who speaks a smattering of English, French and German. 'Cheap, with inside toilet. First class' is his description. The **Pension Tripolitis** (tel 23196) with its blue and white trim is marginally more upmarket. Food is mainly fish, very fresh.

Beaches

Pserimos' crowning glory is a wide, shallow bay, one of the best beaches to be found in the Dodecanese. The sea is perfect for children, blissfully clear and only shoulder-deep even when a 100m off shore.

Rhodes

General character

Perhaps the most 'touristy' island in Greece; one must travel far on Rhodes for peace and solitude. Visitors pour into the island's 1,400sq km by the thousand, attracted by good beaches, duty-free shopping, a wealth of ancient history and a high sunshine rate. From April to September it is best to arrange accommodation in advance; double-booking is a problem, especially in the high season.

Rhodes Town, though still a beautiful city, is severely affected by the crowds and is over-run with tourist shops and package tours. For this reason it is pricey for a Greek island, with value for money often limited to furs and alcohol. That said, Rhodes has ensured that its visitors do not suffer – tourist boards are helpful, buses run to schedule, and timetables, maps and regional information are readily available.

If searching for quiet spots, travel south to Lindos for the evening (after the coach tours have left), or head on to the rugged terrain at the southern tip of the island. Ensure, though, that your car is in good working order, as roads here are untarmacked and primitive. Alter-natively, visit one of the villages on the north-western coast, beyond the airport.

Regional features

The largest island in the Dodecanese, Rhodes is 77km long and 37km wide, and served by a good coastal road system. In mythology, the island belonged to the sun-god Helios, and its unclouded skies are famous. The Roman historian Pliny wrote 'There is not a single day without sun'. Along the entire length of the island is a central mountain range; bare rock gives way to green plains and broad sandy beaches.

History

A strategic location in the busy waters of the Mediterranean has meant that Rhodes has always been a prime target for invaders. From the earliest invasions in 2500BC until the mid-20th century, the island has been frequently attacked by greedy warrior nations. Each conquering power has left its marks, usually on the architecture of the island, beginning with the Minoans of ancient Crete. Rhodes Town was founded in 408BC and in

---

Island chain   Dodecanese
Alternative names   Rodos
Population   87,830
Area   1,400sq km
Area tel code   0241
Tourist offices: City of Rhodes (tel 24888), open 07.30–20.00 Mon–Sat, Apr–Oct. National Tourist Organisation of Greece, 5 Archbishop Makarios/Papagou Sts, tel 23255/23655, open 08.00–14.30 Mon–Fri throughout the year; Airport (no phone), open 09.30–21.00 Mon–Sat, 17.00–21.00 Sun (or whenever flights arrive), Apr–Oct; Harbour (tel 22661), open 07.30–13.30 Mon–Sat, 08.00–12.00 Sun, Apr–Oct. Harbour Police   tel 27634 Distance from Piraeus   174 nautical miles/18–20 hours

Travel information

By air
International airport serving Europe, the Middle East and New York. 3–5 flights daily from Athens, 1–2 daily to Karpathos, Kos and Crete, 2–3 weekly to Santorini, Mykonos and Kassos.

By ferry
Daily from Piraeus all year. Daily in Jul & Aug from Rhodes to Kos, Halki, Symi, Kalymnos, Patmos, Leros; 2 weekly to Kassos, Crete, Karpathos, Tilos, Nissiros; 1 weekly to Lipsi, Kastellorizo, Astipalea, Samos, Chios, Limnos, Ikaria, Amorgos, Paros. Plus weekly boats to Cyprus and Israel; day excursions to Symi. Daily 'Flying Dolphin' hydrofoils to Patmos, Samos, Kos; 2 weekly to Tilos.

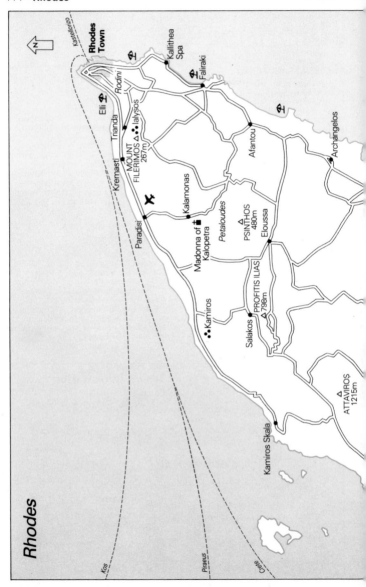

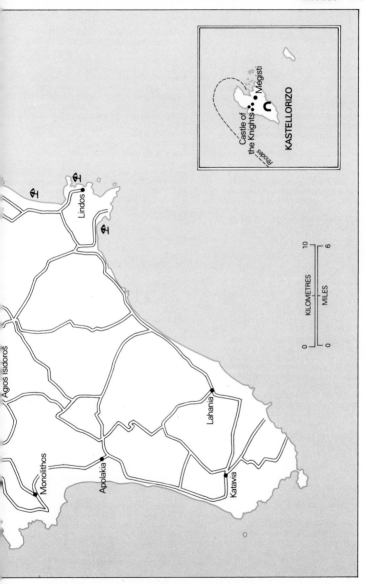

KASTELLORIZO

Megisti

Castle of
the Knights

Rhodes

Lindos

Agios Isidoros

KILOMETRES

MILES

0   10

0   6

Monolithos

Apolakia

Lahania

Katavia

164BC the Rhodians concluded a treaty with the Romans. However, power-struggles within the Roman Empire led Rhodes to be sacked by Cassius in 43BC.

In 395AD the Roman Empire was divided and Rhodes, together with the other Dodecanese islands, became part of the Eastern Empire, under Byzantine rule. During this period the island was sacked and raided many times by the Saracens, Arabs and Venetians. The island was eventually acquired from Genoese pirates by the Knights of St John in 1309. This was to be one of the most prosperous periods in the island's history; many castles and other fortifications were built.

In 1522 the Turks, led by Sultan Suleiman the Magnificent besieged Rhodes for six months and defeated the Knights; for the next 400 years the island was under Turkish rule, long after mainland Greece had won its independence from that country.

Rhodes next passed to the Italians in 1912 and was subsequently occupied by the Germans in 1943, during World War II. After the war the British established a peace-keeping force for two years, until Rhodes was united with the rest of Greece in 1947.

One of the casualties of the island's turbulent past is also a loss to the modern world. The Colossus of Rhodes, one of the Seven Wonders of the Ancient World was cast in bronze by Chares of Lindos around 290BC. A masterful statue of the sun-god Helios, towering to a height of over 30m. It crashed to the ground during an earthquake in 225BC and lay there for eight centuries until the bronze was sold as scrap by the Saracens.

Ports & towns

Rhodes Town

The city of Rhodes is basically divided into two main parts by the medieval city walls surrounding the Old Town. The New Town has grown up around the Old Town and now encloses it.

New Town

An extensive waterfront and wide boulevards are the two main features of the New Town, much of which is now obscured by high-rise hotels. Most of the older buildings of character seem to have become doctors' or dentists' surgeries. The commercial and shopping district has a comprehensive, if mainstream range of goods. It is here that seasoned travellers stock up on the items other islands cannot supply. Have cameras repaired here, replace watches, or take advantage of the excellent health services. One street is almost entirely devoted to discos. No entrance charge, but they all close promptly at 02.00. There are outdoor and indoor cinemas, a casino, and numerous firms offering bicycles, jeeps and cars for hire. The ornate post office has letter boxes labelled 'Germany', 'UK' etc in an attempt to cope with the vast quantities of postcards.

Sights

Mandraki Harbour The most imposing of Rhodes Town's three harbours, it is a delight to both yachtsmen and ferry passengers. At the end of the jetty, the fortress of St Nicholas built in 1464 now functions as a lighthouse. The view from here back towards the town is of minarets, spires and Venetian-Gothic façades. Three medieval windmills line the mole, and flanking the entrance to the harbour are two impressive stone pillars surmounted by statuesque bronze deer. It is thought these massive columns might once have supported the Colossus.

Marketplace/Nea Agora Handsome polygonal building on the waterfront in the south-west corner of Mandraki Harbour. Inside are stalls selling food and cheap souvenirs. The central stall is reserved for fish, arrayed on long marble slabs. Restaurants in the marketplace tend to be quieter than in other parts of town.

Old Town/Kastro

Enclosed by the walls of the medieval citadel, the main thoroughfare of Socratous basically divides the Old Town into two main districts, the Chora and the Collachium, or Castle of the Knights. Socratous is the main bazaar, given over mainly to brass emporiums and shops selling furs, in these days of tourism. Bargain if you wish, but only on small items.

Chora to the south is a pleasant maze of alleyways and arches. A legacy of Turkish rule, six mosques lie within the walls, in various states of disrepair. Best preserved is the Mosque of Suleiman, built in 1523, which stands at the top of Socratous. By comparison with Chora, Collachium is dignified and orderly. Broad avenues with sombre, stately

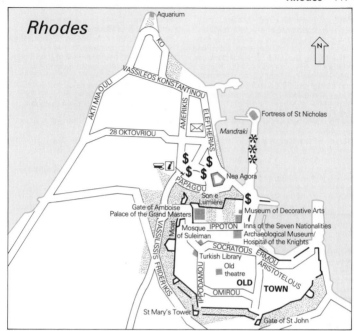

Rhodes

Aquarium

Fortress of St Nicholas

Mandraki

28 OKTOVRIOU

VASSILEOS KONSTANTINOU

AKTI MIAOULI

AMERIKIS

ELEFTHERIAS

KO

Nea Agora

PAPAGOU

Son e Lumière

Gate of Amboise
Palace of the Grand Masters

Mosque
of Suleiman

IPPOTON

Museum of Decorative Arts

Inns of the Seven Nationalities
Archaeological Museum/
Hospital of the Knights

SOCRATOUS

ERMOU

ARISTOTELOUS

Turkish Library

Old
theatre

VASSILISSIS FRIDERIKIS

IPPODAMOU

OLD

OMIROU

TOWN

St Mary's Tower

Gate of St John

buildings, this part of the walled city was occupied by the Knights of St John. Most of the principal sights of the Old Town are to be found here.

Sights

Fortress walls & ramparts

Reconstructed in the early 14thC, during the occupation by the Knights, on the foundations of the original Byzantine walls. When heavier fortifications were needed, the walls were adapted to the new military order of the 15th and 16thC, incorporating massive ornamental gates. The gate of Amboise, built in 1512, is one of the most spectacular, located next to the Palace of the Grand Masters. The coats of arms of the Grand Masters are carved into the walls. Walking the ramparts is a splendid way to view both the Old Town and Mandraki Harbour. Deer graze in the moat, now dry, below. Some of the walls are over 12m thick. Organised tours leave from outside the Palace of the Great Masters at *16.00, Mon & Sat, summer only.*

Just outside the walls, the fortress gardens offer a cool refuge from the searing midday heat. Lofty palms and tropical flowers against a backdrop of towers and minarets.

Hospital of the Knights/

Archaeological Museum Since 1916, this 15thC two-storey building has been the Archaeological Museum. Exhibits include Mycenaean grave treasures, a sarcophagus from the ancient Rhodian city of Ialysos and three rooms of sculpture. *Open 09.30–16.00 Mon–Sat; 10.00–15.00 Sun (longer in summer). Closed Tue.* Charge.

Museum of Decorative Arts/Folklore Museum

Housed in what is thought to be either a disused hospital or arsenal. A large collection of decorative embroidery and traditional island costumes. These are still worn occasionally in isolated parts of the island. *Open 09.00–13.00 Mon, Wed & Fri.* Charge.

Palace of the Grand Masters

Dominating the Old Town, the castellated ramparts of the Palace are the focal point. Originally a 14thC building, it was reconstructed in 1939 using old drawings as a basis. The main halls are located on the upper floor, and many of the beautiful mosaic floors are thought to have come from the island of Kos. The mosaic floor of the Governor's Hall comprises 12 concentric circles with ducks and exotic figures. In the centre of the Hall of Muses is a mosaic depicting the nine Muses. *Open 09.30–16.00 Mon–Sat; 10.00–15.00 Sun (longer in summer). Closed Tue.* Charge.

Street of the Knights The principal street of the Collachium, also known as Ippoton Street, and once a busy medieval thoroughfare, it is the most handsome in Rhodes. Its fine stone buildings have been well restored; the Inns of the Seven Nationalities which make up the Order of St John are ranged on either side of the cobbled street, each with its own coat of arms. That of the Inn of France is most outstanding.

Turkish Library/Library of Ahmed Havouz Built in 1794, and located behind the Mosque of Suleiman, the library houses valuable Persian and Arabian manuscripts including a copy of the Koran. *Open most mornings.*

Activities
Rhodes offers a comprehensive selection of holiday attractions from discos and casinos, to swimming on the excellent town beach. Special events are held throughout the summer months – obtain a list from the City of Rhodes Tourist Office. Also recommended is the seasonal magazine *Where & What* published in three languages.

Aquarium Close to the sea, on the northern tip of Rhodes Town, this aquarium is the only one in Greece. The lower floor is designed to give the impression of being underwater with fish swimming in large tanks around the walls. On the ground floor there are examples of many types of fish and marine animals displayed. Popular with children. *Open most days in summer.* Charge.

Greek folk dances Performances are given in the Old Theatre in Chora, the Turkish quarter of the Old Town. *Summer only 21.15–23.00 Sun–Fri.* Charge.

Son et Lumière/Sound and Light Show Performances in Greek, English, French, German and Swedish in the cool Municipal gardens against the backdrop of the fortress. *Every evening Apr–Oct.* Charge.

Eleoussa
30km SW of Rhodes Town. Pleasant inland village set around a large colonnaded square shaded by palms. At one end of the square is the imposing former governor's palace dating from the Italian occupation.

Kamiros Skala
49km SW of Rhodes Town. Small port serving the island of Halki. Accommodation is limited but good, and its three tavernas serve fresh fish. There is a small beach, and the surrounding countryside is green and fertile, with numerous vineyards. The site of Kamiros, one of the ancient cities of Rhodes, is further along the coast to the north-east.

Lindos
48km SW of Rhodes Town. On a promontory on the west coast of the island below the ancient Acropolis. Lindos is reputed to be the most beautiful village in the Aegean. Sadly its reputation has spread and queues of people, three-deep, line up to join the tour buses from Rhodes Town. During the day it is thronged with tourists and tacky souvenir stalls. Popular with yachtsmen and something of a British enclave, Lindos once surpassed Rhodes Town in importance. Lindos overlooks the only natural harbour on the island – a perfectly formed basin with a good beach. Many of the houses along its narrow cobbled streets date from the 15thC, their architecture a blend of Byzantine, Arabic and local styles, beautifully decorated. One of the most

interesting buildings is the 15thC Church of Panayia, with its 18thC frescos and floor of black and white pebbles.

Trianda/Ancient Ialysos
8km SW of Rhodes Town. This west-coast village, also known as Filerimos, has an 18thC church dedicated to the Assumption of the Virgin Mary, with a finely carved altar screen. 5km south is Mount Filerimos, which rises to a height of 267m. This is the site of ancient Ialysos, one of the Doric cities which together with Lindos and Kamiros, united in 408BC to found the city of Rhodes. Crowned by a 14th/15thC church built by the Knights and a later monastery, all that remains of a Hellenistic temple to Athena are a few stones in front of the church. Near the top of the hill is an early Christian font dating from the 5th or 6thC AD. Down some steps near the entrance to the site is a 4thC BC Doric fountain. *Open 09.00–15.30 Mon–Sat; 10.00–15.00 Sun & hols.* Charge.

Accommodation & eating

Rhodes has over 150 hotels listed in the A–C categories alone; ask for a brochure at the City of Rhodes Information Office. The A class **Colossos Beach Hotel** (tel 85458) near Faliraki offers both studio apartments and bungalows as does the Luxury class **Rodos Palace Hotel** (tel 25222) near Ixia. Near Rhodes Town itself the A class **Doretta Beach Hotel** (tel 41441) has 295 rooms, plus several suites. Determined searching on foot in the Old Town should produce two or three hotels which the New Town cannot match in style. Most delightful is the E class **La Luna Hotel** (tel 25856) with prettily wallpapered rooms and unusual domed showers.

Lindos, too, has a few old-fashioned pensions worth seeking out. The A class **Lindos Bay Hotel** (tel 31212) has a private beach, but is some distance from the village. Hotels abound along the west coast of the island between Rhodes Town and the airport, coinciding with the beaches.

Food is fairly good in both Rhodes Town and Lindos – grilled chicken is a speciality. Many of the restaurants hang octopus out to dry over the balconies and, occasionally, over the chairs too. Freshly squeezed orange juice and cocktails ladened with fresh fruit are luxury drinks, rarely found on less-developed islands.

Sights

Acropolis of Lindos
48km SW of Rhodes Town. The Acropolis today is dominated by the imposing Castle of the Knights. Wear comfortable shoes for the climb or hire a donkey. To the south of the fort is the Sanctuary of the Lindian Athena. From the impressive 5thC BC colonnade, a monumental staircase leads up to the Propylaea; beyond is the small 4thC BC temple. The site offers splendid views of the port of Lindos and the bay. *Open 09.30–13.30, 16.30–18.00 Mon–Sat; 10.00–15.00 Sun & hols. Longer hours in summer. Closed Tue.* Charge.

Kamiros
36km SW of Rhodes Town. Fascinating and extensive ruins of an entire ancient city, which lay buried until discovered by British and French archaeologists in the 19thC. Many of their finds are now in the British Museum, London. Remains include a Temple of Athena dating from the 6thC BC, a row of rooms and shops, and public baths. Also a plumbing system so effective it served 400 families. *Open 09.30–16.00 Mon–Sat; 10.00–15.00 Sun & hols.* Charge.

Petaloudes/Valley of the Butterflies
26km SW of Rhodes Town. A beautiful, densely wooded, narrow valley with lakes and streams. Between June and September, the whole valley is filled with thousands of multi-coloured butterflies. An ascending path leads to the 18thC Monastery of the Madonna of Kalopetra. A pleasant shady walk.

Rodini
3km S of Rhodes Town. Large, cool, wooded park just outside Rhodes Town. Green and flower-filled, a restaurant is open here all summer.

Beaches

It is easy to hire motorboats and sailing boats, ideal for reaching isolated coves; the waters around Rhodes are excellent for snorkelling and diving. Nude sun-bathing is officially prohibited.

Elli
13km SW of Rhodes Town. The municipal beach, which extends from Rhodes Town almost to the airport. The sand nearest the town is somewhat gritty, but amenities are excellent.

Faliraki Beach
20km S of Rhodes Town. Ideal for

children and good for waterskiing.
Kallithea Spa
10km S of Rhodes Town. Here the tiny
bay is ideal for swimming. The spa itself
is enclosed in a curious building – a cross
between Art Deco and something out
of the space age.

Specialities

Wines & spirits

Rhodes produces a large number of
different wines and spirits. Wines include Ilios
(white), Chevalier du Rhodes (red),
Emery demi sec (white and rosé), a
white Muscat and Grand Maître (white
with an attractive label). Belvasia vin de
liqueur and retsina. There is also CAIR
champagne (brut), and a very sweet
liqueur called Colada which comes in
banana and strawberry flavours. There
is a good off-licence in Nea Agora, the
marketplace in the New Town.

Satellite islands

Kastellorizo/Megisti

E of Rhodes. Lying just a few miles
off the coast of Turkey, this small
island with its population of just 222,
is accessible once or twice a week
from Rhodes via the steamer
Panormitis. Similar to the islands of
Halki and Symi, it was once a
wealthy community. Now, the
ruined mansions stand empty under
the dominating façade of a Castle
of the Knights. Best
accommodation is the B class Xenon
Dimou Meghistis Pension (tel 0241
29072). Tavernas are basic, but not
bad. There are no real beaches, but
it is possible to swim from the
rocks.

Symi

General character

Symi is a grand island on a small scale.
Once an important and wealthy centre
for maritime activities, at the beginning
of this century Symi boasted over
30,000 inhabitants – a larger population
than Rhodes Town. Now there is less
than one-tenth of that total. Like its
neighbour, Halki, Symi's elaborate
Venetian houses stand abandoned; relics
of its former glory, now the property of
the island museum. However, due to
good ferry links with Rhodes, Symi is
enjoying something of a comeback. Food
is well prepared and swish bars have
sprung up along the waterfront.
Accommodation is very good. To spend
a few days relaxing in Symi's faded
elegance is a delight. Fresh water tends
to be scarce in high summer.

Regional features

A high ridge encircling Ghialos, the main
port, is crowned with numerous
windmills in various states of disrepair.
Ghialos is actually two towns: the
harbour and shopping area, known as
Ghialos, and the ancient capital at the

Island chain Dodecanese
Population 2,280
Area 53sq km
Area tel code 0241
Tourist office tel 71215 *Open
May–Sep 10.30–13.30, 18.00–
20.00 Mon–Sat. Closed Sun.*
Harbour Police tel 71205
Distance from Piraeus 230
nautical miles/15–18 hours

Travel information

By ferry

At least one daily to Rhodes during
the summer months, less often in
winter. 1–2 weekly to Piraeus,
Astipalea, Amorgos, Kalymnos,
Kos, Leros, Nissiros, Paros, Patmos,
Samos and Tilos.

top of the hill, Chorio. Five hundred steps
in irregular tiers connect the two towns;
finding them amidst the bustle of Ghialos
is part of the charm of staying on Symi.
The island's indented coastline produces
a spectacular array of coves, many

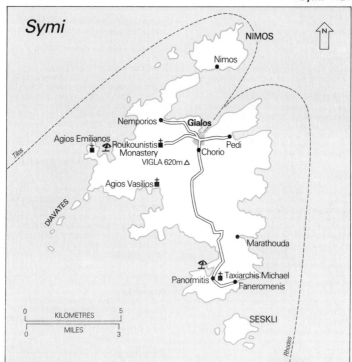

Symi

NIMOS

Nimos

Nemporios ● **Gialos**

Agios Emilianos
⚓ Roukounistis ✝
Monastery   ● Pedi
● Chorio
VIGLA 620m △

Agios Vasilios ✝

DIAVATES

● Marathouda

Panormitis ✝ Taxiarchis Michael
Faneromenis

SESKLI

Tilos

Rhodes

```
0        KILOMETRES        5
0          MILES         3
```

accessible only by boat. Although rugged and picturesque, the beaches, narrow and pebbly, are uninspiring. Those without boats can take one of the many excursions offered by Symi Tours (tel 71307).

Ports & towns

Ghialos/Chorio

The proportions of these twin villages are lovely; their architecture superb. Neo-Classical buildings with tiled roofs and lazy balconies march up the hill to the ancient Kastro, surrounded by windmills and chapels. All activity centres around Ghialos – Chorio is for visiting, but be careful after dark, the steep steps and twisting streets can be bewildering. Without good landmarks it is possible to end up on another part of the island when trying to return to Ghialos. In

Ghialos itself, the ferry from Rhodes docks by the clocktower which houses the Tourist Information Office. The Harbour Master's house nearby, contains the post office. There are two banks, an OTE office, and a sophisticated disco which does not intrude.

Pedi/Pedhi

3km E of Ghialos. With its minute harbour and secluded cafés, Pedi is primarily used by Symiotes as a refuge from the trippers in Ghialos. The last bus from the larger port leaves at 20.00.

Accommodation & eating

Symi's two hotels stand side by side on the waterfront. The B class **Hotel Nireus** (tel 71386) is built in the modern, bungalow style, the A class **Hotel Aliki** (tel 71665) is an elegant townhouse with

15 rooms and a roof garden. Self-catering flats and rooms are available in some of the smaller townhouses and the Tourist Office is only too pleased to advise. The Monastery of Taxiarchis Michael Panormitis lets out 200 of its monastic cells to summer visitors (tel 71354).

Eating on Symi is above average in quality. Shrimps are an island speciality and although pricey by Greek standards, worth ordering from any of the numerous tavernas. In the street behind the harbour is a crêperie serving pancakes and cocktails.

Sights

Archaeological Museum

Chorio. This attractive museum is tucked away down a maze of alleyways. Although well signposted, the winding path should not be attempted in a hurry. The museum is located within an old Symiote house, and exhibits include costumes, handicrafts and Byzantine and post-Byzantine sculptures. *Open Mon–Sat 10.00–14.00.*

Chatziagapitos

Chorio. A notable 18th–19thC mansion currently undergoing restoration by the Archaeological Service. Once in complete ruins, this three-storey building boasts faded murals, rooms of grand proportions and wood carvings under the protection of the Archaeological Museum.

Monastery of Taxiarchis Michael Panormitis

Panormitis. 15km S of Ghialos. Accessible on foot or by donkey, but much quicker to go by caique from Ghialos (65-minute journey). Brilliant white monastery set in a horseshoe-shaped gulf on the south-west tip of the island. With its low vaulted stoa, paved black and white courtyard and mock-baroque bell tower built in 1905, this 18thC monastery gives the impression of being a luxury hotel rather than a monastic refuge. Constructed as a monument to Symi's patron saint, the five-room museum contains fine icons and many votive offerings from sailors. The small church in the courtyard, its interior glittering with silver, often holds services to coincide with the visiting tour boats from Rhodes. At this time the monastery becomes too crowded to view properly.

Specialities

Fragosyko
A sweet delicacy, similar to Turkish Delight, using ingredients from the cactus fig tree. Buy it from the delightful shop behind the harbour in Ghialos where it is made.

Satellite islands

Symi Tours (tel 71307) can help with arranging excursions to these islets which are perfect for swimming and fishing.

Diavates
SW of Symi. Collective name for a group of five uninhabited islands – Pidima, Ghi, Megalonisi, Karavalonisi and Marmars – where privacy is assured.

Nimos
N of Symi. Hilly island, rising to a height of 360m, the home of sheep and shepherds. Most locals visit this island on its feast days, *15 and 24 August.*

Seskli
S of Symi. Tiny, fertile island which abounds with fruit and game. It belongs to the Monastery of Taxiarchis Michael Panormitis.

Telendos

General character

Tiny, prosperous, well-kept and bordering on the fashionable, Telendos smells of fish and flowers. It offers a leisurely lifestyle to its few foreign visitors who make the short journey by caique from Kalymnos. Be prepared to share the boat with the local women, dressed in black and carrying huge sacks of supplies.

Regional features

Towering Mount Rathi gives way to a grassy peninsula with pine trees and a cemetery. This small island was part of neighbouring Kalymnos until an earthquake separated the two in the 6thC AD. A village sank into the sea, and it is claimed that the ancient walls are visible in the narrow channel between the two islands. The ruined monastery of Agios Vassileos stands on the northern slopes of Mount Rathi dominated by a castle.

Ports & towns

Telendos

The island's only hamlet huddles under the protection of Mount Rathi. It is a picturesque place; the trim, almost suburban little houses have pots of violets on courtyard walls, and the ruins of a large church stand isolated in the field beyond. There are few shops and no cars; the conscientious dustman rides a donkey through the whitewashed alleys, which lead eventually to a one-room church, painted a lovely Wedgwood blue.

Island chain   Dodecanese
Alternative names   Telentos
Population   90
Area   5sq km
Area tel code   0243

Travel information

By ferry

10–12 caiques a day from Myrties on Kalymnos in Jul & Aug, much less frequently in winter. 20-min journey.

Accommodation & eating

Both are above average in quality. Accommodation is limited to a couple of pensions and a few rooms to let. **The Ailena**, brick-built and well maintained possesses the island's only telephone (0243 47584), but more are expected soon. Nick Nistazo's eight-room pension has marble steps and balconies overlooking the sea. Nick spent time in Australia and is known locally as 'Uncle George'. The island's four tavernas are bordered by pine trees; through these it is possible to see the attractive port of Myrties across the channel, and the wharf where the evening's seafood is unloaded.

Beaches

There are three beaches within a five-minute walk of the village. Hohlakas Beach, sandy and signposted, is beyond the church, with two shingle beaches to the west.

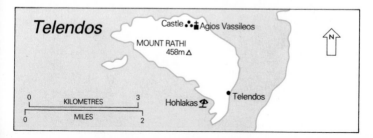

Tilos

General character

Tilos is raw and unsanitised, and may not appeal to all travellers. The island is also poor, and despite increasing numbers of boats from Rhodes, still unaccustomed to tourism; an abandoned air prevails.

Expect to rough it a bit and experience basic island life – goats for the evening meal are often slaughtered on the beach in front of the bathers. The local people are courteous, but aloof; the women still wear traditional dress occasionally.

Regional features

A dry dusty appearance belies the abundance of fresh water; the vegetation is green and aromatic. Watchtowers are a common feature, legacies from the island's long history of

Island chain   Dodecanese
Population   300
Area   63sq km
Area tel code   0241
Distance from Piraeus   290
nautical miles

Travel information

Not accessible directly from Athens.
By ferry
Panormitis service once a week via all the Dodecanese islands; 2 excursion boats weekly from Rhodes, May–Sep; occasional 'Flying Dolphin' hydrofoils from Rhodes. Waters can be rough and boats are often cancelled during the winter months.

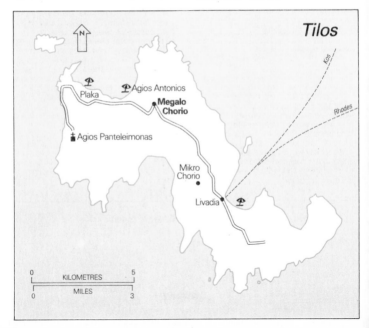

occupation by the Knights of St John, the Turks and the Italians. Transport is minimal and roads are poor; be prepared to walk, cycle or hitch a lift on a donkey to explore this hilly island.

Ports & towns

Livadia/Levadhia

The principal port and capital of Tilos, lying at the edge of a tree-lined bay which extends for almost 1km. The few buildings are surrounded by orchards, and the chirruping of cicadas is deafening. Life is centred around the square, with its elaborately carved fountain of cherubs and animals. The post office is the building with green doors, there is no bank and only a few shops.

Megalochorio

9km NW of Livadia. The island's largest, but almost inaccessible town, is built on the site of the ancient capital. Crowned by a ruined Venetian castle, there are also several churches dotted about. Bicycles can sometimes be hired; enquire locally.

Mikrochorio

1.5km NW of Livadia. An abandoned town with bell towers and tumble-down chapels.

Accommodation & eating

There are rooms to let in Megalochorio and Livadia; the only hotel is the E class **Hotel Livadia** (tel 53202) near the square in the town of the same name. Both towns provide serviceable tavernas; the **Restaurant Irina** in Livadia is right on the beach.

Sights

Agios Panteleimonas

14.5km NW of Livadia. This crumbling 14thC monastery on the north side of the island is more easliy accessible by boat.

Beaches

Livadia beach is comprised of tiny pebbles in an astonishing range of colours – dark wine shot through with marble, rich forest green, pearl flecked with red – they have the appearance of brightly coloured confetti. The water is very clear, and good-sized fish can be speared quite close to the shore. The sea is ideal for snorkelling, but there is no gear available for hire so come prepared. There are also good bathing beaches at Plaka and Agios Antonios.

Evia

Evia

General character

Evia has long been popular with Greek holiday-makers for its excellent beaches, green countryside and easy road access from Athens. Linked by a bridge to the east coast of Attica, Evia is not strictly an island, though neither is it part of mainland Greece. This, coupled with a lack of promotion, has kept foreign visitors away; a pity really, because Evia has much to offer. Beautiful landscapes dominated by Frankish and Byzantine fortifications, winter and summer sports facilities, and more than 30 monasteries scattered through the gently undulating hills. The bus system is adequate, but if time allows, touring by bicycle is an excellent way to reach the more remote areas. Evia is sufficiently densely populated to provide plenty of picturesque villages for rest and recuperation. The road east to Kimi is especially beautiful, with valleys of cypress trees and hill-top townships reminiscent of Tuscany. The north coast is fringed by sandy beaches and little fishing communities. All road signs, bus timetables and menus are in Greek, so pack a phrasebook.

Alternative names   Euboea/Evvia
Population   185,650
Area   3,655sq km
Area tel codes   Khalkis 0221, Karistos 0224, Kimi 0222
Tourist Police   tel (0221) 24662
Harbour Police   tel (0221) 22580
Distance from Athens   1 hour 50 mins by coach

Travel information

By rail
Athens to Khalkis. Information from the Larissa railway station, Athens. Tel 01-8831311.

By coach
Athens to Khalkis, Amarinthos, Eretria & Kimi. Information from the KTEL terminal office in Athens. Tel 01-8317163.

By ferry
1–4 daily to Karistos from Rafina; 1–3 daily to Marmari. Tel Rafina Port Authority for information (0294) 23300. 1–6 weekly to Skyros from Kimi.

Regional features

Running from north-west to south-east, Evia snakes along the coast of Attica for almost 160km, closely following the contours of the shoreline. Once part of the mainland in prehistoric times, it is now separated by the narrow Euripos Straits. The currents in the straits change direction six or seven times a day and have puzzled academics for centuries. Evia is a hilly island, the highest peak, Mount Dirfis, rises in the centre to 1,743m, the southern tip is dominated by Mount Okhi, 1,475m. The mountains give way to fertile plains where corn, figs, olives and vines are grown. The Lelantine Plain between Eretria and Khalkis is particularly productive.

History

A strategic location and a wealth of mineral resources including copper and

iron meant that Evia soon rose to a
position of importance. Inhabited since
prehistoric times, the cities of Khalkis
and Eretria were great rivals from as
early as the 8thC BC. Both sought control
of the fertile and productive Lelantine
Plain.

In 506BC Khalkis was conquered by
the Athenians, and following the Persian
Wars c490BC the whole of Evia became
subject to Athenian rule. In 338BC the
island fell to the Macedonians, then to
the Romans in 194BC, later coming
under the jurisdiction of Byzantium. The
Franks came to Evia in 1204 when
Constantinople was sacked, and in 1209
the island was divided into the three
medieval baronies of Khalkis, Karystos
and Oreos.

During the 14thC the Venetians
gradually assumed control of the island
they called Negroponte. The Turks
seized Evia in 1470, and it remained part
of the Ottoman Empire for 350 years
until finally becoming part of Greece in

1830 after the conclusion of the War of
Independence.

Ports & towns

Khalkis/Halkida/Chalki
Built at the point where the Euripos
Straits are only 60m wide, a swing
bridge connects the town with the
mainland. There has been a bridge at
this point since the 5thC BC and Khalkis
was a wealthy, thriving town long
before the rise of Athens or Sparta. The
modern capital of Evia, it plays an
important role in the daily life of the
island, being the commercial, industrial
and shipping centre.

Rather an unattractive town today, the
Turkish quarter with its mosque and
marble fountain will be of most interest
to the casual visitor. The mosque now
houses the Medieval and Modern
Museum, *open most mornings*. There
is also an archaeological museum in
Khalkis. Near the mosque is the church

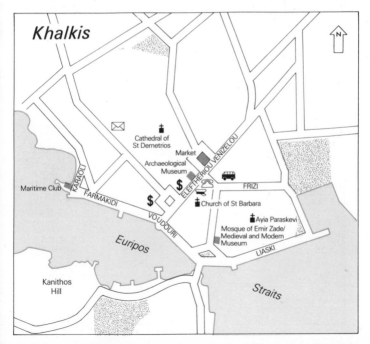

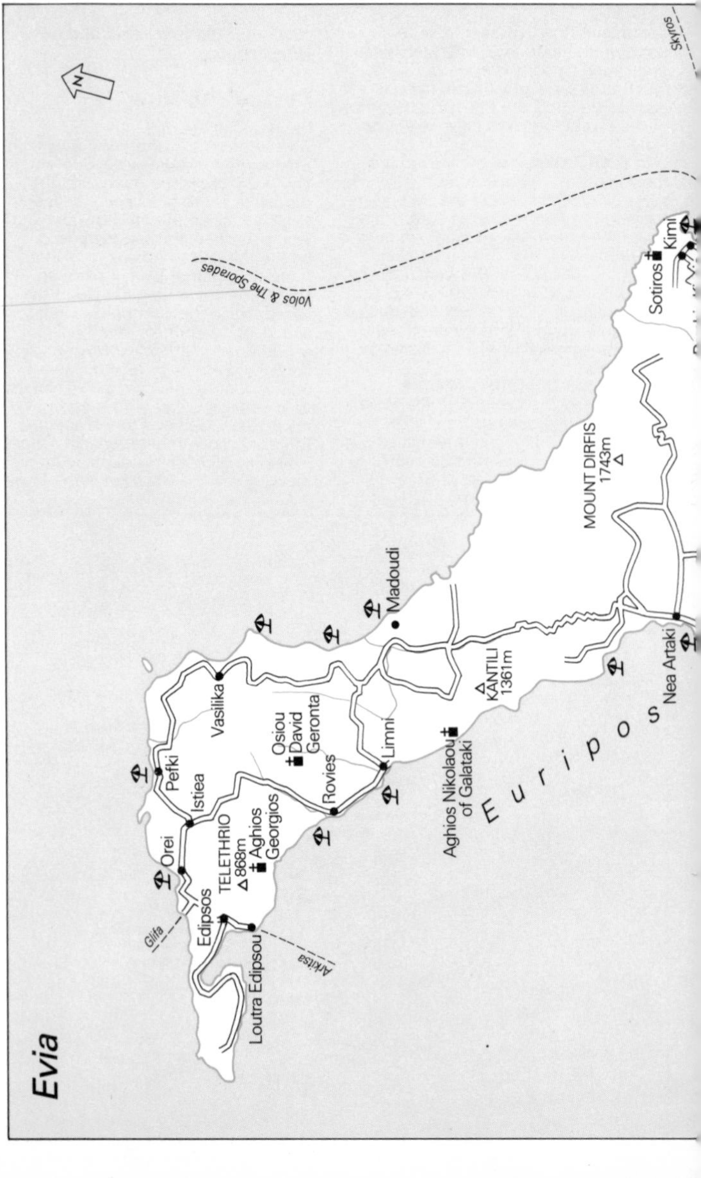

Evia

N

Skyros

Volos & The Sporades

Sotiros
Kimi

MOUNT DIRFIS
1743m

Madoudi

KANTILI
1361m

Vasilika

Osiou
David
Geronta

Limni

Pefki

Rovies

Nea Artaki

Istiea

Aghios Nikolaou
of Galataki

Orei

TELETHRIO
△ 868m
Aghios
Georgios

E u r i p o s

Gilfa

Edipsos

Arkitsa

Loutra Edipsou

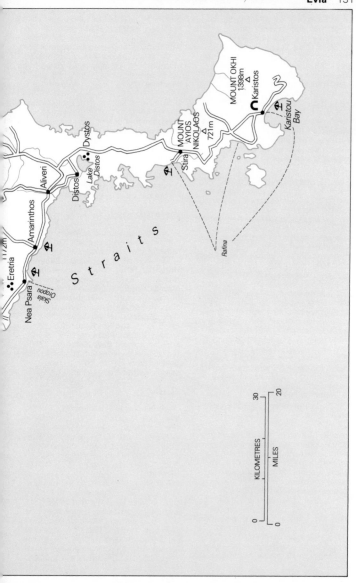

of Ayia Paraskevi, an attractive building with pointed arches which was converted into a cathedral by the Crusaders in the 14thC. The Turkish fortress on the hill above the town was built in 1686.

Khalkis has a post office and several banks. The bus station for services to/from Athens and the other island towns is just off Eleftheriou Venizelou. The office of the Tourist Police is located here. A pleasant residential suburb has grown up on the mainland, just across the bridge. Centred on Kanithos Hill, there are some small hotels here and plenty of shady trees.

Karistos

128km SE of Khalkis. Located on Karistou Bay on the southern tip of the island, this clean, modern resort with its two sandy beaches is one of the most attractive on Evia. Easily reached by boat from Rafina on the mainland, Karistos is also a good base from which to explore the southern part of the island. Crowned by the ruins of the Venetian Castel Rosso (Red Castle) dating from the 13thC, which was later occupied by the Turks. Far-better preserved is the 13thC fort of Bourtzi, a hexagonal building with crenellations and cannon ports,it was strategically positioned right on the sea to defend the harbour. The interior of the 19thC Cathedral of St Nicholas is lavishly painted. The town has good hotels and restaurants and a busy nightlife. Interesting excursions from Karistos include the three-hour climb to the summit of Mount Okhi (1,398m) with its ancient ruins. Near the village of Ayia Triadi, a one-hour journey to the north, is an impressive stalactite cave. Take a torch.

Kimi

93km NE of Khalkis. A pretty town in a thickly wooded area standing 250m above the sea. With a large population even before the Trojan War, Kimi later became a centre for the arts, and its Folklore Museum, *open most mornings*, is housed in a lovely neo-Classical building. The cathedral is large, with several red-tiled cupolas. The port of Paratia Kimis lies 4km to the east at the end of a zig-zagging mountain road. This is the principal port for ferries going to the Sporadean island of Skyros. There is a sandy beach just south of the harbour.

Orei

136km NW of Khalkis. Harbour village on the north coast just beyond Istiea. The ruins of a Venetian Kastro stand on the site of the ancient Acropolis, together with remains of a temple. The focal point of the village square is a statue of a bull rescued from the sea, which dates from the Hellenistic period. There is a good beach nearby.

Stira

103km SE of Khalkis. The Greek writer Homer refers to the ancient city of Styra, the site of this picturesque village, set amongst lemon groves. There is a splendid view of the village from Mount Ayios Nikolaos nearby. On its northern slopes are three ancient buildings, thought to have been either Archaic temples or maritime beacons. Constructed of massive stones, they are known locally as the 'Dragon's houses'.

Accommodation & eating

Evia's resorts and major towns contain numerous hotels and guest-houses. Most villages have rooms to let. Hotels in Khalkis include the A class **Lucy Hotel** (tel 23831), the B class **Hilda Hotel** (tel 28111) and the C class **Manica Hotel** (tel 28922). In the mainland suburb of Kanithos are the C class **Hotel Chara** (tel 25541) and the D class **Morfeus** (tel 24703). In Karistos try the B class **Apollon Resort** (tel 22045) and the C class **Plaza** (tel 22337); in Kimi the C class **Beis Hotel** (tel 22604). Eating is in tavernas, traditional and very Greek. Major resorts have a good selection of seafood restaurants.

Sights

Archaeological Museum

Venizelos Av, Khalkis. Exhibits include fine marble sculptures from the pediment frieze of the Temple of Apollo Daphnephoros at Eretria. *Open 09.00–13.00 Mon–Sat, 10.00–14.00 Sun. Closed Tue.* Charge.

Dystos

60km SE of Khalkis. Near the modern village of Distos, the remains of this 5thC BC city lie at the end of an overgrown farm track on the east side of a swampy lake. The city walls, 3m high and 2m thick, had 11 towers. The remains of houses can be seen on the slopes leading up to the ancient Acropolis, also the site of a Venetian fortress. Keep a look out for snakes here.

Eretria
22km SE of Khalkis. The modern holiday resort of Nea Psara now covers much of the ancient city. Parts of the site have been excavated, revealing extensive remains. These include a 4thC BC palace, a Gymnasium and a Macedonian tomb containing two marble funeral couches. Only seven rows of seats remain intact in the ancient theatre dating from 430BC. Both Doric and Ionic features have been identified in the Temple of Apollo Daphnephoros dating from the 6thC BC. There is a good view of the new town from the site of the ancient Acropolis, a 20-minute uphill climb. On the north-west outskirts of the town is a museum exhibiting finds from the excavations. Charge.

Monasteries
There are over 30 monasteries and convents on Evia. Most are in idyllic settings and can be visited by the public.

Aghios Georgios
107km NW of Khalkis. Situated in a valley on Mount Telethrio in the windswept north-west of Evia, this monastery offers a fine view out across the sea. Amongst its treasures are some fine Byzantine icons and a carved altar screen.

Aghios Nikolaou of Galataki
93km NW of Khalkis. On the coast just south of Limni, this is the island's oldest monastery, dating from the 8thC AD. Beautifully positioned on the lower slopes of Mount Kantili, overlooking the sea and surrounded by pine trees and olive groves. It is built on the site of an ancient temple dedicated to Poseidon. The Byzantine frescos in the chapel date from 1567.

Osiou David Geronta
96km NW of Khalkis. In the foothills of Kavalaris, north-west of Limni. This 15thC monastery, decorated with frescos dating from the 17thC was badly damaged by the Turks in 1824.

Sotiros
97km NE of Khalkis. Just beyond Kimi, on the cliffs overlooking the sea, is this secluded, peaceful monastery. Although probably on the site of an earlier Byzantine monastery, the present building dates from 1643.

Beaches

Evia is ringed with good beaches, but amongst the best are to be found on the north coast from Orei to Pefki (107km NW of Khalkis). Much of the east coast is inaccessible because of the steep cliffs, but there are several beaches between Vasilika (95km NW of Khalkis) and Madoudi (58km NW of Khalkis) which can be reached. There is a beach at Nea Artaki just north of Khalkis. At Limni (85km NW of Khalkis) the beach is surrounded by olive groves. Other beaches on the Eupiros Straits include the town beach at Amarinthos (31km E of Khalkis) and Sitra down in the south where there is a beautiful expanse of sand.

Sports

Skiing
The Greek Alpine Club, tel (0221) 25230, has ski lifts and a rest hut at Liri (42km NE of Khalkis) on Mount Dirfis, at an altitude of 1,150m. The headquarters in Athens is at 7 Karageorgi Servias St, tel 01-3234555.

Waterskiing
Beginners can train at the Khalkis Maritime Club, Karaoli St/Demetrious St. Tel (0221) 26456.

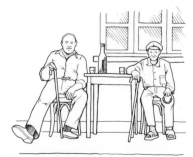

The Ionian
Islands

Corfu

General character

Corfu has long been considered the most beautiful Greek island. Immortalised by Shakespeare, Laurence Durrell and Henry Miller, Corfu's unrivalled scenery cannot fail to captivate. Olive groves of almost preternatural beauty shimmer silver in the moonlight, and the sun on the distant mountains creates patterns which change hourly. Corfu's ethereal greeness – more like the English countryside than a sunburnt Greek island – can be attributed to abundant rainfall. July and August are the only truly dry months; if arriving in autumn especially, expect short, torrential showers followed by brilliant sunshine. During the summer months the pleasures of Corfu must be shared with hundreds of fellow tourists. In the last decade the island has seen an unparalleled explosion in popularity and in the 1980s, villas, snack bars, high-rise hotels and souvenir shops are threatening to take over. It is a noisy, rowdy, fun-loving crowd who congregate on Corfu. For those who want a cheap and cheerful holiday in the sun the island is superb. Nightlife is good – each resort offers a choice of discos and inexpensively priced drinks. Watersports of all descriptions are well catered for. Many roads are tarmacked, and frequent buses run to some of the best beaches in Greece. There are excursions and tours galore.

Anyone desiring a more private holiday will have to be cunning. A good tip is to, stay in Corfu Town itself, a quiet, elegant city which echoes at night to the sound of horse-drawn carriages. Hire a car or moped in one of the innumerable agencies and head off in the morning for one of the sandy strips along the southern coast, or the secluded coves of the north. Alternatively, take one of the boats which run daily to neighbouring Paxi throughout the year.

Corfu was ruled by the British from 1759 to 1864, and in certain ways still feels like an outpost of the Empire. Corfu Town is noted for its ginger beer, and a cricket match is held annually between British and Corfiot players. Some of the finest buildings on the island were

Island chain Ionian
Alternative names Kerkira
Population 96,500
Area 592sq km
Area tel codes Corfu Town 0661, Kassiopi 0661, Paleokastritsa 0663, Perama 0661, Sidari 0663.
Tourist offices: NTOG office, Administration Building, Corfu Town. Tel 39730 *Open Mar–Oct 07.00–14.20, 17.30–19.30 Mon–Fri; 09.00–12.00 Sat. Closed Sun & winter.*
Tourist Police tel 39503
Harbour Police tel 39602
Distance from Athens 11–12 hours by coach & ferry

Travel information

By air
International airport serving Europe. 3–6 flights daily to/from Athens.
By coach
2–4 daily from Kifissou Street Station, Athens to Igoumenitsa on the mainland, connecting with ferry.
By ferry
New Port: large car ferries and cruise ships. Daily to Brindisi in Italy; every hour to Igoumenitsa in summer, every two hours in winter. Plus numerous cruise ships to/from the mainland. 3 weekly to Kefalonia, & Patras on the mainland during summer; 1 weekly in autumn; none in winter.
Old Port: small car ferries to/from the mainland and direct to Paxi. Daily to Paxi at 14.30, returning next day, throughout the year. Seas often rough and boats cancelled.

designed by British architects and there is a British cemetery in the southern part of Corfu Town.

History

Corfu, once known as Corcyra, is traditionally the island where Odysseus was washed ashore after being shipwrecked on his return to Ithaca from the Trojan Wars. The Corinthians colonised the island in 734BC, but hostilities soon developed due to the success and prosperity of Corcyra. The Greek historian Thucydides, records a battle which took place in 665BC as being the first naval battle to be fought in Greece. Eventually, the struggles between Corcyra and Corinth led to the Peloponnesian War.

Corcyra never regained its former power; its strategic position in the busy trading waters of the Mediterranean ensured a succession of conquerers and ruling nations. Conquered by the Romans in 229BC, and ruled by them until the decline of the Empire in the 4thC AD, Corfu then came under the jurisdiction of Byzantium. During the Crusades, the Norman knight Robert Guiscard took the island in 1081; it subsequently passed backwards and forwards between the Venetians and Genoese until a period of relative stability was achieved under Venetian rule, lasting almost 400 years. During this period – in 1716 – the Turks besieged the island for six weeks, but were eventually thwarted. This was the last siege undertaken in Europe by the Ottoman Empire, and earnt Corfu the distinction of being the only part of Greece which never fell to the Sultans.

Whilst under Venetian domination, Italian became the official language and the Greek Orthodox religion was shunned in favour of Catholicism. The Venetians were also responsible for planting Corfu's olive groves; an economic mainstay for centuries to come. When Venice lost power in 1797, Corfu was given to the French, only to be taken over by allied Russian and Turkish troops shortly afterwards.

The Treaty of 1800, supposedly gave the Ionian islands a measure of independence; forming them into a separate state known as the Septinsular Republic. Terror reigned, however, and the islanders protested; seven years later under the Treaty of Tilsit in 1807, Corfu was once again ceded to the French. Following the defeat of Napoleon in 1813, the island was handed over to the British for protection. This was the first time for almost four centuries that the speaking of Greek was permitted.

The first British Lord High Commissioner of Corfu was Sir Thomas Maitland. Maitland's 'reign' from 1817–1824 was controversial but prosperous. A comprehensive network of roads was constructed; aqueducts, harbours and educational establishments – including a university – were also built. By 1830, following the Greek War of Independence, there was considerable resentment towards the British, and an atmosphere of unrest continued. With the Treaty of London in 1864, Britain withdrew voluntarily from Corfu, which at last became part of Greece.

In 1923, under Mussolini, the Italians occupied Corfu and returned again during World War II. German forces arrived in 1943 and there was heavy fighting. Part of Corfu Town was destroyed, including a number of fine churches and the 70,000-volume library of the University. The Germans evacuated the island in 1944. The only invasion which has taken place since is that of tourism.

Regional features

Corfu is the most northerly of the Ionian islands, lying less than 3km off the coast of Albania. Lush and green, the island is well-watered and fertile with a mild climate. Lemons, oranges and figs grow in abundance, but it is the olive trees, gnarled and twisted into strange configurations, which are most prolific – over four million are grown in Corfu. Vast quantities of olive oil are produced. The highest mountain, Pantokrator, rises in the north to a height of 906m.

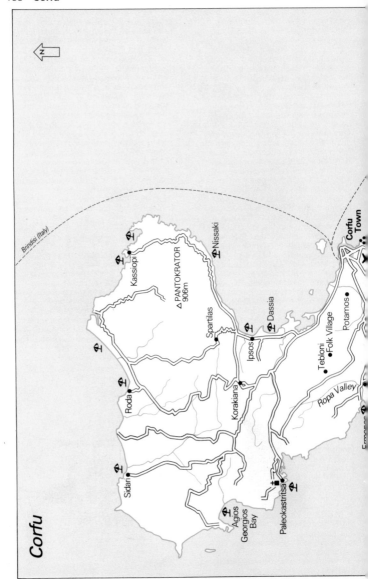

Corfu

Brindisi (Italy)

Corfu Town

Kassiopi

Nissaki

△PANTOKRATOR
906m

Spartilas

Dassia

Ipsos

Potamos

Tebloni
Folk Village

Korakiana

Ropa Valley

Roda

Sidari

Agios
Georgios
Bay

Paleokastritsa

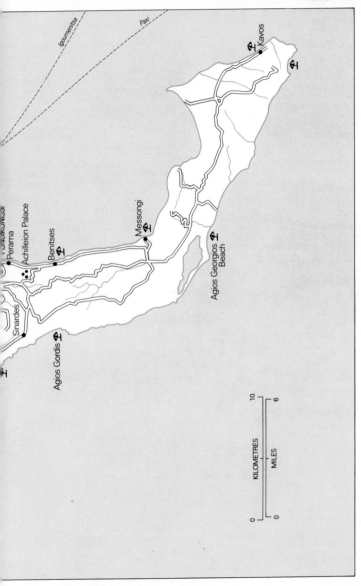

Ports & towns

Corfu Town

A lovely place, the most elegant and
sophisticated of all the island towns.
The mixture of architectural styles, wide
avenues, broad squares and an
expansive waterfront promenade give
the town an overall feeling of space and
harmony. Some of the houses have
arches and colonnades, some look like
English mansions built during the
Georgian period. There are Venetian
steps and monuments, French balconies
and windows, Byzantine churches and
dark, gloomy fortresses.

Although delightful, Corfu is a difficult
town to come to grips with
geographically. Confusion arises over the
fact that there are two ports and two
forts, both 'Old' and 'New'. The Old Port
is nearest to the New Fort, thus
compounding the difficulty. Basically, the
town is divided into two main districts

– Garitsa to the south and Agios Nikolaos
to the north.

Most places of interest to the visitor
are in Agios Nikolaos, around the
beautiful park-like square called the
Esplanade (Spianada) – the large
expanse of greenery which separates the
Old Fort from the town. Cricket is played
here and the small neo-Classical Ionic
Rotunda in the Spianada is dedicated to
Sir Thomas Maitland the island's first
British High Commissioner. Dominating
the north side is the early 19thC Palace
of St Michael; to the west is an elegant
arcade of tall houses built by the French
in 1810. Called the Liston, its open-air
cafés are a popular spot for after dinner
coffee and sweets. The shopping area
is directly behind the Esplanade, with
regimentally straight streets crossed by
twisting alleyways. The NTOG office,
friendly and well informed, is located in
a square further west, but the Tourist
Police are housed in a waterside office
near the New Fort. Bus timetables can

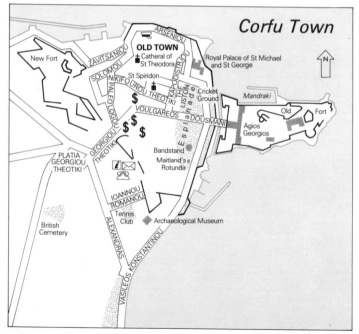

Corfu Town

be obtained from the NTOG office, but these overcrowded vehicles are inclined to depart before the stated time. It is best to arrive at the bus station (next to the New Fort) well in advance.

Sights

Archaeological Museum
Vasileos Konstantinou. Good, purpose-built museum displaying local finds. Amongst the outstanding exhibits are the restored Gorgon pediment from the west front of the Temple of Artemis dating from c590BC, and the carved stone lion from the tomb of Menekrates, wonderfully intact, from the 6thC BC. *Open 09.00–15.30 Mon–Sat; 10.00–15.00 Sun. Closed Tue.* Charge.

Cathedral of St Theodora
The Orthodox Cathedral, built in 1577, is located near the Old Port. Also called the Metropolitan, it has a valuable collection of Byzantine items. In an ornate silver casket lie the headless remains of St Theodora Augusta.

Mon Repos
Located just to the south of the Garitsa district, this royal villa was the summer residence of the British Lord High Commissioners. Built in 1824, Prince Philip, the Duke of Edinburgh, was born here almost 100 years later in 1921. It is not open to the public, but it is possible to swim from the beach nearby.

Museum of Asian Art
Housed in the former staterooms of the Palace of St Michael and St George, this elegant museum contains over 10,000 items of Chinese, Indian and Japanese art. Particularly beautiful is the porcelain from the Ching dynasty (1644–1912). *Open 09.00–15.30 Mon–Sat; 10.00–15.00 Sun. Closed Tue.* Charge.

New Fort
Now used as a Greek naval base, the fortress was begun by the Venetians around 1580. Later added to and finally completed in 1645 it was built to protect the Corfiots living outside the walls of the Old Fort from the Turkish raiders. Admission is restricted, but walks can be taken around its walls.

Old Fort
The two hills on which this fort lies gave the island its name. Corfio is the Greek word for 'twin peaks'. The Venetians began the moat in the late 14thC and two centuries later added the bastions on the west tower. The island's subsequent occupation by the French, the Russians and the British saw new additions, but later, the fort was almost destroyed. Only a few barracks and a Venetian bell tower now remain. The walk to the top through the pine trees is a pleasant one, and the view is superb. A café just inside its walls has a splendid view. *Son et lumière* are held here *May–Sep.* Gates open 08.00–sunset.

Royal Palace of St Michael & St George
Imposing building constructed for the first British High Commissioner in 1819. It has a splendid portico of 32 Doric columns and two arched gateways (one dedicated to St Michael and one to St George). When viewed from the Esplanade, emblems denoting each of the seven Ionian islands also can be seen; a statue of Britannia also once stood here. The magnificent staterooms can be viewed whilst visiting the Museum of Asian Art which is housed in the palace.

St Spyridon Church
Right in the heart of the shopping district of the Old Town, this church was built in the late 16thC. The elaborate silver casket containing the remains of the island's patron saint is progressed round the town on feast days four times a year. The bell tower, the highest building on Corfu, was erected in 1590.

Benitses
12.5km S of Corfu Town. Former fishing village now transformed into a community of hotels, tavernas and discos. A place for the young and energetic. There is a small beach nearby.

Kassiopi
36km N of Corfu Town. Excavations have shown there was a city on this site as early as the 1stC BC. Although later occupied by the Romans and serving as a major harbour, subsequent invasions reduced Kassiopi to little more than a hamlet. Now it exists as a low-key tourist resort offering many rooms to let, motorboat hire, pony trekking and day excursions to other sites.

All that remains of historical interest is the church of Panagia Cassopitra, built in 1590, and a ruined castle incorporating several architectural styles. There are good sandy beaches 10 minutes' walk to the north, and more around the southern headland. Kassiopi also offers the best views of Albania, only a short distance away across the Corfu Straights.

Perama
8km S of Corfu Town. Surrounded by olive groves, Perama is a wealthy resort

with luxurious hotels and villas, many of which can be rented. Pondikonissi, or Mouse Isle is only a short distance away, and all around the sweet scent of sub-tropical flowers pervades the air.

Sidari
37km NW of Corfu Town. Together with Roda, this resort is a good base from which to explore the lovely north coast. The sandstone cliffs to the west are deeply indented with caves, coves and hidden beaches. The best-known cave is the Canal D'Amour, a passage worn through a cliff. At Sidari itself there are shallow beaches good for children, also the remains of a Neolithic settlement.

Accommodation & eating

Both are good on Corfu, but many hotels get fully booked for the summer months. However, the constant building of new hotels should ensure a room for all. Although Corfu Town has a number of large, modern hotels it is more fun to stay in a refurbished Venetian house. Try the B class **Archontico** (tel 37222) in Garitsa or the charming C class **Calypso** (tel 30723) opposite the Archaeological Museum. For a touch of urban grandeur the Luxury class **Astir Palace** (tel 91490) cannot be bettered. In Perama try the A class **Alexandros** (tel 36855), the B class **Aeolos** (tel 33132) or the C class **Fryni** (tel 36877). In Sidari is the C class **Aphroditi Beach Hotel** (tel 31247); in Kassiopi the B class **Balari** (tel 81220). The Luxury class **Corfu Hilton** (tel 36540) near Mouse Isle is one of the best in the Hilton chain, offering private bungalows in secluded gardens and its own beach.

Food is tasty, fresh and abundant. Although outside Corfu Town variety is limited, the fish will have been locally caught or brought in from neighbouring islands. Corfu Town offers an enormous choice, including hamburgers, hot dogs and a very good French crêperie called **Asterix** at the top of Filarmoniki Street. The well-signposted **Faliraki Restaurant** is right on the beach and serves both Greek and Chinese food. Harbourside tavernas cook excellent pizzas. There are also numerous establishments where traditional Greek food can be eaten.

Sights

Achilleion Palace
10km S of Corfu Town. Constructed in 1890 for the fascinating character, Elizabeth, Empress of Austria. The house and its Italian-style grounds reflect two main themes – dolphins and the ancient Greek hero Achilles. There are a number of statues and motifs of each. Particularly interesting is the statue by the German sculptor Ernst Herter called The Dying Achilles done in 1884. Following the assassination of the Empress, the Palace was bought by Kaiser Wilhelm II of Germany. Since December 1962 it has functioned as a state-run casino. *Open 19.00–02.00 Mon–Fri, 19.00–03.00 Sat.* However, the gardens and a ground-floor museum can be visited during the day. *Open 08.00–18.30 Mon–Sat, 09.00–18.30 Sun.*

Folk Village
13km W of Corfu Town. Take the main road to Potamos and then follow the signs. A Venetian village has been reconstructed using original materials. Includes a church, a museum, workshops, houses and a restaurant. Good for children. Charge.

Kaiser's Throne
15km W of Corfu Town. Near the village of Pelekas. Small watch tower with a telescope, named after Kaiser Wilhelm II of Germany. The Kaiser, who used to spend spring in Corfu at his residence, the Achilleion Palace, would come here to watch the sunset. Still a favourite spot; the sunsets are spectacular.

Paleokastritsa Bay
25km NW of Corfu Town. One of Corfu's best-known beauty spots, combining shimmering scenery, towering mountains and dense forests. There are six coves along its length, each with its own sandy beach. From the bus stop, a path ascends to the Monastery of Paleokastritsa, exquisitely sited on a promontory amongst cypress trees. The monks' cells are centred around a church with a lovely tower and many bells. Originally founded in 1228 on the site of an ancient Kastro, it was destroyed by fire in 1537 and subsequently rebuilt. Also within walking distance of Paleokastritsa are the ruins of Angelokastro. This 13thC Byzantine castle is 300m above the sea, and it is interesting to note the reservoir hewn out of the solid rock.

Pondikonissi/Mouse Isle
4km S of Corfu Town. This famous islet, with its 13thC chapel of Agios Pnevmatos is indeed enchanting. Its sister islet with the picturesque convent of Panaya Vlancherina is now connected to the mainland by a causeway. The convent covers most of the tiny island. Inside, one cool blue-painted room containing icons and candles is open to the public. Pondikonissi is a 15-minute boat ride from Panaya Vlancherina; numerous vessels moored along the causeway vie for custom.

There is a good view of both islets from the viewing terrace on the mainland which has a café. What the postcards do not show, but is all too apparent from here is the close proximity of the airport runway; planes come in very low over the islands. Take the No 2 local bus from Corfu Town and ask for the Kanoni stop.

Beaches

Corfu has some excellent beaches. Head for Perama (7km S of Corfu Town), or further afield to the extensive beach at Messongi (25km S of Corfu Town) which has tourist amenities and hotels.

On the west coast, Paleokastritsa (25km NW of Corfu Town) has lovely sandy coves as does Glifada (17km SW of Corfu Town) and Agios Gordis (19km SW of Corfu Town). The finest beaches of all are to be found on the north coast; less crowded and less developed. There are many secluded sandy bays here. Hire a car or moped, head for Kassiopi, then drive west towards Roda and Sidari (both 37km NW of Corfu Town). Diligence will be rewarded.

Specialities

Wines & spirits
Red and white Theotoki wines. Kum Kwat, a bright orange liqueur made from small Cantonese oranges.

Sport

Cricket
A legacy from the days of British rule, cricket is a popular game on Corfu. Those wishing to join a club as temporary members are invited to apply to Gymnastikos Syllogos – The Gymnastic Association – tel (0661) 38726.

Golf
Near the village of Vatos (13km W of Corfu Town) is an 18-hole course at Ropa's Meadow (Livadi tou Ropa). Follow the road down to Ermones (15.5km W of Corfu Town) for a swim. This sandy beach is reputed to be where Odysseus was washed ashore after being shipwrecked.

Sailing
There is a yacht supply station in Corfu Harbour, plus a 500-berth NTOG marina at Gouvia on the west coast (8km NW of Corfu Town). Small sailing boats, motorboats and yachts can be hired. Enquire at tourist agencies in Corfu Town.

Tennis
Many resorts have tennis courts. The Tennis Club in Corfu Town (tel 37021) is located on Ioannou Romanou St. Open to non-members.

Watersports
Corfu is a well-known watersports centre. There are several waterski schools along the west coast of the island and para-gliding is also becoming increasingly popular. It is possible to hire windsurfers, surf boards and scuba diving equipment at all the major resorts. The clear water and abundant fish make snorkelling enjoyable.

Ithaca

General character

Ithaca's appeal lies as much in myth as in reality. It was to this small rocky isle that the hero of the Homeric epic, Odysseus, was returning after the Trojan War. His 10-year journey from Troy to the western isles forms the basis of *The Odyssey*. In chapter nine, Odysseus states 'My home is under the clear skies of Ithaca. Our landmark is the wooded peak of windswept Neriton. . . . It is a rough land but a fit nurse for a man. And I, for one, know of no sweeter sight for man's eyes than his own country.'

In reality this 'rough land' is a low-key, peaceful place. Despite the myths, it attracts few tourists and few facilities are provided. Its beaches are unimpressive as are the local sights. The charm of this 'own country' lies in its hospitable people and a lifestyle which revolves around animals and the sea. Goat's bells and church bells are often heard, and donkeys provide a sound form of transport. Scattered throughout the hills are numerous ancient sites attributed to the Homeric period. Archaeologists may dispute this, but locals remain convinced. For proper exploration, sturdy shoes and a torch are required; directions can be gleaned along the way.

Regional features

Ithaca is actually two peninsulas joined by a narrow isthmus on which there is barely room for the island's one main road. The view from this road is superb. To one side open sea and the purple mountains of Kefalonia, on the other the still, turquoise waters of the Molos Gulf. The town of Vathi is located at the end of this fjord-like finger of water. Silent, brooding, and backed by steep green hills, much of the gulf is in shadow. When the sun does strike its surface there is lovely interplay of light and shade.

Ports & towns

Vathi/Ithaki Town
After the silent ferry journey through the Molos Gulf, Vathi appears like a vision.

Island chain   Ionian
Alternative names   Ithaki
Population   3,650
Area   96sq km
Area tel code   0674
Tourist Police   tel 32205
Harbour Police   tel 32909

Travel information

By ferry
1–4 weekly connecting with the other Ionian islands; occasional day excursions from Kefalonia during the summer months.

Pretty white buildings with terracotta-tiled roofs surrounded by green, conical hills. In the middle of the bay lies Lazareto, an islet of pine trees. It is said Lord Byron used to swim here on his visits to Ithaca. On closer inspection, Vathi is less attractive. Modern bungalows are much in evidence, though there is a Venetian-style government building with an ornamental fish pond. Bicycles and scooters can be hired. There is also a bus service running to Stavros, Frikes and Kioni. Vathi holds an annual drama festival during the months of August and September.

Stavros
17km NW of Vathi. For centuries there has been gentle rivalry between north and south Ithaca, each claiming the right to be Odysseus' true home. Stavros, with only one main street and a small square is the commercial centre of the north. A beautifully proportioned church is the only building of interest; a modern fresco is painted on the wall opposite. Several village men speak English as a consequence of years at sea in foreign waters.

Accommodation & eating

Stavros, and the hamlets dotted around, offer rooms to let, but Vathi has the only hotels. On the far side of the harbour, the B class **Mendor** (tel 32433) is the nicest. The E class **Aktaeon** (tel 32387) is more convenient when disembarking from the ferry. The best place to eat is in the cafés which line the quayside.

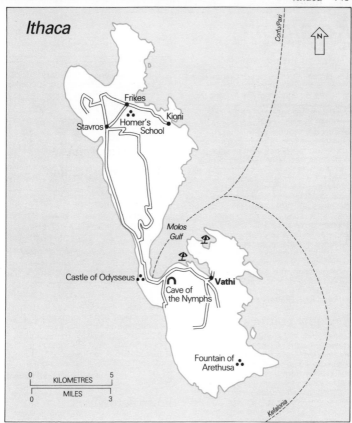

Sights

Archaeological Museum

Vathi. Houses a large collection of 8th–6thC BC vases. *Open most mornings 09.30–12.30.*

Cave of the Nymphs

3km W of Vathi. Near the bay of Dexia, where Odysseus is believed to have secreted his Phaecian treasure from Corfu. Also known as Marmarospilia, a narrow entrance leads into a large stalactite chamber.

Fountain of Arethusa

5km S of Vathi. Named after a nymph of Diana, who on hearing of the death of her son, wept so much she turned into a fountain. The water is good to drink and this is a popular spot for picnics.

Castle of Odysseus

7km W of Vathi. Also known as Kastro Piso Aetos. All that now remains are some fragmented walls and a crumbling tower.

Homer's School

20km NW of Vathi. Just north of Stavros, the ruins of this imposingly-sited ancient building jut out over the valley on a huge rock. Although the trek makes an interesting walk, there is little evidence to connect the ruined 6thC BC tower with the poet.

Kefalonia

General character

The largest and most mountainous of the Ionian islands, Kefalonia is not immediately appealing. Devastated by an earthquake in 1953 which also destroyed neighbouring Zante, Kefalonia shunned extensive rebuilding in favour of expedient rehousing. It is for this reason that most of the island's major towns are functional; with unattractive prefabs and concrete replacing typical island architecture. The countryside, too, is bold and slightly forbidding.

Although the bus network is extensive, high mountain ridges and long distances preclude short outings to the most interesting sights, and many people do not linger long enough to discover them. A pity really, for hidden away under Kefalonia's rough exterior is an island of distinction. For the walker, the explorer, the intrepid sightseer with good transport, the island is an undiscovered delight, and what the towns lack in charm is compensated for in hospitality. The beaches are excellent.

Regional features

Mount Enos in the south rises to a towering height of 1,628m. Its slopes are covered with a type of rare tree known as the 'Cephallonean fir'. The bus journey from Sami, the port to the capital town of Argostoli is a hair-raising experience – riding along a mountain

Island chain   Ionian
Alternative names   Cefalonia/
Cephallonia
Population   27,650
Area   780sq km
Area tel code   0671
Tourist Police   tel 22222
Harbour Police   tel 28083
Distance from Athens   8 hours by
bus & ferry

Travel information

By air
1–2 flights daily to/from Athens; 2 weekly to/from Zante
By ferry
1–4 weekly connecting with the other Ionian islands; daily to/from Kilini on the mainland in the summer, less often in winter; daily to/from Patras on the mainland in summer; less often in winter.

road just level with the tree tops in the ravine below. The view is stunning; sun-dappled valleys and far-off plains give the landscape of Kefalonia a unique and fragmented appearance. The Eparhia Palis peninsula, west of Argostoli, is scattered with olive groves, as is the southern tip of the island around the village of Poros – the greenest part of Kefalonia.

Ports & towns

The island's two major ports are both located on the eastern coast.
Poros
44km E of Agrostoli. An attractive port, and a minor resort in its own right. Boats from Poros land at Kilini on the mainland for connections to Zante and Athens.
Sami
24km E of Agrostoli. The destination of the car ferries from Corfu and Ithaca. Sami is a serviceable town backed by pines.
Argostoli
Life in this flat, grey capital town centres around Valianos Square, which is due south of the harbour. Spacious, brightly-lit and fringed with trees, on a warm summer's evening, the atmosphere in

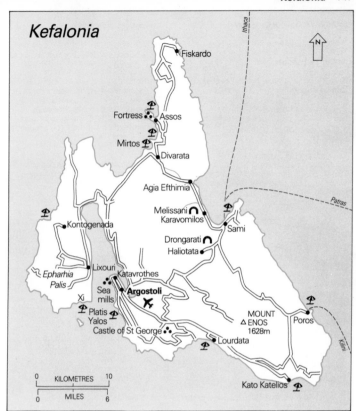

Kefalonia

Fiskardo

Fortress · Assos

Mirtos

Divarata

Agia Efthimia

Melissani
Karavomilos
Sami

Drongarati
Haliotata

Kontogenada

Lixouri
Katavrothes
Epharhia
Palis
Sea
mills · **Argostoli**
Xi
Platis
Yalos
Castle of St George

MOUNT
△ ENOS
1628m
Poros

Lourdata

Kato Katelios

Ithaca

Patras

Kilini

```
0          KILOMETRES        10
0              MILES            6
```

the square is relaxed; locals strolling, tourists eating in the outdoor cafés and old men drinking oúzo as their teenage sons roar around on motorbikes or in souped-up cars. Just south of the square is the Tourist Office. *Open most mornings Jun–Sep.*

Assos

39km N of Argostoli. Attractive village standing on a promontory jutting out into the sea. Further along the road are the remains of a Venetian fortress. This isolated building was used as a prison at one stage – a Greek Alcatraz – but now all is calm and peaceful. The view from its crumbling walls offers a stunning panorama.

Fiskardo

53km N of Argostoli. A picturesque little port, the only village to have survived the earthquake of 1953, it is a favourite with yachtsmen and, more recently, with tour operators. Its streets, lined with 18th and 19th century Venetian houses, are very attractive but often teeming with visitors during the summer months.

Accommodation & eating

Argostoli is good for eating out, but poor for accommodation. The island's two best hotels, both A class, are situated near beaches on the outskirts of Argostoli: the **Mediterranee** (tel 28760)

and the **White Rocks Hotel** (tel 28332).
There are also three campsites.

The restaurants around Valianos
Square in Argostoli are quite good. The
Italian Lagondola café serves 'eight
different types of spaghetti'. The best
Greek food is served in the **Taverna
Demosthenes** around the corner,
where the service is cordial and food
very fresh and reasonably priced. It also
has a shaded garden at the rear.

Sights

Archaeological Museum
Diathohou Konstantinou St, Argostoli.
This museum houses an interesting
range of prehistoric exhibits including a
splendid collection of late Mycenean
pottery. *Open in summer 08.00–13.00,
15.00–18.00 Mon–Sat; 09.00–13.30,
16.00–18.00 Sun & hols. Closed Tue.
Open mornings only in winter.*

Castle of St George
9km SE of Argostoli. The town which
once surrounded this castle was the
medieval and Venetian capital of the
island, but was abandoned in favour of
Argostoli following an earthquake. The
original Castle of St George was built in
1264; the fortress which now stands
here is Venetian and was rebuilt around
1500. The round tower contains a spring-
chamber, reached by a flight of steps.
There is an excellent panoramic view
from the castle. *Open in summer
08.30–12.30, 16.00–18.00 Mon–Sat;
09.00–18.00 Sun & hols. Closed Tue.
Fewer hours in winter.*

Caves
Two of the most spectacular caves in the
Ionian chain are located near Sami on
the eastern coast of Kefalonia.
Drongarati
19km NE of Argostoli. Close to the
village of Haliotata en route to Sami.
This cavern has wonderful acoustics and
impressive stalagmites and stalactites.
Open all day in summer. Charge.
Melissani
29km NE of Argostoli. Near the village of
Karavomilos beyond Sami. This strange
and magical cave also boasts impressive
stalagmites and stalactites. There is a
salt-water lake in the centre which
catches the light in dazzling ways. It is
possible to take a boat onto the lake.
Open all day in summer. Charge.

Katavrothes Sea Mills
3km NW of Argostoli. Just behind the
Katavrothes nightclub is a rock garden
with bridges spanning a stream. To one
side is a restored corn mill. The salt-
water stream emerges here at
Katavrothes after a remarkable 16km
journey underground (it was, in fact, only
in the late 1960s that the source was
discovered to be on the other side of the
island). In the 19thC the current was
sufficiently strong for mills to be built to
harness the power, but due to changes
in land levels following an earthquake,
this is no longer the case. At night it is
very attractive and the nightclub provides
both cabaret and plate smashing until
the small hours.

Koryalenios Historical and Cultural Museum
Argostoli. Housed in the public library,
with exhibits labelled in Greek and
English this museum is a fine example
of its kind. Interesting exhibits include a
display of musical instruments, antique
tableware and old photographs. *Open
08.00–12.00, 16.00–20.00 Mon–Sat.
Closed Sun.*

Beaches

Kefalonia is blessed with many good
beaches. Three are listed below.

Platis Yalos
3km S of Argostoli. One of the best is
just a short bus-ride away from the
capital. Platis Yalos is a smooth, sandy
beach, good for children and surrounded
by lush vegetation. Beach umbrellas are
available for hire; in the summer buses
leave Valianos Square approx every
hour.

Mirtos Beach
30km N of Argostoli. Another sandy
beach reached from the main road by a
narrow, winding lane. Deep turquoise
bay encircled by steep cliffs.

Xi Beach
43km W of Argostoli. A very long journey
by road, but only a short caïque trip from
the capital. Dramatic beach of red sand
backed by tall white cliffs. No shade, so
take an umbrella and provisions.

Specialities

Local wines
Calliga rosé, very tart.

Paxi

General character

The smallest in the Ionian chain, Paxi can easily be explored on foot, and as there is little else to do except eat and lie in the sun, walking is a pleasant pastime. The olive groves south of the capital town of Gaios provide a shady refuge from the midday sun; the more energetic could tackle the 8km route from Gaios to the tiny port of Lakka in the north. Whitewashed churches dot the route.

There are organised excursions by caique to wonderful beaches, or the sea caves on the west coast. Until fairly recently most of Paxi's visitors were Italian, but villa holidays, day trips and an increase in the number of ferries from Corfu have made it popular with the British as well. There is a yacht refuelling station at Gaios; more limited boat supplies can be obtained in Lakka. Beaches are numerous, and reasonably secluded.

Regional features

Paxi lies 48km south of Corfu and 16km from the Greek mainland. A charming, verdant island, it is only 10km long and 4km wide. Gently hilly, the highest point is only 270m and there is plenty of fresh water. The main agricultural crop is olives, and many of the groves are extremely old; the trunks of the trees are gnarled and twisted like serpents entwined upon a wooden column.

Ports & towns

Gaios

Gaios is a picturesque port, sheltered by an islet of pine trees in the middle of the bay. When disembarking from the car ferry at the new port (1km beyond on the northern coast of the bay), the town is hidden altogether; smaller boats are, however, able to put in at the harbour. Although Gaios has the feel of a village it actually looks like a town, with several three-storey buildings and a main square. It is a civilized place, pleasant and beguiling; many people return to Gaios year after year. There are bicycles and scooters for hire, plus organised excursions to neighbouring islets and beaches.

Island chain   Ionian
Alternative names   Paxoi/Paxos
Population   2,250
Area   25sq km
Area tel code   0662
Tourist Police   tel 31222
Harbour Police   tel 31259

Travel information

By ferry

2–4 weekly from Corfu; 3–7 weekly from Parga on the mainland; several day-long excursions each week from Corfu during the summer months.

Lakka

8km N of Gaios. Tiny port located on a peaceful, near-circular bay, protected from the open sea. There are tavernas and a few shops providing necessities; the shingle beach offers safe bathing.

Accommodation & eating

Accommodation on Paxi is difficult to secure. A number of companies rent out villas for one- to two-week periods, but these must be arranged from Britain or Corfu. The island's two hotels, the lovely

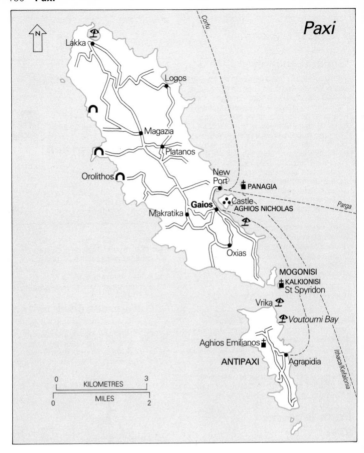

Paxi

B class bungalow-style **Paxos Beach** (tel 31211) and the D class **Aghios Georgios** (tel 31223) are often booked solid. There are 20–30 rooms to let around the island; enquire in Gaios. Do not plan to stay on Paxi without having booked beforehand.

The abundance of self-catering villas limits the number of tavernas and restaurants to be found. Although few in number, the quality is excellent; locally caught lobster and wine from neighbouring Antipaxi are recommended.

Sights

Coastal scenery

An impressive and much-photographed natural feature on the west coast of the island is Ortholithos – a giant limestone stack which towers above the waves. There are also several spectacular sea caves along the western coast of Paxi whose black mouths loom ominously against steep grey cliffs. An organised excursion from Gaios is the best way to view them.

Satellite islands

Aghios Nicholas

E of Paxi. Small island in Gaios Bay densely covered with pine trees. The remains of a ruined Venetian castle, built in 1423, are preserved here.

Antipaxi

S of Paxi. 50 mins by boat from Gaios. Antipaxi is the largest of the islets in the choppy waters surrounding Paxi. Clean, peaceful and with a population of only 126, there are no proper villages on the island and no tourist accommodation. Most people visit Antipaxi on a day trip from Gaios or Corfu; bays and secluded coves are numerous, excellent local wine and fish provide a good lunch.

Voutoumi Bay, on the east coast, has one of the loveliest beaches of all the Ionian islands; sandy, long and curving, and splendidly isolated until the tour boats arrive. Try to hire a dinghy in Mogonisi and arrive first.

Kalkionisi

E of Paxi. Located close to Mogonisi just beyond the south-eastern tip of Paxi. The small chapel of St Spyridon is close to the sea.

Mogonisi

E of Paxi. At one point the channel between the two islands is very narrow. Mogonisi is a lively, active resort, where it is possible to hire sailing boats. There is a bar and a restaurant.

Panagia

E of Paxi. Tiny islet to the north-east of Aghios Nicholas in Gaios Bay. On 15 August hundreds of pilgrims arrive on the island to celebrate Dormition Day at the Monastery of Panagia. Festivities last all day and night.

Zante

General character

Zante is a land of perfume and poets. Homer and Pliny both wrote of its charms, and the Venetians, who occupied this graceful island for more than 300 years, set about building a town to rival that of Florence in their native land. Zante has suffered several earthquakes during the course of its history, the most recent in 1953, which also hit neighbouring Kefalonia, causing widespread devastation. The two islands subsequently adopted radically different rebuilding programmes. The Kefalonians migrated, or rebuilt their towns in squat, functional style; Zakinthians, on the other hand, embarked on a vast, meticulous scheme to reconstruct their buildings in the original Venetian mode. For this reason Zante Town is typified by broad avenues and tree-lined squares; it is the most elegant of island towns, cultured and dignified; the same might be said of the island as a whole.

Zante is an enormously pleasing place to holiday – undemanding, unobtrusive

Island chain	Ionian
Alternative names	Zakinthos
Population	30,000
Area	405sq km
Area tel code	0695
Tourist Police	tel 22550
Harbour Police	tel 22417
Distance from Athens	7 hours by bus & ferry

Travel information

By air
International airport serving Europe and the UK. 2–5 flights weekly to/from Athens; 2 weekly to/from Kefalonia.

By ferry
1–3 daily to/from Kilini on the mainland.

and highly attractive. The sights can be easily reached or ignored altogether and most of its principal points of interest lie in the capital itself. Always popular with

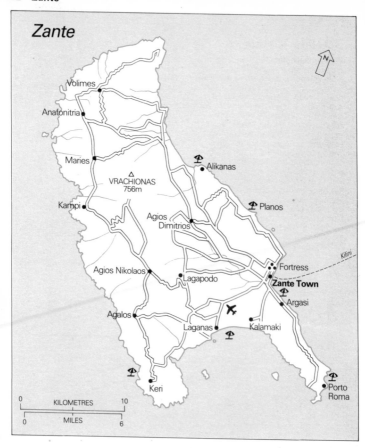

Greek tourists, it is only in the last few years that other nationalities have discovered its delights. English is less widely spoken than on other equally large islands, so invest in a phrasebook and a map. The locals are relaxed and friendly, seemingly enchanted with their island, and with the clever tourist for discovering it.

Regional features

Southernmost of the four main Ionian islands, an abundance of springs and wells have meant the valleys of Zante are fertile and green; earning the island the sobriquet 'Flower of the Levant' from the Venetians. In many respects the countryside is similar to the English landscape; country lanes twist and turn against high banks of wild flowers; garden flowers grow in profusion around houses which are tidy and neat. Most of the south-eastern region is flat or gently hilly, and bicycles and scooters are ideal transport. By contrast, the north-western region is mountainous; good for climbing and exploring.

Ports & towns

Zante Town
A town of distinction, still keeping to its original grid-pattern layout, with a waterfront fully 3km long. At one end of the harbour is the free-standing campanile of the church of Zante's patron saint Ayos Dionissios; outlined in lights at night, it is a landmark from both land and sea. At the other end lies Solomas Square, broad and stately, housing one of the town's two museums. In between are two cinemas, a supermarket stocked with sophisticated produce, tavernas and shops. The other museum is located in St Marks Square – the hub of island nightlife, which is lined with restaurants. All around is a feeling of spaciousness and elegance; shops sell local or imported perfumes, fashions are Italian, and there are also several antique shops. All types of transport can be hired. The bus network is good, but schedules, unfortunately, are only in Greek.

Laganas
7km S of Zante Town. The island's principal beach resort; tavernas, hotels and restaurants situated around 9km of soft sand and shallow clear waters.

Porto Roma
17km E of Zante Town. Idyllic hamlet consisting of one taverna, one restaurant and one shop on a clifftop above the beach.

Accommodation & eating

There are many hotels in both Laganas and Argasi, two of the island's main beach resorts. Two hotels in Zante Town are the B class **Strada Marina** (tel 22761/3) and the C class **Hotel Bitzaro** (tel 23644) opposite the Lido. Several less expensive pensions line the streets behind the harbour. Eating is in the beachside tavernas or the restaurants around St Marks Square, many of which serve Italian-style pizzas or Greek 'fast-food'.

Sights

Neo-Byzantine Museum
Solomas Sq, Zante Town. Opposite a bust of the national poet, this museum exhibits the religious work of the 'Zakinthos School of Art' which flourished in the 16th and 17th centuries.

Open all year 09.00–15.30 Mon–Sat, 10.00–15.00 Sun. Closed Tue.

Solomas Museum
This stately museum is dedicated to the poets of Zakinthos, including Dionyssios Solomos, who, in 1823 wrote what was to become the Greek National Anthem. His tomb lies on the ground floor of the museum. *Open 09.00–13.30, 18.00–20.00. Closed Tue.*

Venetian Fortress
1km N of Zante Town. It was around these stone ramparts that the town of Zakinthos huddled during its years of turbulence with the Turks and other invaders. The remains of a Classical city have been discovered beneath the fortress, but the interior is now a virtual pine forest – cool and refreshing. The view alone was worth fighting for; its walls look down over the wonderful roofscape of Zante Town to the pale turquoise of Zakinthos Bay. Very windy. *Open 08.00–20.00 Mon–Sat, 10.00–20.00 Sun. Closed Tue.* Charge.

Specialities

Perfume
Zante produces several types of locally made perfumes. For thirty years the Razi family has created fragrances from the flowers and spices grown in their garden. Buy one of the five eau de toilettes, or two colognes for men in the chemists in Zante Town.

Local wines
White Verdea, and Comouto rosé. Also island brandy, oúzo and a strawberry liqueur.

NE Aegean
Islands

Lemnos

General character

Lemnos is a low-lying, low-key island, strategically sited at the entrance to the Dardanelles. This location gives access to the ports belonging to both Russia and Turkey, and for this reason Lemnos plays a vital role in Greece's defence scheme. Although the island's beaches and archaeological sites attract a few tourists, it is too remote, too poorly equipped, and not sufficiently exciting to ever qualify as more than a minor resort. Military installations are placed in key positions around the island, and the planes landing at the airport are as likely to be carrying bulky cargo as tourists in a holiday mood.

On the plus side, Lemnos' lack of immediate appeal ensures it is mercifully free of commercialism, and the inhabitants in its many villages have a traditional lifestyle which is rapidly vanishing on other islands. Pleasures are simple and the people friendly. The beaches are good and the principal port of Myrina is pleasantly attractive.

Regional features

Lemnos lies in the middle of the north Aegean, halfway between Asia Minor and Athos on the Greek mainland. Two deep inlets practically bisect the island, giving Lemnos its characteristic butterfly shape, with the Bay of Pournia in the north and the Gulf of Moudros in the south. There are two lakes in the eastern part of the island, a fertile region where tobacco and foodstuffs are grown; the west is rocky, rising to a height of 470m near Skopia in the north-west. There are thermal springs near Kornos with a constant temperature of 35°C.

Ports & towns

Myrina/Mirina

Myrina is the shipping, administrative and commercial capital of Lemnos. Most hotels and reasonable restaurants are here, as well as banks and the post office. The Kastro is its dominating feature; a ruined Byzantine fortress on a volcanic hill which has sandy bays on each side. The bay to the south serves

| Island chain   NE Aegean |
| Alternative names   Limnos |
| Population   15,750 |
| Area   476sq km |
| Area tel code   0276 |
| Tourist Police   tel 22200 |
| Harbour Police . tel 22823 |
| Distance from Piraeus   186 |
| nautical miles/19 hours |

Travel information

By air
2–3 flights daily to/from Athens. Daily flight to/from Thessaloniki on the mainland.
By ferry
2–3 weekly to/from Kavala (6 hours), often linking with Lesbos, Aghios Efstratios & the Sporades. 1 weekly to/from Piraeus via Lesbos. Occasional services to Kimi on Evia, also Chios, Samos, Ikara, Leros, Kalymnos, Rhodes & Crete.

as the port, the one to the north is quieter and more residential. Scooters, bicycles and cars can be hired here.

Moudros

28km E of Myrina. The island's second largest town is primarily a military base, and of little interest to the casual visitor.

Tsimandria

23km E of Myrina. The closest thing to a tourist resort on Lemnos, with restaurants and weekend nightlife consisting of eating, drinking and dancing – often in the streets.

Accommodation & eating

The **Akti Myrina** (tel 22681) is a Luxury class hotel built, and primarily frequented, by Swiss businessmen. Not only does it have a private beach, tennis courts and swimming pools, it also boasts four restaurants. Less expensive in Myrina is the B class **Kastro Beach** (tel 22772), the C class **Lemnos** (tel 22153) or the D class **Thraki** (tel 22617). Rooms to let are available in other villages. Undoubtably the best food is served at the **Akti Myrina**, whose high-class restaurants are open to the public. There is a good fish restaurant in Tsimandria.

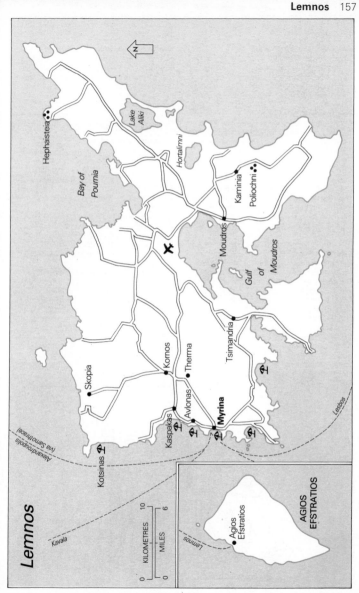

Lemnos

Sights

Archaeology Museum
Myrina. This 10-room museum is housed in and elegant mansion, and displays finds from the ancient cities of Hephaisteia and Poliochni. *Open most mornings Mon–Sat. Closed Tue & Sun.* Charge.

Hephaisteia
38km NE of Myrina. In Classical times this was the most important city on Lemnos; conquered by the Venetians in 1204, it was later destroyed by a landslide in 1395. The earliest ruins are of a necropolis dating from the 8thC BC and a sanctuary. Traces of Byzantine churches and a theatre, remodelled by the Romans, can also be seen. The site, located on a headland in the Bay of Pournia, can be difficult to find; ask locally for directions.

Poliochni
39km E of Myrina. Located near the village of Kaminia, the earliest levels of this ancient site are thought to predate Troy, having been constructed during the 4th millennium BC. Excavations conducted by the Italian School in the 1930s discovered four ancient settlements, built one on top of the other. The later of the two Neolithic cities was found to possess the earliest-known stone baths in the Aegean. A fortified city with impressive town walls lies above, dating from the pre-Mycenean period, and above that an unfortified Early Bronze Age town (1500–1000BC).

Beaches

The two sandy beaches close to the port of Myrina are both suitable for bathing, although the one to the north is larger and offers more shade. Both have cafés nearby. Further north, there are sandy strips at Avlonas, Kaspakas and Kotsinas.

Satellite islands

Aghios Efstratios
S of Lemnos. Accessible by caique from Lemnos and by occasional ferry from Kavala on the mainland. Aghios Efstratios is a remote, secluded fishing community with one village – the port of Aghios Efstratios – and only one road. The village is constructed on several tiers which are connected by steps; some buildings are little more than concrete huts, erected hurriedly after an earthquake devastated the island in 1967.

There is one guest-house with less than a dozen rooms, and food is primarily fish, as is to be expected. Locals can be initially aloof as foreigners are uncommon, but become friendly and generous with time. The bathing is excellent for those willing to walk – as a reward for a 1½-hour trek there are some excellent beaches around the coast. The beach at the port is also perfectly serviceable.

Lesbos

General character

The third largest Greek island, and a popular destination with Greek holidaymakers for some time, Lesbos has only recently been discovered by foreign tourists. Its charms are considerable – spectacular scenery, golden sandy beaches and a rich historical and cultural tradition documented in almost a dozen museums. Homer mentions Lesbos in both the *Iliad* and the *Odyssey*, but it is as the birthplace of the Greek poetess Sappho that the island is best known in international circles.

Lesbos is not an island for everyone, however, and some foreigners have been known to return home disappointed. Its attractions are low-key, almost tucked away, and distances so great as to require private transport or plenty of time to spend idly waiting for buses. Although most villages can be reached by bus from Mytilene, the capital, returning again can involve several transfers and take almost a day. Much of the interior is mountainous and uninspiring. Local architecture, although often splendid, can equally be dull. Lesbos is best when appraised in parts, rather than taken as a whole. For artists, scholars and adventurers it is ideal; this is not the kind of island where martinis and chips will be found.

Regional features

Lesbos lies very close to Asia Minor, and boat trips are often available; shaped like a broad horse-shoe, the island is almost bisected by the Gulf of Kallonis. Another arm of water, the Gulf of Geras, penetrates the south-eastern corner. The eastern region is fertile and largely given over to dense olive plantations; the west is barren and rocky. In the north-west of the island, beyond Eressos, are the extensive remains of a petrified forest.

Ports & towns

Mytilene/Mytilini

The island's capital is a large, sprawling town, built amphitheatrically on several low hills, below a lovely 13thC castle. It

Island chain   NE Aegean
Alternative names   Lesvos/Mitilini/ Mytilene
Population   88,600
Area   1,630sq km
Area tel code   Agiassos 0252, Eressos 0253, Molyvos 0253, Mytilene 0251, Petra 0253
Tourist Police   tel (0251) 22776
Harbour Police   tel (0251) 28647
Distance from Piraeus   188 nautical miles/15 hours

Travel information

By air
International airport serving Europe. Up to 6 flights daily to/from Athens; 6–7 weekly to/from Thessaloniki on the mainland.

By ferry
4 weekly to/from Piraeus; 2–4 weekly to/from Lemnos & Chios. Regular ferries to Turkey.

is a practical, rather than picturesque port, with the northern side of the wide harbour given over to cargo and military ships. Surprisingly little English is spoken, although sign language is sufficient for purchasing fresh fish and vegetables in the long, narrow marketplace just behind the harbour. Cars and scooters can be hired from several firms, also jeeps – the ideal form of transport for reaching far-flung places.

Most of the island's museums and two ancient sites are to be found in Mytilene. The ruins of a theatre and a marketplace are buried deep in the suburbs to the north, and much searching is required, even with a town map. Dating from the Hellenistic period, the theatre, in the north-west of the town, was one of the largest in ancient Greece. The area known as Kioski, just below the castle, is an old, aristocratic district, and some fine, traditional mansions still remain. The Tourist Police are located around a dangerous bend in the road at the far end of the harbour – pedestrians beware. The staff in the office are particularly charming and helpful. A friendly place.

Lesbos

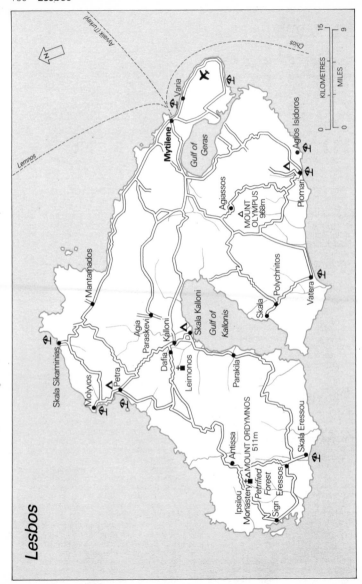

Agiassos/Ayiasos

27km W of Mytilene. Traditional village on the slopes of Mount Olympus. Cobbled streets lead past whitewashed houses with red-tiled roofs; all around are pine, plane and chestnut trees. The village has its own theatre and folklore collection – there is a long tradition of wood carving, weaving and pottery-making here. Agiassos is also known for the Church of Our Lady of Agiassos which houses a famous icon attributed to St Luke. It was brought to the village from Jerusalem in AD803. Each year on 15 August, the feast day of the church, the village is crowded with pilgrims.

Eressos

89km NW of Mytilene. The birthplace of Sappho. This village, with its busy market and large plane tree by the square, is now a cultural and artistic centre. Performances and lectures are often held in what used to be the agricultural school. A small archaeological museum displays finds from Ancient Eressos, the site now occupied by the resort of Skala Eressou, 4km south, on the coast. An attractive village with numerous restaurants, a long sandy beach and rooms to let.

Molyvos/Methymna

62km NW of Mytilene. Friendly, cultured tourist town dominated by the façade of a Byzantine castle. The narrow streets are filled with fish restaurants, shops and bars; buildings are of local stone. The pebble beach is a disappointment, but during the season buses run four times a day to the sandy beach at Petra. One of Lesbos' many archaeological museums is located in the Town Hall. *Open 09.00–14.00 Mon–Sat. Closed Tue.* The library is excellent. *Open 09.00–14.00 Mon–Fri.* The Picture Gallery holds exhibitions by local and other well-known artists. *Open 09.00–13.00, 17.00–21.00 Mon–Sat. In winter 09.00–13.00 only.*

Petra

55km NW of Mytilene. This small residential village is the site of the first women's agricultural-tourist cooperative. Local women have opened their homes to visitors, who are welcome to join in with the daily activities of cooking, grape-picking or fishing. It is also enjoyable merely to sit on the beach and watch the glorious sunsets. The scheme is promoted by the National Tourist Organisation of Greece in an attempt to achieve economic independence for women living in rural areas. For information on the cooperative, tel (0253) 41238.

Accommodation & eating

Hotels in Mytilene include the B class **Blue Sea** (tel 23994) and the C class **Sappho** (tel 28415). Apartments are also available in the surrounding area (tel 23693). Most of the popular villages have pensions, guest-houses or rooms to let: in Agiassos try the B class **Aghia Sion** (tel 22242); in Skala Eressou the C class **Sappho the Eressia** (tel 53233); in Molyvos the A class **Molyvos Pension** (tel 71386). Camping is allowed near Molyvos and also near Plomari on the south coast. Food throughout the island is traditional and Greek. The fish is caught locally, and most vegetables come from one of Lesbos' numerous market gardens.

Sights

Archaeological Museum

Mytilene. Housed in an attractive mansion, the museum exhibits ancient coins, sculpture and ceramics from all over the island. *Open 09.00–19.00 Mon–Sat; 10.00–14.00 Sun. Closed Tue.* Charge.

Byzantine Museum

Mytilene. Located on the ground floor of the Philanthropic Society building, this museum contains all the important icons no longer in the churches. *Open 09.00–13.00 daily.*

Castle of the Gattelusi

Mytilene. Thought to date originally from 1260, this well-preserved fortress was renovated by the Genoese Francisco Gattelusi in 1373. The Turks, who conquered Lesbos in 1462, added a seminary and defensive walls to the north. Several of the walls, built from a pinkish stone, contain fully intact marble plaques. The one in the south wall is a relief of an eagle and a set of scales – the device of the Gattelusi family. The Queen's Tower and several domes and cells are clearly visible.

The view from the battlements is splendid; the shady pine forest below, the town of Mytilene beyond, and across the sea, the Turkish mainland.

Folklore Museum

Mytilene. Exhibits items of popular arts and crafts on the island including paintings and pottery. Also regional costumes. *Open 10.00–12.00, 15.00–19.00 daily.*

Ipsilou Monastery
81km NW of Mytilene. Sited beyond the village of Antissa on the road to Sigri. High on the slopes of Mount Ordymnos, the monastery has a commanding view. It was founded around AD800 by Theophanes the Sigrian and rebuilt in the 12thC. Its museum contains many ecclesiastical relics, including crucifixes studded with precious stones and some ingenious portable altars. *Open mornings only 09.00–13.00.*

Leimonos Monastery
45km NW of Mytilene. Near the village of Dafia, just north of Kalloni. A lovely red-stone building constructed in 1523. A secret school was held here during the years of Turkish rule, and under the altar, in a clandestine setting, are some lovely frescos by the monk Nikolaos of Mount Athos. The museum contains treasures from all over Lesbos; its library houses over 2,500 books, including rare 9thC manuscripts. *Open mornings only 09.00–13.00.*

Old Mytilene House
Mytilene. An exact replica of a 19thC island home, with a working kitchen and several other rooms, all meticulously furnished. For an appointment to view tel 28550. *Open 10.00–12.00, 17.00–19.00.* Charge.

Petrified forest
85km NW of Mytilene. Beyond the Ipsilou Monastery, between the villages of Eressos and Sigri is this remarkable natural phenomenon. The trees, mainly conifers including sequoia – the Californian giant redwood – were buried under volcanic ash and other material,

following the eruption of Mount Ordymnos. Gradually petrification took place. Experts differ in their opinions on the age of the trees, but they may have stood here for millions of years. Some of the remaining trunks stand as high as 6.5m with circumferences of up to 8m. It is an offence to remove any rock fragments from this area, which is accessible only by jeep or on foot.

Teriade Museum of Modern Art
Varia. 4km S of Mytilene. Purpose-built museum standing in the grounds of the family home of the Parisian art critic Teriad. This private collection is of the highest quality, including five books illustrated by Chagall, and Pierre Reverdy's 'Song of the Dead', illustrated by Picasso. *Open 09.00–14.00, 17.00–20.00 daily in summer; mornings only in winter.* Charge.

Theophilus Museum
Varia. 4km S of Mytilene. Built with money provided by Teriad, who also founded the Modern Art museum in Varia. Five-room museum containing 86 works by the Greek folk painter Theophilus. Teriad used his considerable influence to stage an exhibition of Theophilus' work at the Louvre in Paris. Sadly, the painter did not live to see his success, having died in poverty in 1934. *Open 09.00–13.00, 17.00–19.00 Mon–Sat in summer; mornings only in winter.* Charge.

Specialities

Wines & spirits
Red and white Epom wine; Epom retsina. Six different types of oúzo: Arvaniti, Epom, Fino, Kefi, Pitsiladi and Veto; Fino brandy.

Samos

General character

Samos is pretty and verdant – one of the greenest of the eastern isles. Settled as long ago as the third millenium BC, Samos boasts throughout its long history, a distinguished list of artists, writers, philosophers and seafarers amongst its sons. Pythagoras, the father of trigonometry, was born on Samos around 580BC; the Temple of Hera and

the Tunnel of Eupalinos were wonders of the ancient world. Samian wine is celebrated throughout Greece for its ripe, fruity taste, and the island's beaches, although often crowded now, are excellent.

In the last few years Samos has enjoyed a rise in popularity, and excursion boats from Patmos swell the number of summer visitors enormously. The ancient and attractive port of

Pythagorion is a well-known haunt for yachtsmen, with the waterside restaurants and bars correspondingly expensive. New construction is going on in the wooded valleys between Pythagorion and Samos Town. Samos has been conquered by many invaders over the years, and should continue to weather the tourist invasion with equal grace.

Regional features

Lying just 3km from the coast of Turkey, Samos is the most easterly of the North-East Aegean islands. Long stretches of the north coast are rocky and inaccessible; the southern shores accommodate a series of sandy beaches. Much of the interior is devoted to the vineyards which yield the famous Samian wine; also thickly wooded valleys irrigated by natural springs. Crumbling windmills and other ruined buildings dot the horizon.

Island chain   NE Aegean
Population   31,650
Area   476sq km
Area tel code   0273
Tourist Police   tel 27980
Harbour Police   tel 27890
Distance from Piraeus   174
nautical miles/12 hours

Travel information

By air
International airport serving Europe. 1–3 flights daily to/from Athens.
By ferry
3–7 weekly to/from Piraeus; 3–7 weekly to/from Ikaria; 3 weekly to/from Paros in summer; 2 weekly to Chios & Leros. Excursion boat to/from Patmos 4 times weekly during summer; daily caiques to Turkey Jun–Aug – check beforehand with Harbour Police.

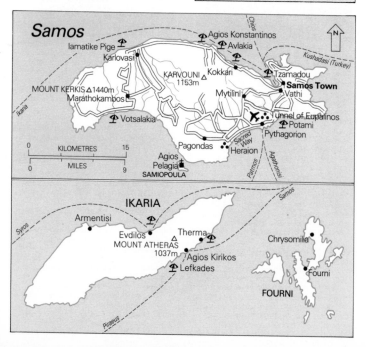

Ports & towns

Samos Town/Vathi

Samos is the name given to the port district of this capital town; Vathi is the older quarter, rising up the gentle slopes of the hill. A superb view of Samos can be gained from this hill – attractive red-tiled roofs more typical of Italy than Greece. In the teeming streets it becomes clear Samos is a working town with little time for sophistication. The best place to rest from the midday sun is behind the harbour in the City Garden. This tropical refuge is also a small zoo. Between June and August boats leave daily from Samos Town for nearby Turkey.

Karlovasi

51km NE of Samos Town. Ferries from Piraeus sometimes call at this serviceable port on the north coast, rather than going on to Samos Town. There are hotels, tavernas and buses to other destinations, but the latter are lamentably infrequent.

Pythagorion

12km S of Samos Town. Formerly known as Tigani, the name was changed in honour of Pythagoras, the renowned mathematician. Elegant, tree-lined spot on the site of ancient Samos. The quayside is colourful and sophisticated; the food in the tavernas delightfully fresh. The remarkable Church of the Transfiguration of the Saviour rises to one side, with its brightly painted, Swiss-style clock tower; a touch of whimsy next to the sombre façade of the Castle of Logothetes. The castle was built in 1824 on the site of an earlier fortress. A small museum just behind the harbour contains a row of 6thC BC tomb columns as well as marble reliefs and statues. *Open most mornings.* There are beaches on either side of the bay. Pythagorion is best visited out of season or after sunset when it is less crowded and its considerable charms can be appreciated.

Accommodation & eating

Pythagorion has many guest-houses and rooms to let, as well as larger hotels such as the A class **Doryssa Bay** (tel 61360) on the outskirts of town, and the B class **Acropole** (tel 61261). Samos Town has less accommodation; the most attractive hotel – obscured from the sea by flowers – is the B class **Hotel Xenia** (tel 27463). Three hotels in Karlovasi are the B class **Merope** (tel 32650), the D class **Astir** (tel 33150) and the D class **Morpheus** (tel 32672). Pythagorion offers a wide choice of eating establishments; as well as the quayside restaurants there are small, less expensive cafés in the back streets.

Sights

Archaeology Museum

Samos Town. Next to the Town Hall, the museum has two floors of exhibits dating mainly from the 6thC BC. The upper storey contains a rich collection of finds from the Temple of Hera. *Open 09.00–13.00, 16.00–18.00 Mon–Sat; 10.00–14.00 Sun. Closed Tue.*

Byzantine Museum

Samos Town. Housed in the Palace of the Metropolis. Six showcases display ecclesiastical objects including icons, manuscripts, vestments and chalices. *Open most mornings 09.00–13.00. Closed Tue.*

Heraion/Temple of Hera

21km SW of Samos Town. On the south coast of the island west of Pythagorion, the history of this site can be traced in detail. The first great temple, built in the 6thC BC, was claimed by Herodotus (the Greek historian who lived on Samos around 450BC), as one of the largest temples ever constructed. It was 100m long and 50m wide; a second temple, built around 525BC after the first was destroyed by fire, was longer but narrower. Two smaller temples dating from the Roman period lie to the east of the great temple; to the north is a Hellenistic stoa or portico. *Open daily. Charge.*

The road between Pythagorion and Heraion is known as the Sacred Way, and was once lined with statues, some of which are now housed in the Archaeology Museum, Samos Town.

Palaeontology Museum

Mytilini. 12km W of Samos Town. Rare in Greece, the museum exhibits a range of palaeontological material, including the fossilised bones of prehistoric animals. *Open most mornings 09.00–13.00. Closed Tue.*

Tunnel of Eupalinos

13km SW of Samos Town. Just north of Pythagorion. A major feat of engineering, the tunnel, 1,026m long was hewn from solid rock. The teams worked from each end, meeting in the

Satellite islands

Fourni

SW of Samos. Most easily accessible by caique from Ikaria during the summer months, a 1½-hour journey. Fourni, has just over a thousand inhabitants, most of whom live in the two main villages of Fourni and Chrysomilia. Few tourists visit Fourni and rooms can be hard to come by. There are both sand and pebble beaches on the island.

Ikaria

SW of Samos. Ikaria is 143 nautical miles from Piraeus, and shares the same ferry links as Samos. It is noted for its thermal springs, which attract visitors who book for a series of treatments. The port of Agios Kirikos, surrounded by hills, has an air of decaying grandeur; it is possible to swim off the rocks here. Walking and secluded bathing are the main activities in the north-west around Armentisi. Buses from Agios Kirikos to Armentisi are fairly frequent, but returning can cause problems and it's easy to get stranded. Best to share a communal taxi with the local women, ladened with shopping.

Samiopoula

1km S of Samos. Lying just beyond the southern tip of the main island, Samiopoula is tiny. The chapel of Agios Pelagia is on the north coast, and there is a resident population of just five.

middle; remarkably, there was only a few metres difference in level between the two excavations. Completed in 524BC during the Tyranny of Polycrates, when Samos was at the height of its prosperity, Eupalinos was Polycrates' chief engineer. Running through a mountain, it was constructed as an escape route. As yet the tunnel has no illumination so bring a torch.

Beaches

Two of the island's best beaches are at Votsalakia near the resort of Maratho-kambos, and further north at Iamatike Pige, outside Karlovasi. There is a long pebble beach at Kokkari, and another further west at Tzamadou, where unofficial camping is tolerated.

Specialities

Wines & spirits

Of Samian wine the most popular is Samaina, dry, light and good. Fokianos is a dry rosé. Other locally-made drinks include brandy, vermouth and a vin de liqueur, with a pleasant aftertaste – very sweet.

Samothrace

General character

Samothrace is a remote, dramatic island dominated by Mount Fengari – the Mountain of the Moon – whose towering peak is used as a landmark by the sailors who navigate the often stormy seas. Frequented mostly by archaeologists interested in the impressive ancient site of Paleopolis, and those seeking the simple life, Samothrace has few obvious tourist attractions; its beaches are indifferent and amenities are few. Accommodation is also fairly limited, despite all the new construction which is taking place.

Surprisingly the island attracts a large number of visitors each year; perhaps they are lured by Samothrace's reputation of being the most mysterious island in the Aegean because of the mists which swirl around its rocky hills. They may also be drawn by the 'unspoilt' nature of the island. It is possible to observe Greek customs on Samothrace which are dying out on more popular islands, and traditional dress is still worn in outlying hamlets.

More suited to pedestrians than motor

Island chain   NE Aegean
Alternative names   Samothrake/ Samothraki
Population   2,870
Area   178sq km
Area tel code   0551
Tourist Police   tel 41203
Harbour Police   tel 41305

Travel information

By ferry
Daily to/from Alexandroupolis on the mainland (which has an airport); 1 weekly to/from Kavala on the mainland.

vehicles, Samothrace is an island for walkers. If mountain climbing appeals, it is best to take a local guide as the paths up Mount Fengari are difficult to follow. It is a five-hour walk, but camping is allowed on the summit. The view is breathtaking – all of Asia Minor lies below; Homer wrote that Poseidon sat here to observe the Trojan War.

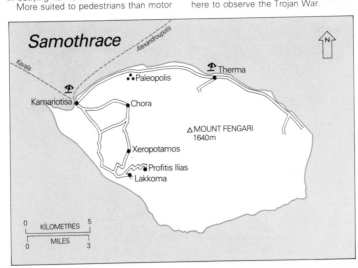

Regional features

Samothrace is a very mountainous island; its low-lying land is confined to small fertile areas where olives and wheat are grown. The road system is improving; tarmacked surfaces will soon run to all the major villages, already connected by frequent buses.

Ports & towns

Kamariotisa

The island's port, but with no natural anchorage, only a long concrete pier. Consisting of a few shops and tavernas, development is beginning to take place. It is also the starting point for two buses – one bus goes north and the other south, covering most of the island. To one side is a steep pebble beach with a shower and changing rooms.

Chora/Samothrace Town

5km E of Kamariotisa. Charmingly sited island capital on the foothills of Mount Fengari. Here, village life remains intact, centred around its few pensions and tavernas; built in traditional Thracian style, the houses have balconies and red-tiled roofs weighted down with large stones. The main road snakes upwards past a bank and a tiny post office. Located just below the lonely ruins of a Byzantine fortress are the headquarters of the Tourist Police.

Therma

13km NW of Kamariotisa. Taking its name from the thermal springs in the town, Therma is a low-key holiday resort set amongst shady trees; at its entrance is a small, well-attended spa. The beach, with a shower and changing rooms, is a short walk away.

Accommodation & eating

The island's two hotels are the B class **Xenia** (tel 41230) and the C class **Niki Beach** (tel 41561). Rooms in private houses can be found in the larger villages, although overall, accommodation is limited. Food is standard Greek, with the emphasis on meat and rice; most fresh vegetables have to be imported.

Sights

Archaeology Museum

Paleopolis. 6km NW of Kamariotisa. Laid out as an aid to understanding the ancient city of Paleopolis, a visit to the museum is recommended before going to the site itself. There are reconstructions of many of the buildings and statues, including a copy of the 'Nike'; commonly known as the 'Winged Victory of Samothrace'. A guidebook is available in English. *Open 09.00–15.30 Mon–Sat, 10.00–15.00 Sun. Closed Tue.* Charge.

Paleopolis

6km NW of Kamariotisa. Of particular interest amongst the extensive ruins of this ancient city are the Hellenistic city walls. Also the Sanctuary of the Great Gods, the pagan worship-place of the cult of the Kaberoi – the Great Gods – whose mysteries and sacrifices attracted pilgrims from all over the Aegean. In 700BC Greek colonists took over and enlarged the city, erecting the impressive Rotunda Arsinoeion, the largest circular building in Greece. The outline of an amphitheatre can still be determined. *Open 09.00–15.30 Mon–Sat, 10.00–15.00 Sun.* Charge.

Thassos

General character

Lying just a one-hour journey off the coast of north-east Greece, Thassos has long been a popular holiday spot for locals from the mainland. Luxuriously green, with pretty inland villages and sophisticated ports, Thassos is an ideal place for a family vacation; an excellent beach with full amenities is never far away.

A good tarmac road rings this almost circular island; buses to the larger villages are frequent and bicycles, cars and scooters can be hired to explore the smaller ones. Most road signs and menus are in Greek only, and little English is spoken, even by those who deal with the public; so learn a few phrases before you go. As Thassos is little known outside its own country, all amenities are reasonably priced.

Regional features

Thassos is the most northerly Aegean island, only 12km from the mainland. Over half the total area is wooded, principally with plane, oak, cedar, pine and olive trees. Water is abundant, as are rich veins of marble; in antiquity, Thassos was also famed for its gold and silver. Mount Hypsarion rises to a height of 1,204m in the centre.

Ports & towns

Thassos Town/Limenas/Limen
Built on the site of an ancient settlement, this busy port and capital has a cinema, discos, hire agencies and tavernas. The Tourist Police and several hotels occupy the waterfront area; parallel to it is the main shopping street where camping and beach goods can be bought. In the old harbour area, not far from the Archaeological Museum, is the lovely, disused Monastery of St Nicholas, soon to be converted into a folklore museum.

Limenaria
45km SW of Thassos Town. Surrounded by trees and with a large sandy beach nearby, Limenaria is the island's second largest town and the main tourist resort. Less urban in feel than Thassos Town, Limenaria boasts a fair share of local Thassian architecture. The large cream building with its red-tiled roof which

Island chain   NE Aegean
Population   13,100
Area   379sq km
Area tel code   0593
Tourist Police   tel 28500 s.o.
Harbour Police   tel 21355

Travel information

By ferry
20 daily in summer from Kavala on the mainland; 6 daily in winter. Journey time 1 hour. 6–20 daily throughout the year from Keramoti on the mainland. Journey time 45 mins.

dominates the skyline is, however, German. It was constructed by a mining executive in 1903, and is known locally as the Palataki or 'Little Palace'.

Theologos
58km S of Thassos Town. One of the island's picturesque inland villages, with buildings capped by distinctive grey-slate roofs. One has been converted into a museum of local crafts, known as the Popularity Museum, where hand-woven carpets can be admired. In the high season re-enactments of the traditional wedding ceremony take place.

Accommodation & eating

Hotels, guest-houses and rooms to let are common, but many people prefer to camp. Four hotels include the A class **Roula** (tel 22905) and the C class **Lido** (tel 22929) in Limenas; the C class **Menel** (tel 51396) in Limenaria and the C class **Thassos** (tel 51596) in the village of Pefkari. Three campsites on Thassos are all situated near beaches: **Golden Beach Camping** is the cheapest, but often lacks shade (tel 61472); **Pefkari Camping** (tel 51595) is attractive, but sometimes crowded; **Camping Ioannidis** (tel 71377) has 180 pitches and many amenities.

Food is Greek and traditionally cooked; expect to walk into the kitchens of the tavernas to choose from the day's selection of dishes.

Sights

Archaeological Museum

Thassos Town. Located in the old harbour area, this charming museum has statues of lions in the gardens and five rooms of local finds. Of note are antiquities from the Temple of Artemis, including a lion's head carved in ivory dating from the 6thC BC, and a bronze statuette of the goddess herself. *Open*

09.00–15.30 Mon–Sat; 10.00–15.00 Sun. Closed Tue. Charge.

Archangelou Monastery

38km S of Thassos Town. Screened from the main coast road by a high wall, this monastery has a grey-slate roof, tiny arched windows and a wonderful sea view. Inside is a small chapel containing icons. Long trousers and skirts can be hired for those dressed in beach clothes.

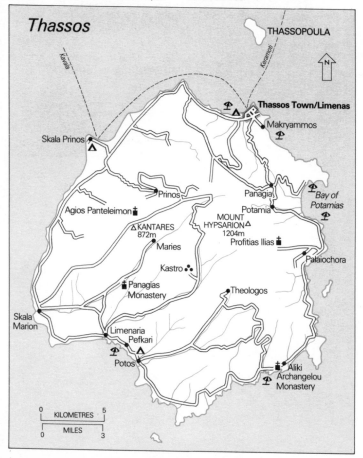

Thassos

THASSOPOULA

Kavala

Keramoti

N

Thassos Town/Limenas

Makryammos

Skala Prinos

Prinos

Panagia

Bay of Potamias

Agios Panteleimon

Potamia

MOUNT HYPSARION
1204m

△KANTARES
872m

Maries

Profitias Ilias

Kastro

Palaiochora

Panagias Monastery

Theologos

Skala Marion

Limenaria
Pefkari

Potos

Aliki
Archangelou Monastery

0   KILOMETRES   5

0   MILES   3

Other monasteries include Agios Panteleimon high in the hills of Kantares; Panagias Monastery en route to the village of Maries, and the deserted Profitis Ilias near Palaiochori.

Kastro

50km S of Thassos Town. This mountain village was abandoned in the 19thC, when most of its residents moved to more accessible Limenaria. Recently some of the houses have been refurbished to provide rough accommodation for tourists; enquire locally at Kastro or with the Tourist Police.

Thassos Ancient City

Thassos Town. The walls date from 412BC and take approx two hours to tour. Several gates still remain, bearing original Archaic bas-reliefs. In a wood of holm oaks lies the amphitheatre which dates from the 4thC BC. Classical performances are given during the summer months. Further up the hill is the Acropolis; a relief of a funeral feast in the outer wall dates from the 5th or 4thC BC. Also dating from the 5thC BC are the foundations of the Temple of Athena nearby. The ancient Agora lies in the town near the Archaeological Museum.

Beaches

Limenas has a sandy town beach with cafés close by; Aliki has a series of pleasant beaches, including one where nudism is accepted. The Bay of Potamias is an extensive 3km of soft, pale sand; the villages of Potos and Pefkari also have sandy strips, the latter with trees almost down to the water's edge.

Satellite islands

Thassopoula

During the summer, caiques make the short trip from Limenas to the islet of Thassopoula. A desolate place, covered with low-growing vegetation and known for its snakes. Pack sturdy shoes.

The Saronic
Islands

Aegina

General character

Lying only 30 minutes by hydrofoil from Piraeus, Aegina is one of the most visited of all the Greek islands; its beaches are reasonable and the food quite good. Although pleasant enough for a day trip from Athens, Aegina – with its flat terrain and smooth ashphalted roads – is a bland island. It can, however, be justifiably proud of the Temple of Aphaia, one of the finest examples of Doric architecture in Greece. Its donkey carts carry more tourists than local labourers, and if a local ventures out in native dress it is obviously for the benefit of camera-happy crowds. Aegina is very popular with American tourists.

Close proximity to Athens and a strategic position in the trading waters of the Mediterranean ensured from ancient times, a social, political and economic sophistication far removed from the simplicity of comparable islands. Some of the earliest European coinage was minted on Aegina in 650BC. A tradition which continued, as the first modern drachmas were also minted here around 1828 when Aegina was the temporary capital of Greece. The first prison to be established in Greece was also on Aegina.

The centre of the island's ancient civilization was located in the area known today as Kolona. The present-day port of Aegina Town is built over most of this site; in its heyday, wealthy merchants commissioned the building of a marvellous theatre and three temples, of which only one column now remains.

Regional features

Aegina is equidistant from Piraeus and the island of Poros. Triangular in shape, much of the island is covered by low rocky mountains – the highest, Mount Profitis Ilias in the south, rises to only 532m. Pistachio nuts, figs, almonds, grapes and olives are grown in a small fertile valley in the south-west. Many churches and chapels are dotted around the bare brown hills. Because it is so dry some of the island's water has to be brought over from the mainland.

Island chain   Saronic
Population   11,200
Area   83sq km
Area tel code   0297
Tourist Police   tel 22391
Harbour Police   tel 22328
Distance from Piraeus   17 nautical miles/1½ hours

Travel information

By ferry
8–10 daily from Piraeus; 30-min hydrofoil service from Zea Marina throughout the year. Aegina/Poros/Hydra daily throughout the year.

Ports & towns

Aegina Town

Aegina is a bustling port, its wide marina providing safe anchorage for boats of every description. There is safe bathing on either side – at the town beach just to the north and the Vithania Beach Club to the south. The offices of both Tourist Police and Harbour Police are situated on the waterfront. The cathedral and a good local museum can be found in the narrow backstreets behind the harbour. Horse-drawn carriages vie for right of way with tour buses and motorcars; cars and scooters can be hired, but bicycles are best for independent travel. For most direct routes the bus system is good; buses leave from the Temple of Apollo in Kolona, to the north of town.

In 1828, seven years after Aegina was liberated from the Ottoman Empire, the island became the capital of free Greece. The first governor, John Capodistrias, ordered the construction of many of the fine buildings which make a stroll through the town at twilight very pleasant. Several mansions belonging to leading 19thC statesmen still remain; the library is housed in the former governor's office. At the southern end of the town stands Capodistrias' greatest monument, the Orphan Asylum. In its time it was not only a welfare centre but provided training and education to more than 500 orphan children.

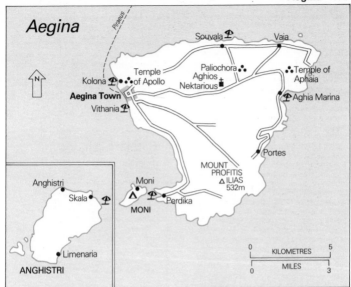

Aegina

Aghia Marina
14km E of Aegina Town. Popular beach resort on the eastern coast, half an hour by bus from Aegina Town. There are also occasional steamers from Piraeus (1½-hour journey). Well-equipped hotels overlook a sandy beach backed by pine trees.

Perdika
9km SE of Aegina Town. Picturesque fishing village, still relatively unspoilt. Its restaurants serve fresh fish, and there is a reasonable bathing beach. The tiny island of Moni is just offshore.

Souvala
8km NE of Aegina Town. This small town was once the most important port on the island, and a major trading centre of the Mediterranean. Now it is a lively resort town with numerous guesthouses and hotels.

Accommodation & eating

Hotels, bungalows and guest-houses abound on Aegina. These get booked up not only in the high season, but during the warm spring and autumn months as well. Visitors are advised to reserve accommodation well in advance. Three

B class hotels in Aegina Town are the **Danae** (tel 22424), the **Nausika** (tel 22333) and the **Pavlou** (tel 22795). Three hotels in Aghia Marina include the B class **Apollo** (tel 32271), the B class **Argo** (tel 32266) and the C class **Isidora** (tel 32414). In Souvala try the C class Ephi (tel 52214).

Eating is above average in standard. Aegina's popularity ensures a rapid turnover of food, which, if not locally grown, is shipped daily from the mainland. The resorts all offer a wide choice of tavernas; Perdika is the best place to eat fresh fish. Many larger hotels have dining rooms which are open to the public.

Sights

Museum of Aegina
Aegina Town. Housed in a 19thC building, the museum contains relics found in the 5thC temples of Apollo (formerly attributed to Aphrodite) and Aphaia, as well as many other finds. The clay casks dating from the middle Hellenic period are particularly interesting. *Open 09.00–15.30 Mon–Sat, 10.00–15.00 Sun. Closed Tue.* Charge.

Monastery of Aghios Nektarious
7km E of Aegina Town. Pilgrims from all
over Greece come to worship at this,
the resting place of the most recent
Greek Orthodox saint. St Nektarious
was canonised in 1961.

Paliochora
8km E of Aegina Town. Former
Byzantine and medieval capital of the
island, Paliochora is now in ruins.
Founded in the 9thC AD, it is said that
there were once 365 churches here,
though now only some 25 remain.
Several of these churches, built from the
13thC onwards are cruciform in shape
and contain some lovely frescos.

Temple of Aphaia/Aphaea/Afea
11.5km NE of Aegina Town. Situated
high on a pine-covered hillside, with a
commanding view of much of the island,
this beautiful Doric temple is thought to
have been built between 510–480BC.
Dedicated to Aphaia, goddess of
wisdom and light, it is built in the Doric
style and 25 of its original 32 columns
are still intact. The pediment sculptures
depicting scenes from the Trojan War in
Parian marble were acquired for King
Ludwig of Bavaria at the beginning of
the 19thC and are now in Munich. It is a
lovely temple in a lovely setting,
certainly the finest to have survived on
any of the islands.

Unfortunately the atmosphere
surrounding the temple today is that of
a three-ring circus. Sightseeing coaches
block the narrow road, and the jabbering
of tour operators in a multitude of
languages obscures much of the magic.
Avoid mid-morning at all costs, as the
cruiseships make a half-hour stop-over.
Instead, opt to stay overnight or until
twilight, when a majestic tranquillity
returns to the site. The temple itself will
be closed but a sacred air prevails. *Open
09.00–15.30 Mon–Sat; 10.00–15.00
Sun.* Charge.

Satellite islands

Anghistri
W of Aegina. Several boats daily
leave from Aegina Town for the
island of Anghistri. It covers an area
of 13sq km and its 650 inhabitants
are settled in four communities.
Guest-houses and tavernas are
scattered throughout the island.
Skala is best for swimming.

Moni
W of Aegina. Just off the coast from
Perdika, Moni was once run by a
monastic order; now the National
Tourist Organisation of Greece is
responsible for its wooded acres.
During the high season the NTOG
operate a campsite here; details
from the Tourist Police in Aegina
Town.

Hydra

General character

Third port of call for the one-day cruise ships from Piraeus, Hydra manages to retain a touch of dignity despite the barrage of tourists. Perhaps it is because historic Hydra has always been a 'discovered' island; mentioned by Herodotus in the 5thC BC, settled by refugees from Albania who, in time built up a mighty merchant fleet, later a haunt for artists and writers. The capital and main port is attractive, with several distinguished mansions built by wealthy Hydriots. As with the other Saronic isles, Hydra is geared for tourism – ask a price in one of Hydra Town's chic boutiques and it will be quoted in dollars. Cocktails and hamburgers are common fare; even the donkeys respond to commands in English. Still, the streets are prettily cobbled, food is excellent, and the cosmopolitan flavour of Hydra comes into its own at nightfall, when the strains of bouzouki and rock music mingle in a tuneful din.

Island chain   Saronic
Alternative names   Ydra
Population   2,750
Area   50sq km
Area tel code   0298
Tourist Police   tel 52205 s.o.
Harbour Police   tel 52279
Distance from Piraeus   38 nautical miles/3 hours

Travel information

By ferry

5–8 daily to/from Piraeus; frequent service to/from Ermioni on the mainland; daily hydrofoil service from Zea Marina, Piraeus, throughout the year. 1-day cruise Aegina/Poros/Hydra, throughout the year.

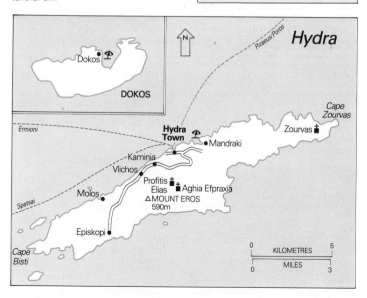

Regional features

Hydra is dry, mountainous, often suffering from a water shortage later in the season. Long and narrow, it is 20km from Cape Zouvras in the north-east to Cape Bisti on the south-western tip of the island. Many of the beaches along Hydra's barren, indented coastline are inhospitable; the better ones often organised into resorts. No cars are allowed; transport is by donkey, scooter or bicycle, all of which can be hired along the waterfront in Hydra Town.

Ports & towns

Hydra Town

The only proper settlement on the island, Hydra Town is built amphitheatrically on the steep slopes of the hills which encircle a natural harbour. This harbour, entered by a narrow channel, is the primary source of island activity, both commercial and social. Boats, steamers and yachts of every description sail into its placid waters all year round; cafés and tavernas are packed with short-term residents eager to observe the new faces. The town's famous pastel-coloured buildings, featured in many brochures, have, on the whole, been repainted white; the effect is neat. An air of dignity is added by the grey stone mansions which dominate the harbour area. Restaurants are sophisticated, the discos lively, and the range of boutiques selling clothes and souvenirs are amongst the best to be found on any Greek island. There is a yacht supply station, and an open-air cinema shows films throughout the summer months.

Kaminia

2km SW of Hydra Town. Small harbour with one or two tavernas and shops. It is possible to swim off the rocks here.

Mandraki

4km NE of Hydra Town. Village built along the bay which provides the island's best beach. Although pebbly, facilities are good, with paddle boats and windsurfing equipment available for hire.

Accommodation & eating

Due to its popularity, accommodation on Hydra must be booked well in advance. The best hotel on the island is the A class **Miramare** (tel 52300) close to Mandraki beach. The B class **Amaryllis** (tel 52249) and the C class **Hydra** (tel 52102), are two pensions in Hydra Town. One of the oldest restaurants in Hydra Town is the **Xeri Elia-Douskos**, which has tables under the trees in an attractive square. Pizzas, fast-food and ice cream are much in evidence; for a pre-dinner drink and *mezédes*, go to the **To Laikon** ouzeri located on the ground floor of the Merchant Marine building, itself an old mansion house.

Sights

Mansions

Several wealthy Hydriots built three- and four-storey houses on the outskirts of Hydra Town. These fortress-like homes, built of heavy local stone have beautiful interiors, often the work of decorators brought from Italy. Permission to view the privately-owned homes must be obtained from the Town Hall, but two have been turned into public institutes and access is freely given. The great house of the Tsamados family is now the School of Merchant Marine, the oldest school of its kind in Greece. The mansion of Emmanuel Tombazis has become a School of Fine Art.

Monasteries & convents

Seven monasteries and convents can be discovered in the hills around the capital. Most are either abandoned now, or home to a small number of monks or nuns. The Monastery of Assumption of the Virgin Mary, built in 1774, situated on the waterfront in Hydra Town, is now an administration building. The Monastery of Profitis Elias, one and a half hours by donkey south from Hydra Town, and the Convent of Aghia Efpraxia just below, are both worth a visit.

Satellite islands

Dokos

W of Hydra. Situated between Hydra and the mainland is the little islet of Dokos, known for a type of marble – Marmaropita – very hard, and used for construction purposes. With a population of just nine people, its main attraction is a long, practically deserted beach. It is a one-hour boat ride from Hydra, but caiques must be privately hired.

Poros

General character

According to the Greek historian Strabo, writing in the 1stC BC, the capital town of Poros was originally called Poseidonia, after the god Poseidon. The god's precise relationship with this gently wooded island is unclear, but his influence has been considerable. The Sanctuary of Poseidon, located between the mountains of Profitis Elias and Vigla, can be visited today.

Although sharing the load of day cruises, Poros lacks the 'glamour' of its more famous neighbours, Aegina and Hydra. Its main town is prettily formed around undulating hills, but the shops lack variety, the restaurants style. Less crowded are the wooded bays to the north, a popular destination for British package tours.

Regional features

Poros is actually two islands connected by a bridge. The larger of the two,

Island chain   Saronic
Population   3,950
Area   23sq km
Area tel code   0298
Tourist Police   tel 22462 s.o.
Harbour Police   tel 22274
Distance from Piraeus . 31 nautical miles/2 hours

Travel information

By ferry
5–8 daily from Piraeus, frequent service to/from Galata on mainland; daily hydrofoil service from Zea Marina, Piraeus throughout the year; 1-day Aegina/Poros/Hydra cruise throughout the year.

Kalavria, has the smaller population and is lush with olive and pine trees. There are sandy beaches here. Sferia is the volcanic islet forming the southern tip of Poros. Most of the island's inhabitants

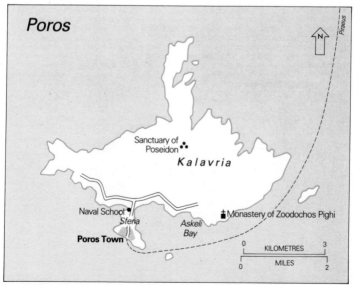

Poros

Piraeus

N

Sanctuary of Poseidon

K a l a v r i a

Naval School
Sferia

Askeli
Bay

⛪ Monastery of Zoodochos Pighi

Poros Town

| 0 | KILOMETRES | 3 |
| 0 | MILES | 2 |

live here in Poros Town, the island capital. Poros itself means 'ford' or 'passage', appropriate for an island separated from the mainland by less than 400m.

Ports & towns

Poros Town

Built amphitheatrically around several gently rolling hills, the tendency, when arriving at this busy port, is to look upwards. The skyline there is dominated by the blue clock tower, Poros' famous landmark; on nearby hills it is the pointed spires of the cypresses. Steps connect the narrow streets; one, parallel to the harbour, doubles as an open-air market. To the left of the harbour, when facing the sea, the jumble of alleyways and shops give way to a gracious seaside boulevard. A few handsome houses line this street; one with a particularly interesting façade is now the National Bank of Greece.

Accommodation & eating

On a promontory facing the town is the B class **Poros Hotel** (tel 22216) with its lovely, sweeping views. The B class **Sirene Hotel** (tel 22741) is located near the monastery of Zoodochos Pighi. There are rooms to let in Poros Town. Most of the major hotels have restaurants open to the public; by the square in town where the ferry docks is the **Seven Brothers** taverna which is, indeed, run by brothers. Further west is another, called the **Three Brothers**.

Sights

Monastery of Zoodochos Pighi

7km NE of Poros Town. This attractive white 18thC building stands in a deeply wooded area overlooking Askeli Bay. Two of its notable features are the iconostasis of finely carved wood, and the cemetery enclosed within its walls. An English officer who fought in the Greek War of Independence is buried here.

Naval Training School

Poros Town. Housed in the old arsenal built by Kapodistrias, which in 1830 was the first naval arsenal in Greece. Now a naval training school for boys, it is located at the head of the Sferia peninsula.

Sanctuary of Poseidon

12km N of Poros Town. Although once perhaps as magnificent as the Temple of Aphaia on Aegina, sadly little remains of the sanctuary today. One Doric column found in the vicinity places the date of construction at around 500BC, but now only a few stone walls can be seen.

The mainland

Galatas, on the Peloponnese mainland, is only a five-minute boat trip from Poros Town across the Straits of Poros. From Galatas it is possible to make day excursions to interesting sites in the Peloponnese. These include the impressive ancient theatre at Epidauros dating from the 3rdC BC and the lemon forest known as Lemonodassos. Almost 30,000 lemon trees grow on the slopes here.

Salamis

General character

Lying opposite the port of Piraeus,
Salamis is the most northerly island in
the Saronic Gulf and was the site of a
famous sea battle in 480BC between
the Greeks and the Persians. Salamis is
a dry, dusty island, unwelcoming and
unprepared for tourists; its beaches are
gritty and the water muddy. The
architecture is similar to that of present-
day Athens, with functional, cube-
shaped houses, petrol stations and
supermarkets.

   The bus service is quite good,
connecting both ports with the capital
town and most small villages;

Island chain Saronic
Alternative names Salamina
Population 28,600
Area 95sq km
Area tel code 01
Tourist Police tel 4651100
Harbour Police tel 4653252
Distance from Piraeus ½ hour

Travel information

By ferry
5–8 daily from Piraeus; shuttle
service to/from mainland town of
Perama, approx 20 a day.

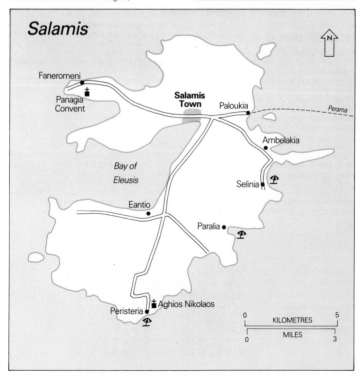

unfortunately there is little for the visitor to see or do after disembarking. Female visitors, especially, are made to feel uncomfortable on Salamis. Older men leer from the tables of kafeneíons; younger ones pursue from the safety of motorbikes.

Regional features

Salamis is a crescent-shaped island with the large, sheltered Bay of Eleusis on the west coast. Salamis Town, in the north-east corner of the bay, is surrounded by limestone hills, the highest of which is Mount Profitis Elias. From the summit there is an impressive view over the Saronic Gulf to Piraeus. Although a dry, rocky island, some areas are pine-forested and vines are grown. The most scenic part of the island is the south-east, beyond the village of Eantio.

Ports & towns

Salamis Town
The island's capital and commercial centre extends around the bay for approx 3km. The road parallel to the harbour is the main shopping area, but there is also much gossiping and activity around the large fish stalls to the left of the harbour (when facing the sea). Neatly planted trees separate the gritty beach from the pavement cafés, adding a welcome touch of style.

Eantio/Mouliki
7km SW of Salamis Town. The island's main resort is surrounded by green hills and offers a wide, sweeping view of the southern peninsula and the sea. The promenade which stretches along the rocky shore is a popular spot from which

to admire the sunset. Discos and tavernas abound.

Paloukia
3km E of Salamis Town. The island is so narrow at this point that the two ports on opposite coasts are only a short bus-ride apart. Ferries from the mainland port of Perama land at Paloukia, and there is a strong naval presence here. There are several waterside restaurants, tavernas and cafés.

Selinia
7km SE of Salamis Town. A second small port on the east coast of the island. The most impressive building is a church close to the quayside with pale, sun-bleached blue walls and several domes. There are a few pensions and tavernas and a muddy beach.

Accommodation & eating

The only listed hotels on the island are both C class, the **Gabriel** (tel 4662275) in Eantio and the **Selinia** (tel 4653424) in Salamis Town. However, there are numerous pensions and rooms to let. The smart ice cream parlour in Salamis Town can provide a good end to a taverna meal.

Sights

Panagia Convent
8km NW of Salamis Town. Close to the village of Faneromeni, a frequent bus service from Salamis Town makes it easily accessible. Situated amongst pine trees, this fortress-like convent dates from 1661. The walls of its church are decorated with impressive large-scale frescos, with more than 3,000 figures painted in fine detail. *Open most mornings & late afternoon.*

Spetsai

General character

The most southerly of the Saronic Gulf islands, Spetsai exudes character and charm. Although popular with Athenians for summer weekends, overcrowding is not a problem, and outside the high season, the island still bustles with local industry. Tourism is the most important economic contribution; in many ways adding, rather than detracting from the general appeal.

Spetsai Town brims with good restaurants and shops; tiny red and white water taxis buzz from the nearby mainland to Dapia Harbour with scenic regularity. Two-thirds of the island is covered with pine trees owned by the Anargyros Trust. The resin collected from these trees is used in the making of retsina. There are pleasant beaches on the western and south-western coasts, accessible only by caique or donkey; motor vehicles are not allowed on this tranquil isle.

Regional features

Spetsai is oval in shape and the landscape gently undulating. Lying only 2km from the Argolid peninsula on the mainland, ferry links are extremely good. In the 2ndC AD it was known as Pityoussa – literally pine tree island – these evergreens still grace much of the countryside today. Figs, oleander and pistachio nuts are also grown. The climate is mild and several species of orchid bloom in spring.

Ports & towns

Spetsai Town

Located in the north-eastern corner of the island, the town extends for some 3km along the coast. The atmosphere in Spetsai's only town is genial and gay. The focal point is Dapia Square; still dotted with cannons from the War of Independence of 1821, but also now festooned with coloured lights. These combined with the glow of candlelight from the cafés make it very picturesque at night. Attractive buildings with red-tiled roofs and some elegant 19thC mansions line the waterfront, amongst them, the Possidonion Palace hotel,

Island chain	Saronic
Alternative names	Spetses
Population	3,700
Area	22sq km
Area tel code	0298
Tourist Police	tel 73100 s.o.
Harbour Police	tel 72245
Distance from Piraeus	53 nautical miles/4 hours

Travel information

By ferry

5–8 daily to/from Piraeus, frequent service to/from Costa & Porto Heli on the mainland; daily hydrofoil service from Zea Marina, Piraeus throughout the year.

once the site of glittering masked balls. Horse-drawn carriages ferry visitors from one end of town to another; the clip-clop of hooves on the promenade is the most distinctive late-night sound. Just off the square is a place which hires out bicycles. Behind the square are several more 19thC houses, including the former home of Lascarina Bouboulina; a heroine of the War of Independence, she captained her own ship and was the mother of nine children. House not open to the public.

Many of the narrow, cobbled alleyways threading through the town are inlaid with designs of mythical marine figures made from different-coloured pebbles. These are a well-known feature of the island. On a plateau just north-west of Spetsai Town is the area known as Kastelli, which has several notable churches.

Accommodation & eating

Spetsai Town has several pensions, hotels and rooms to let in private houses. The A class **Kasteli** (tel 72161) offers both hotel rooms and bungalows to let, but the best accommodation is provided by the elegant A class **Possidonion Palace** (tel 72208). The interior is bare and echoing, but rooms are clean and the atmosphere unbeatable. The food in most of the tavernas is above average in quality.

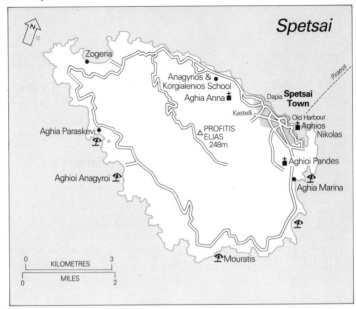

Spetsai

Sights

Anargyrios and Korgialenios School
2km W of Spetsai Town. Named after
two philanthropists, this imposing
school, opened in 1927, is modelled on
an English public school. It has a
stadium, tennis courts and an open-air
theatre. The English novelist John
Fowles based his book *The Magus* on
Spetsai and, in particular, this school.

Monastery of Aghios Nikolas
1km E of Spetsai Town. Located next to
the old harbour, this early 17thC
monastery is now used to store archives.
Its campanile of smooth white marble
can be seen for some distance and
dominates the square in which the
church lies. The square itself is covered
with pebble mosaics, including one of
Bouboulina.

Two other monasteries, on the
outskirts of Spetsai Town, are worth a
visit. The simply-built **Monastery of
Aghioi Pandes**, containing rich icons,
and the **Monastery of Aghia Anna**, a
modern church designed by the local
artist Byron Kesses.

Spetsai Museum
Spetsai Town. This museum is situated
in the former house of Hadziyannis
Mexis, an 18thC Spetsiot shipbuilder. It
exhibits the work of local 19thC artists
and relics from the War of Independence
of 1821, including Bouboulina's casket
which contains the bones of the heroine.
An archaeological room displays finds
from local excavations. *Open
10.00–14.00 daily. Closed Tue.*

Satellite islands

Spetsopoula
Only 800m separates this tiny island
from the east coast of Spetsai.
Spetsopoula is owned by the Greek
shipping magnate Stavros
Niarchos, who has turned it into an
exotic game reserve. Not open to the
public.

The purchase of Spetsopoula
prompted Niarchos' arch rival
Aristotle Onassis to buy the Ionian
island of Skorpios.

The Sporades

Alonnisos

General character

In certain ways the least interesting of the Sporades, Alonnisos is more barren and less green than its neighbours. Its appeal lies in the romantic old capital high on a hill above the port, and the attractive offshore islands which are perfect for snorkellers and swimmers. Alonnisos is hungry for the visitors which converge on its prettier neighbours; however, when the new airport is completed, package tours from Scandinavia, Britain and the Continent are confidently expected. Outside the high season, little English is spoken.

Regional features

Alonnisos is long and narrow, most of its industry and all of its 10km of roads are

Island chain   Sporades
Alternative names   Halonnisos
Population   1,530
Area   64sq km
Area tel code   0424
Tourist Police   tel 65205
Harbour Police   tel 65480
Distance from Athens   5 hours by bus to Volos; 62 nautical miles/5½ hours by boat to Alonnisos.

Travel information

By air
International airport due for completion 1985/86.
By ferry
2–5 daily to/from Volos connecting with Skiathos & Skopelos; occasional services to/from Ag Konstandinos (mainland) & Kimi (Evia); 1–4 weekly to/from Skyros.

concentrated in the south-western corner. Many of the inhabitants are shepherds or sailors; there is a rough-and-ready appeal to the island which is ideal for some tourists, but may be off-putting to others. Alonnisos has been plagued throughout the years by earthquakes, which have left numerous small islets in their wake. These can be reached by daily excursions organised during the high season.

Ports & towns

Patitiri

Devastated by an earthquake in 1965, Patitiri, which once boasted graceful buildings similar to those still seen in Old Alonnisos, has been rebuilt in flat, functional style. However, the amenities are good; there is a bank, an OTE office, a doctor and many rooms to let in the buildings which meander haphazardly up the hillside.

The most attractive area is to the left of the quay (when facing the sea); a pine-fringed path ascends the hill where there are small hotels and a pretty taverna. Take a torch at night as the path is unlit. Patitiri also serves as a base for over 100 fishing boats; from here it is possible to hire windsurfers,

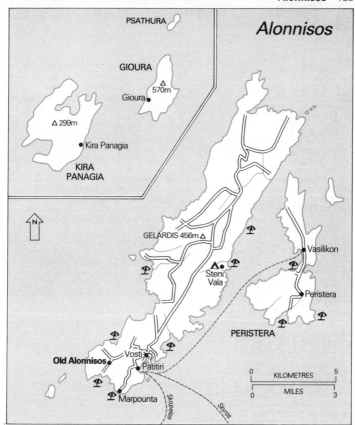

motorboats, a bicycle or a motorcycle. There is a waterski school nearby.

Old Alonnisos

5km NW of Patitiri. From the port below, the old town is an intriguing sight; a splash of white peeping from a crevice in the bare brown hills. This former capital, deserted for many years, has an atmosphere of romantic abandon about it. Many of the lovely buildings have lost their roofs, and interiors are exposed to sunshine and rain; iron balconies, twisted with age, surround courtyards overgrown with vegetation. Tiny gargoyles hang above sagging doorways, and the flagstone paths are now more suited to the chickens and donkeys which use them. As the town is high in the hills, the view it commands is impressive; the distinctive slate roofs of the dilapidated buildings – like coins tossed in a heap – and lacy ethereal foliage give way to mottled green and gold hills stretching down to a calm blue sea.

In very recent years Old Alonnisos has been 'discovered' by outsiders, and some of the houses are now undergoing renovation. At the moment there are still only a couple of tavernas and shops and a few rooms to let, but this is changing as the property speculators move in.

Accommodation & eating

Most accommodation is centred around Patitiri; the construction boom indicates that the island is gearing up for tourism. The **Hotel Liadromia** (tel 65521) is pricey for an E class hotel but has large rooms and a roof garden. Up the wooded path to the left of the harbour in Patitiri, there is a restaurant offering a splendid view out across the water; at the **Taverna Aloni** in Old Alonnisos one of the taxi drivers plays the bouzouki.

Satellite islands

Gioura
NE of Alonnisos. Gioura is home to a species of wild goat, known only to its shores. It also boasts a Cave of the Cyclopes which can be reached by boat; take a torch to view the multi-coloured stalactites and stalagmites.

Kira Panagia/Pelagos
NE of Alonnisos. The island has good beaches and was used as a base for divers, who in the last decade discovered the wrecks of several Byzantine ships just off its shores.

Peristera
E of Alonnisos. Divided from Alonnisos by a narrow stretch of water, Peristera has a population of just 15 people. The beaches are better than those on Alonnisos; a day excursion to this island is very pleasant, but take a picnic basket as facilities are minimal.

Psathoura
SE of Alonnisos. Only two people live on this isolated island, where the remains of an ancient city have been discovered just below the surface of the water. When the sea is calm, traces of the streets and houses can be seen from above. Snorkellers should find plenty to explore, but come prepared as there is little equipment available for hire in Alonnisos.

Skiathos

General character

With up to seven flights daily from Athens, Skiathos is in no way undiscovered. As late in the season as October, scores of tourists flock to the island, attracted by fine green scenery, a pretty port and numerous beaches. It is one of the few islands outside the Cyclades which is popular with Americans; German travellers are of course everywhere. If arriving in the high season, be sure to have booked accommodation in advance. The airport is tiny and unable to cope with the large number of people, so luggage is deposited in the car park to be collected at random. However, an airport under construction on the nearby island Alonnisos should in time relieve the congestion.

Despite the overcrowding, Skiathos is a genial place; the locals are pleasant to

Island chain   Sporades
Population   4,130
Area   48sq km
Area tel code   0424
Tourist Police   tel 42392
Harbour Police   tel 42017
Distance from Athens   5 hours by bus to Volos; 41 nautical miles/3 hours by boat to Skiathos

Travel information

By air
3–7 flights daily to/from Athens.
By ferry
2–5 daily to/from Volos; occasional services from Ag Konstandinos & Kimi. 1–2 daily to Skopelos & Alonnisos; 1–4 weekly to/from Skyros.

the tourists, the tourists themselves good-humoured and respectful. Skiathos Town is busy and bustling, and in spite of several high-rise hotels the landscape is still the property of grazing donkeys. Sights to see are of a pleasing rather than stunning nature – visiting them is not obligatory and most people prefer to spend their time beach-hopping. Skiathos is in every way an 'easy' Greek island; every conceivable excursion is offered every single day, including day trips to the islands of Alonnisos and Skopelos. The food is very good and beaches, of course, are superb.

Regional features

Skiathos is a picturesque little island, very green, with lots of pine trees and olive groves slipping down to the sea. The western side consists of a steep mountain range accessible only on foot or by mule; the east is a plain which is served by the island's only paved road, basically running from Skiathos Town to Koukounaries beach. Buses ply this route every half-hour; motorscooters or bicycles can be hired to travel the dirt paths which disappear into the hills.

Ports & towns

Skiathos Town/Chora
Although resorts have sprung up alongside the major beaches, Skiathos is the only real town on the island. Attractive buildings with red-tiled roofs slope between two hills, one crowned by a domed clock tower, the other by a decorative church steeple. Jutting into

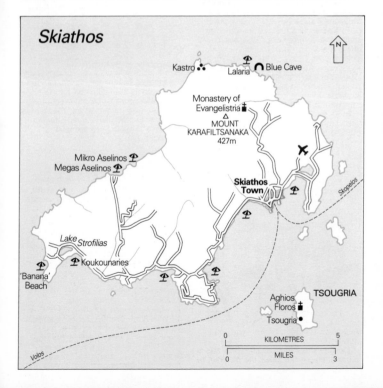

the sea is the wooded Bourtzi peninsula, at the entrance to which stands a bust of the novelist Alexandros Papadiamantis, who was born nearby in 1851. The town's only street is named after this local hero and a museum dedicated to him is awaiting transferral to the large former schoolhouse on the peninsula. Criss-crossing Papadiamantis Street are paths and paved alleyways which house the post office, a bank, an OTE office and the Tourist Police.

The waterfront glitters with boutiques, seafood restaurants, bars and tasteful antique shops; patronised by foreigners and locals alike. The atmosphere is lively and noisy, but late at night serenity returns to Skiathos.

Accommodation & eating

Two of the largest hotels overlook golden Koukounaries Beach, the Luxury class **Skiathos Palace** (tel 42242) and the B class **Xenia** (tel 42041). Both are open spring and summer only. Skiathos Town offers many pensions and rooms to let, including the C class **Akti** (tel 42024) and the E class **Australia House** (tel 42488) – testimony to the island's cosmopolitan appeal. Furnished apartments are also available; enquire locally. There is a campsite at Kolios.

Food, by Greek standards, is uncommonly good – shrimp and crab in the waterfront restaurants, fresh fruit, yoghurt and freshly squeezed orange juice in the cafés. Tucked behind the harbour in Skiathos Town is a small take-away crêperie.

Sights

Blue Cave
On the N coast, approx 45 mins by boat from Skiathos Town. Many tour boats pause at this cavern, but most are too large to navigate the channel into it. To hire a small boat, enquire locally, and take a strong torch.

Kastro
On the N coast, approx 70 mins by boat from Skiathos Town. It is also possible to walk to this ancient walled town, but the journey takes two to three hours. Situated 500m above the sea, during the 16th century the entire population of Skiathos lived within these walls and the only access was by drawbridge. Today, winding stone steps lead up from the pebble beach to its crumbling walls. Originally they enclosed some 300 houses and 22 churches, two of which can still be visited.

Monastery of Evangelistria
5km N of Skiathos Town. Tucked under the looming Mount Karafiltsanaka, the monastery is accessible on foot (a one- to two-hour trek) or by motorscooter; there are also organised excursions. Inside is an attractive carved altar screen and several icons from the post-Byzantine period.

Beaches

There are almost 60 beaches tucked into the jagged shores of Skiathos; some sandy and surrounded by trees, others pebbly and backed by bold red cliffs. Some of the more interesting beaches are listed below.

'Banana' Beach
14km SW of Skiathos Town. Situated on Krassas Bay just 1km west of Koukounaries Beach, this is the island's nudist beach. Boats leave every morning from Skiathos Town; alternatively take the bus to Koukounaries and then walk.

Koukounaries Beach
13km SW of Skiathos Town. A smooth, curving crescent of sand backed by lush green pines. Directly behind the trees is Lake Strofilias, a large fresh-water lagoon. Unfortunately, this paradise is now highly developed, with hotels and

tavernas all around. However, the atmosphere is not claustrophobic, and out of season Koukounaries is lovely. Beach umbrellas, a kiosk and shallow water make this beach perfect for children. Bus every half-hour from Skiathos Town.

Lalaria Beach

On the N coast, approx 1 hour by boat from Skiathos Town. Dramatic pebbly beach enclosed by high white cliffs. At the eastern end of the bay is a feature known as 'Tripia Petra' (which literally means perforated stone); a much-photographed natural arch in the cliff, through which it is possible to swim or pilot a small boat. Lalaria is a popular spot with tour operators, but beware, most only pause long enough for a quick swim, and the beach is almost impossible to reach overland. Take shoes as the pebbles hold the heat well.

Megas Aselinos

On the W coast. Accessible by caique or on foot. Sandy cove backed with bamboo and surrounded by gently rolling green hills. There is a taverna with a covered verandah here. Approx 2km to the north-east is Mikro Aselinos Beach which offers more privacy, but gettting there involves a stiff climb.

Satellite islands

Tsougria

SE of Skiathos. There are no fewer than nine uninhabited islands surrounding Skiathos; several are used only as lighthouse stations. Tsougria is the largest, and has a chapel known as Aghios Floros, two beaches and a small yacht marina.

Skopelos

General character

Skopelos, although larger, is less developed than its neighbour Skiathos, but has a similar atmosphere. Pine trees cover much of its hilly slopes, and as there is only one paved road, boats are common transport. The island is long and narrow; the roads are so poor that ferries plying the Sporadian route call at two separate ports, allowing locals to use the boats as a 'bus service'. What Skopelos lacks in sandy beaches is compensated for by lovely local architecture. Skopelos Town is the most beautiful port in the island chain, growing more sophisticated every year.

Regional features

According to tradition, the first olive trees on Skopelos were brought from the city of Knossos on Crete. Today these groves of silver-leaved trees can be seen throughout the island, interspersed with pine. At the beginning of the 5thC BC the island was wealthy enough to mint its own money; ancient ruins thought to date from this period have been discovered in the south-western part of Skopelos.

Island chain   Sporades
Population   4,500
Area   95sq km
Area tel code   0424
Tourist Police   tel 22235
Harbour Police   tel 22182
Distance from Athens   5 hours by bus to Volos; 58 nautical miles/4½ hours by boat to Skopelos

Travel information

By ferry
2–5 daily to/from Volos; occasional services from Ag Konstandinos & Kimi. 1–2 daily to Skiathos; Alonnisos; 1–4 weekly to Skyros.

Ports & towns

Skopelos Town/Chora

A beautiful, graceful port; white three-storey houses follow the contours of the hills on which it lies. On the far left of the harbour (when facing the sea), three picturesque churches gleam in the sun. Over one-third of the island's 360 chapels are located in the tiny streets or

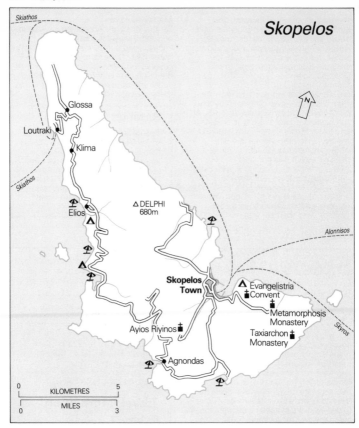

Skopelos

private courtyards of this capital town; many were built by sailors rescued from near-death in the often stormy seas. Buildings are packed close together and occasionally the upper storeys are linked by bridges which span the narrow streets. The traditional white walls are relieved by splashes of colour on shutters, balconies and doors. Flower-pots in front of the houses are so prolific as to create a virtual avenue of potted greenery leading to the Venetian Kastro above; donkeys, cats and Germans are much in evidence. Only two things mar the loveliness of Chora; the town beach

is unsuitable for swimming, and around the harbour, a fishy smell of the most unpleasant kind would seem to be a permanent fixture. Although the impact dies away, the smell is noticeable for the first few hours.

Glossa/Loutraki

20km NW of Skopelos Town. Although Glossa is the name given by ferries as the destination in northern Skopelos, the boat actually docks in the village of Loutraki at the foot of the hill. Loutraki is a sleepy port with an attractive square dominated by a domed church. Glossa, the commercial centre of northern

Skopelos, tumbles down the hillside 10 minutes' walk above; a sprinkling of white and orange houses on the green slopes. Loutraki has a small stoney beach.

Accommodation & eating

In Skopelos Town there are furnished apartments for rent (tel 22517), as well as rooms to let and hotels such as the B class **Amalia** (tel 22688) and the C class **Aeolos** (tel 22233). The C class **Avra** (tel 33550) is the only listed hotel for Glossa, although rooms in private houses can be found. Food is predominantly fish in the waterfront tavernas of Skopelos Town; the **Rania Restaurant** in Glossa has a balcony overlooking the port. A jazz club in Skopelos claims to serve wholefood-type meals, a rarity in Greece.

Sights

Kastro
1km up the hill from Skopelos Town. The road to the Kastro is a long dusty one, frequented more by donkeys and goats than by people. Although to some the ruins might not be worth the effort, a sweeping panorama of the town and harbour far below is stunning, especially when the ferries dock.

Churches
Many of the island's 360 churches can be visited. If they are locked, enquire in the nearest available building for the key; leave a votive offering.

Convents & monasteries
Twelve religious houses on Skopelos are open to visitors; many are set high in the hills, offering breathtaking views of the surrounding countryside.

Evangelistria Convent
3km E of Skopelos Town. Still in use, and offering a splendid view across the bay to Skopelos Town. *Open mornings and evenings.*

Monastery of Ayios Riyinos
3km S of Skopelos. A lovely, multi-domed brick building set in peaceful countryside.

Specialities

Prunes
Skopelos is noted for its prunes; a visit to the factory where the fruit is cooked, wrapped and packed can be arranged. Enquire locally.

Skyros

General character

Skyros is an island of character and charm with a distinctive capital tumbling down the hillside, a friendly local population and reasonable sandy beaches. It also boasts two fine traditions which, in spite of increasing tourism, seem determined to survive. These are the breeding of miniature horses which are similiar to Shetland ponies, and the carving of elegant wooden furniture. The latter can be seen in workshops around the town, in one of the two excellent museums, or on hot summer afternoons by peeping into the open doorways of many of the island homes. The Athenian hero Theseus spent his last days on Skyros, and the English poet Rupert Brooke, was buried, at his request, in a leafy olive grove on a remote corner of the island in 1915.

Island chain Sporades
Alternative names Skiros
Population 2,760
Area 209sq km
Area tel code 0222
Tourist Police tel 91274
Harbour Police tel 91475
Distance from Athens 4–5 hours by bus to Kimi on Evia; 2 hours by boat to Skyros.

Travel information

By air
1 flight daily to/from Athens in the high season, less often in winter

By ferry
1–2 daily from Kimi on island of Evia; occasional boats from Volos. 1–4 weekly to Skiathos, Skopelos, Alonnisos

Regional features

Skyros is kidney-shaped, its two halves distinctly different from each other. The northern half is fertile, covered with dense pine forests and fruit trees. The southern region is arid, rocky, and used primarily as grazing land for the herds of ponies who roam freely.

Ports & towns

Skyros Town/Horio

An attractive cluster of whitewashed houses cascading down the slopes of a hill, nestling under the protection of the castle and the Monastery of St George on the craggy summit. An earth tremor in 1983 destroyed much of the interior of the monastery, but it is slowly being rebuilt. The island seems especially popular with discerning British travellers, although little English is spoken out of the high season, when many of the workers return to Athens.

The town is a large one, extending from the top of a hill to the shores of a sandy beach. It is easy to get lost in the narrow sidestreets, where the flagstone paths and whitewashed houses all look confusingly alike. Skyros Travel, on the main pedestrian thoroughfare, can arrange tours around the island, plus windsurfing and sailing.

Linaria

12km SW of Skyros Town. A simple port consisting of a cluster of houses, a few tavernas, and telephones which often do not work. Miniature horses occasionally graze in the churchyard on the hill. It is from Linaria that the boats depart for the island of Evia.

Accommodation & eating

There are rooms to let in both Linaria and Skyros Town, although most are concentrated in the larger town. The most lavish hotel is the B class **Xenia** (tel 91209), right on Magazia beach below Skyros Town. Eating is mainly in the tavernas and cafés lining the main pedestrian street of the capital.

Sights

Three of the main places of interest on Skyros all lie within a few hundred metres of each other, close to the centre of Skyros Town. However, they are not signposted and can be difficult to find if trying to follow the confusing maze of streets. The simplest way is to head directly for the ringroad overlooking the beach and then ask for directions.

Archaeology Museum

Skyros Town. Beautifully situated museum built in 1963 to house an impressive range of artefacts. Amongst the most interesting are a pair of vases shaped like birds, dating from 950–800BC; also a male torso, possibly Apollo, from the late Hellenistic period. A typical Skyrian room has been reconstructed in the museum, with an intricately carved low wall on top of which lies the family bed. *Open 09.00–15.30 Mon–Sat; 10.00–16.30 Sun & hols. Closed Tue.* Charge.

Faltaits Museum

Skyros Town. Charming folklore museum overlooking the sea. Inside are hand-painted copies of traditional island embroidery for which Skyros is renowned; also some of the original embroideries, decorated with peacocks and princes. There are many shelves of old books including, incongruously, leather-bound copies of *The Spectator* magazine. *Open in summer 10.00–13.00, 17.30–20.00; opening hours in winter are erratic.* Charge.

Monument of Eternal Poetry

Skyros Town. This statue to Rupert

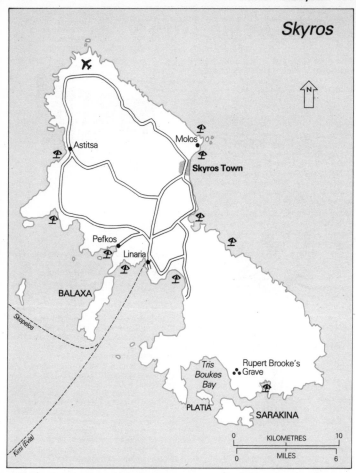

Skyros

Molos

Skyros Town

Astitsa

Pefkos

Linaria

BALAXA

Stopelos

Kimi (Evia)

Tris Boukes Bay

Rupert Brooke's Grave

PLATIA   SARAKINA

| KILOMETRES | 0 | 10 |
| MILES | 0 | 6 |

Brooke is sited on a headland looking out to sea. A naked athlete standing 1.8m high, it is in the Classical style. The money to erect it was collected from poets throughout the world, to honour the memory of this young English poet. The unveiling of the statue was a cause for great ceremony on the island.

Rupert Brooke's grave

Approx 30km SE of Skyros Town. It is possible to reach the grave by road; an easier method is to take a boat from Linaria to Tris Boukes bay and then walk. Located on the remote southern tip of the island, the simple monument is surrounded by olive groves.

Art & architecture

With the introduction of metal-working techniques from the Near East at the beginning of the Bronze Age, Greece underwent a period of rapid cultural development. Distinct cultures began to emerge, associated with individual islands or island groups. The availability of two important natural resources – clay and marble – provided the raw materials for the manufacture of the stylised idols of the Cycladic culture (2700–1400BC). Made on Naxos and Paros, these carved figurines were exported throughout the Aegean. However, by far the most important culture to emerge at this time was the Minoan civilization of Crete.

Tapering columns – Knossos

Cycladic idol

Minoan (2600–1450BC)

Many small settlements grew up in the eastern part of Crete, and the richness of the grave treasures indicates a prosperous and flourishing society. This wealth provided the basis for the development of the great Minoan Palatial civilization from 1900BC, when the palaces of Knossos, Malia and Phaistos were built. Numerous rooms, varying in size but all rectangular in shape, were laid out around central courtyards in a labyrinthine network. Monumental staircases, shady colonnades with their columns tapering

towards the base, and advanced plumbing are all characteristic features of the Minoan palaces. Decoration was also important. Many of the royal apartments were painted with fine, subtly coloured frescos, some of which can still be seen today. Themes tended to be naturalistic with animals, birds, fish and flowers. Similar Late Minoan frescos were discovered at Akrotiri on Santorini, again concentrating on naturalistic themes.

The skills of the potter were well advanced during this period. The polychrome Kamares ware with its pale designs painted on a dark background was made from c2000BC. Plants and marine animals, particularly the octopus, were frequently represented.

Mycenean (1600–1200BC)

The Mycenean civilization, centred on the Peloponnese mainland, had little effect on many of the Aegean islands. Evolving as a result of close contact with the Minoans, the buildings of this period were also on a grand scale. However, greater emphasis was placed on fortifications and the construction of massive Cyclopean walls such as those at Mycenae. The citadel rather than the courtyard now provided the focal point around which the other buildings were gathered. The success and wealth of the Mycenean culture is demonstrated in the rich grave goods and their skill in working gold.

Geometric/Homeric (1200–700BC)
The Dorian invasions led to the collapse of the Mycenean world. This turbulent period saw the development of the typical Hellenic city, centred originally on a strongly defended Acropolis. Later it was the agora or marketplace on the plain below which provided the focal point of the city with the Acropolis becoming a religious site.

Temple of Aphaia – Aegina

Archaic (700–480BC)
The age of the Greek temple. Masterpieces of architecture and decoration, with intricately carved stonework, ornate friezes and elaborate pediments. Built between 510 and 480BC, the Temple of Aphaia on Aegina with its rectangular cella, colonnades and pediment sculptures, must have been one of the most beautiful of the temples built in the Doric order. The Ionic order, with a similar ground plan but more elaborate columns and capitals, was also in use at this time.

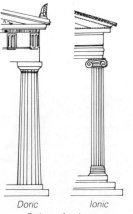

Doric   Ionic
Orders of columns

Kore

The Archaic period saw the beginnings of Greek monumental sculpture. Imitating the Egyptian and Near-Eastern style, life-sized statues were first made in Crete. Facilitated by the excellent stone from the marble quarries of Naxos, the Cyclades were also one of the earliest centres of Greek sculpture. The naked male figures, known as *kouros*, are characterised by stiff limbs and stylised hair. The females – *kore* – again with stiff limbs and stylised hair, have almond-shaped eyes and were usually draped. Later, as techniques evolved, greater attention was paid to anatomical detail and the suggestion of life and movement. One of the earliest examples is the Kouros of Flerio on Naxos, dating from the 7thC BC. Also as a result of Egyptian and Near-Eastern influence, lions were a popular subject for the Archaic sculptors. The magnificent Terrace of the Lions on Delos dates from the 7thC BC, the Lion of Kea from the 6thC BC.

By the end of the 7thC BC, the use of black-figure work on terracotta pottery had been universally adopted. The development of red-figure work in the mid 6thC BC was a complete reversal of this technique. It made possible a much

Archaic lion

freer decorative style as additional detail could be added in black to the red figures.

Classical (480–330BC)
Sculpture became freer and more expressive. The works of Pheidias and Polykleitos in both marble and bronze are particularly outstanding during this, the greatest period of Greek sculpture. The Classical age was also the heyday of Greek architecture. The rotunda or round temple is a typical feature of this period. The rotunda on Samothrace, with a diameter of 20m, was the largest circular building in Greece. On the island of Sifnos are the remains of over 40 round towers built in Classical times.

Hellenistic (330–146BC)
The mid 4thC BC saw the widespread introduction of the Corinthian order in architecture, though it differed only slightly from the Ionic. Mosaics became an increasingly popular style of decoration. The island of Delos is a great monument to the art and architecture of the Hellenistic period. Many of the great amphitheatres such as at Epidauros, and on Lesbos and Kos date from this period. The theatre on Lesbos, later remodelled by the Romans, was once the largest in Greece.

The mighty Colossus of Rhodes, one of the Seven Wonders of the Ancient World, was cast in bronze by Chares of Lindos c290BC. A statue of the sun-god Helios, it towered to a height of over 30m, but was destroyed by an earthquake in 225BC.

Corinthian order

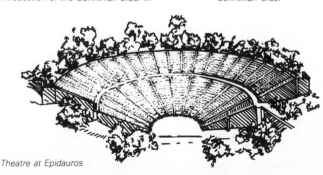

Theatre at Epidauros

Roman (146BC–AD330)

With the destruction of Corinth in 146BC, Greece became a Roman province. Roman influences on the northern part of Greece were more pronounced. In the south and on the islands, there is little architecture that is typically Roman. However, some fine examples do exist and their remains can be seen today. The ancient town of Gortys on Crete was the Roman capital of the island and also the North African province of Cyrenaica. Outstanding ruins include the Praetorium – the residence of the Roman governor, and a Nymphaeum, or shrine of the Nymphs, both dating from the 2ndC AD. The Odeon was built in AD100. Also of interest are the 1stC AD Roman baths of the Asklipeion, Kos and the aqueducts on Lesbos. Many large public buildings including stadiums, gymnasiums and theatres date from this period.

The predominant trend in sculpture was to continue the traditions of the earlier Classical works. There was, however, increased attention to detail on the head, creating a more realistic portrait.

Byzantine (AD300–14thC)

Constantine the Great transferred the Roman capital to Byzantium (Constantinople) in AD300. With the coming of Christianity to Greece in the 6thC AD, the earlier Classical temples either fell into disuse or were converted into churches. The churches and monasteries built by the Byzantines were the supreme architectural achievement of this period; characterised by the typical cross-in-square ground plan, attractive stonework and terracotta-tiled domes. One of the oldest and most important churches in Greece is the Church of One Hundred Doors (Ekatontapyliani) in Parikia, Paros, which was commissioned by the Emperor Justinian in the 6thC AD.

The predominant theme running through all Byzantine art is that of the religious. Mosaics and frescos adorned the walls and ceilings of the churches. Carved iconostases – screens made from wood or marble – separated the sanctuary from the main body of the church. Ornate, richly decorated icons were hung on the iconostasis.

From the beginning of the 13thC the Byzantine empire began to decline, though Byzantine traditions of art and architecture in Greece continued to flourish. This period also saw the emergence of the basic cube-shaped houses with their flat roofs. Now whitewashed, they are still the most typical feature of island architecture today.

Gate of St John – Rhodes Town

Knights of St John, Venetian & Turkish (14thC–1821)

Fortifications feature prominently in the architecture of this turbulent period. Many fortresses were built on the site of earlier Byzantine castles. The Knights of St John, who occupied the islands of Kos and Rhodes for over 200 years, protected their cities by constructing the so called 'Castles of the Knights'. Another fine example of the architecture of this period can still be observed in Ippoton St, Rhodes Town – the Street of the Knights – with its well-preserved stone Inns and houses.

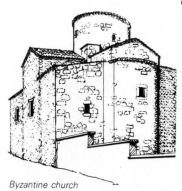

Byzantine church

The Venetians created citadels, surrounding whole towns with massive walls. Those at Heraklion in Crete can still be seen today, and are up to 29m thick in some places. The remains of numerous smaller fortresses can be found throughout the islands. The long-term occupation of many of the islands by the Venetians brought prosperity and stability. Elegant mansions, public buildings, churches and bell towers in the Venetian style are still an attractive feature of many island towns. Some of the best examples are to be found on Halki, Kea, Symi, Naxos and throughout the Ionian group.

The centuries of Turkish domination were culturally oppressive and little indigenous development took place. Many churches were converted into mosques, but new mosques were also built. Their distinctive minarets still figure prominently today on the skyline on Kos, Crete and Rhodes.

Venetian buildings – Corfu Town

Vocabulary

Greek alphabet

Α α	álfa		Ι ι	yóta		Ρ ρ	ró	
Β β	víta		Κ κ	káppa		Σ σ ς	sígma	
Γ γ	gámma		Λ λ	lámda		Τ τ	táf	
Δ δ	délta		Μ μ	mí		Υ υ	ípsilon	
Ε ε	épsilon		Ν ν	ní		Φ φ	fí	
Ζ ζ	zíta		Ξ ξ	xí		Χ χ	chí	
Η η	íta		Ο ο	ómikron		Ψ ψ	psí	
Θ ϑ	thíta		Π π	pí		Ω ω	oméga	

Numbers

0	midén	μηδέν	17	dekaeptá	δεκαεπτά	
1	éna	ένα	18	dekaoktó	δεκαοκτώ	
2	dío	δύο	19	dekaenniá	δεκαεννέα	
3	tría	τρία	20	íkosi	είκοσι	
4	téssera	τέσσερα	21	ikosiéna	εικοσιένα	
5	pénde	πέντε	22	ikosidío	εικοσιδύο	
6	éxi	έξι	30	triánda	τριάντα	
7	eptá	επτά	40	saránda	σαράντα	
8	októ	οκτώ	50	peninda	πενήντα	
9	ennéa	εννέα	60	exinda	εξήντα	
10	déka	δέκα	70	evdominda	εβδομήντα	
11	éndeka	έντεκα	80	ogdónda	ογδόντα	
12	dódeka	δώδεκα	90	eneninda	ενενήντα	
13	dekatría	δεκατρία	100	ekató	εκατό	
14	dekatéssera	δεκατέσσερα	500	pendakósia	πεντακόσια	
15	dekapénde	δεκαπέντε	1,000	chília	χίλια	
16	dekaéxi	δεκαέξι	5,000	pénde chiliades	πέντε χιλιάδες	

Useful words

yes	né	ναί	morning	proí	πρωί
no	óhki	όχι	afternoon	apógevma	απόγευμα
please	parakaló	παρακαλώ	evening	vrádi	βράδυ
thank you	efkharistó	ευχαριστώ	night	níkta	νύκτα
sorry/			today	símera	σήμερα
excuse me	signómi	συγγνώμη	tomorrow	ávrio	αύριο
I don't	dén kata-	δέν κατα-	next week	tín áli	τήν άλλη
understand	lavéno	λαβαίνω		vdomáda	βδομάδα
Greek	Elliniká	Ελληνικά			
I am	íme	είμαι	here	edó	εδώ
English	'Anglos	'Αγγλος	there	ekí	εκεί
American	Amerikános	Αμερικάνος	north	vória	βόρια
help	voíthia	βοήθεια	south	nótia	νότια
hello	yásou	γειά σού	east	anatoliká	ανατολικά
goodbye	adío	αντίο	west	ditiká	δυτικά
good			walk	perípatos	περίπατος
morning	kaliméra	καλημέρα	road	drómos	δρόμος
good			path	monopáti	μονοπάτι
afternoon	kalispéra	καλησπέρα	street	odós	οδός
good night	kaliníkta	καληνύκτα	square	platía	πλατεία
early	norís	νωρίς	open	aniktó	ανοικτό
late	argá	αργά	closed	klistó	κλειστό
			entrance	íssodos	είσοδος

English			English		
exit	éxodos	έξοδος	toilet	toualéta	τουαλέτα
keep out	apagorévete i íssodos	απαγορεύεται η εισοδος	campsite	camping	
danger	kíndinos	κίνδυνος	restaurant	estiatório	εστιατόριο
stop	stóp	στόπ	table	trapézi	τραπέζι
left	aristerá	αριστερά	chair	karékla	καρέκλα
right	dexiá	δεξιά	menu	katálogos	κατάλογος
up	páno	πάνω	bill	logariasmós	λογαριασμός
down	káto	κάτω	church	eklisía	εκκλησία
in front	embrós	εμπρός	museum	moussío	μουσείο
behind	píso	πίσω	bank	trápeza	τράπεζα
slow	sigá	σιγά	cheque	tsék	τσέκ
fast	grigora	γρήγορα	travellers' cheque	travellers' tsék	
big	megálo	μεγάλο	money	leftá	λεφτά
small	mikró	μικρό	post office	takhidromío	ταχυδρομείο
bad	kakós	κακός	telephone	tiléfono	τηλέφωνο
good	kalós	καλός	stamp	grammató-simo	γραμματό-σημο
very good	polí kaló	πολύ καλό			
expensive	akrivó	ακριβό	postcard	kárta	κάρτα
cheap	ftinó	φτηνό	letter	grámma	γράμμα
old	palió	παλιό	film	film	φίλμ
new	néo	νέο	chemist	farmakío	φαρμακείο
easy	éfkolo	εύκολο	hospital	nosokomío	νοσοκομείο
difficult	dískolo	δύσκολο	doctor	yiatrós	γιατρός
man	ándras	άνδρας	dentist	odontoyiatrós	οδοντογι-ατρός
men	ándres	άνδρες			
woman	yinéka	γυναίκα	kiosk	períptero	περίπτερο
women	yinékes	γυναίκες	police	astinomía	αστυνομία
child	pedí	παιδί	tourist police	touristikí astinomía	τουριστική αστυνομία
children	pediá	παιδιά			
what	tí	τί	book	vivlío	βιβλίο
when	póte	πότε	map	khártis	χάρτης
where	poú	πού	newspaper	efimerida	εφημερίδα
how	pós	πώς	bakery	foúrnos	φούρνος
how much	pósso	πόσο	pastry shop	zakharo-plastío	ζαχαρο-πλαστείο
I don't know	dén xéro	δέν ξέρω			
to	prós	πρός	market	agorá	αγορά
from	apó	από	fruit	fruta	φρούτα
and	ké	καί	apple	mílo	μήλο
with	mé	μέ	orange	portokáli	πορτοκάλι
without	horís	χωρίς	lemon	lemóni	λεμόνι
nothing	típota	τίποτα	banana	banána	μπανάνα
hot	zestó	ζεστό	peach	rodákino	ροδάκινο
cold	krío	κρύο	melon	pepóni	πεπόνι
sun	ílios	ήλιος	watermelon	karpoúzi	καρπούζι
shade	skiá	σκιά	figs	síka	σύκα
wind	ánemos	άνεμος	grapes	stafília	σταφύλια
sea	thálassa	θάλασσα	cherries	kerásia	κεράσια
sand	ámos	άμμος	tomatoes	tomátes	ντομάτες
beach	paralía	παραλία	cucumber	angoúri	αγγούρι
cave	spiliá	σπηλιά	potatoes	patátes	πατάτες
inside	mésa	μέσα	onions	kremídia	κρεμμύδια
outside	éxo	έξω	beans	fasólia	φασόλια
hotel	xenodokhío	ξενοδοχείο	water	neró	νερό
room	domátio	δωμάτιο	mineral water	emfialoméno neró	εμφιαλωμένο νερό
single	monó	μονό	lemonade	lemonáda	λεμονάδα
double	dipló	διπλό	red wine	kókkino krassí	κόκκινο κρασί
balcony	balkóni	μπαλκόνι			
bed	kreváti	κρεββάτι	white wine	áspro krassí	άσπρο κρασί
shower	doús	ντούς	beer	bíra	μπύρα
bath	bánio	μπάνιο			

glass	potíri	ποτήρι	chicken	kotópoulo	κοτόπουλο
bottle	boukáli	μπουκάλι	lamb	arnáki	αρνάκι
ice	págos	πάγος	yoghurt	yaoúrti	γιαούρτι
iced	pagoméno	παγωμένο	salad	saláta	σαλάτα
ice cream	pagotó	παγωτό	aeroplane	aeropláno	αεροπλάνο
chocolate	sokoláta	σοκολάτα	airport	aerodrómio	αεροδρόμιο
coffee	kafés	καφές	train	tréno	τρένο
tea	tsái	τσάι	station	stathmós	σταθμός
milk	gála	γάλα	coach	poúlman	πούλμαν
sugar	zákhari	ζάχαρη	bus	leoforío	λεωφορείο
no sugar	skéto	σκέτο	bus stop	stássi	στάση
sweet	glykó	γλυκό		leoforíou	λεωφορείου
honey	méli	μέλι	ship	vapóri	βαπόρι
jam	marmeláda	μαρμελάδα	boat	várka/plío	βάρκα, πλοίο
salt	aláti	αλάτι	hydrofoil	delfíni	δελφίνι
pepper	pipéri	πιπέρι	port	limáni	λιμάνι
oil	ládi	λάδι	ticket	isitírio	εισιτήριο
vinegar	xídi	ξύδι	seat	théssi	θέση
butter	voútiro	βούτυρο	return	met'	μετ'
cheese	tirí	τυρί		epistrofís	επιστροφής
eggs	avgá	αυγά	half-fare	misó	μισό
bread	psomí	ψωμί		isitírio	εισιτήριο
fish	psári	ψάρι	first (class)	próti (thessi)	πρώτη (θέση)
meat	kréas	κρέας	second	défteri	δεύτερη
steak	filéto	φιλέτο	third	tríti	τρίτη

Index